I0034814

Mark D. Packard
Entrepreneurial Valuation

Mark D. Packard

Entrepreneurial Valuation

An Entrepreneur's Guide to Getting into the Minds of Customers

DE GRUYTER

ISBN 978-3-11-075067-6
e-ISBN (PDF) 978-3-11-075080-5
e-ISBN (EPUB) 978-3-11-075084-3

Library of Congress Control Number: 2022934620

Bibliographic information published by the Deutsche Nationalbibliothek
The Deutsche Nationalbibliothek lists this publication in the Deutsche Nationalbibliografie;
detailed bibliographic data are available on the Internet at http://dnb.dnb.de.

© 2022 Walter de Gruyter GmbH, Berlin/Boston
Cover image: Kateryna Kovarzh/iStock/Getty Images Plus
Typesetting: Integra Software Services Pvt. Ltd.
Printing and binding: CPI books GmbH, Leck

www.degruyter.com

Preface

What if everything they taught in business school was wrong? Okay, maybe not *everything*. But much of it. Maybe even most of it. What if most of the business books you've read are full of half-truths and misleading platitudes? What if just about every entrepreneur has been doing it wrong?

We know very well that new venture failure rates are quite high. Actually, scholars can't seem to agree on this rate because we can't agree on what constitutes 'failure.' It's regularly cited that over 50 percent of new businesses fail within 5 years of their start (although many of these 'failures' can barely be called 'businesses' to begin with), and over 70 percent fail by year 10. However you want to define it, entrepreneurs have historically had a high chance of failing.

But what if I told you that the reason that so many fail is because they don't have a clue what they're doing? Maybe that's not a surprise to you. Maybe you can relate. But I don't just mean the average first-time entrepreneur that is drinking in all the ins and outs of new venturing through a fire hose. I also include among these 'no-clue' entrepreneurs the successful ones and even the long-time serial entrepreneurs. Some of them have written books about how to become successful like they did, their books in fact revealing that, although they've indeed learned a lot of valuable knowledge in the process, they really have no clue how they really made it big.

The fact of the matter is this: most successful startups succeed because they're *lucky*.

Successful entrepreneurs might not enjoy hearing this sour-grapes declaration of their own coincidental fortune. And I'm being somewhat facetious. But I believe it to be largely true. Most successful entrepreneurs simply guessed right – or guessed well enough. The bulk of entrepreneurs, those who fail, guessed wrong – or if they guessed right, didn't have the wherewithal to deliver. If you will stick with me through the end of the book (or even through the first few chapters), I'll try to explain why I'm right.

But here's where I'm trying to go with this: you can do better than mere luck. No, I can't guarantee your success. But I *can* teach you how and why most entrepreneurs are 'doing it wrong' and how you can do it 'right.' It turns out that it's mostly economists' fault.

Where Economics Went Wrong

What is an economy? I ask my students this question every semester. I typically have several economics majors in my class, the rest of them business majors. Blank stares, every one of them. How would you answer it?

After a little pushing, some of my students will hazard an answer, often something like 'a system of exchange' or 'supply and demand' or 'buying and selling.' Honestly, they're not bad answers. I've even asked some professional and academic

https://doi.org/10.1515/9783110750805-202

economists this question to essentially the same reactions. It turns out, almost no one ever really defines it. Like the concept of 'time,' we all think we understand it, but when hard pressed to explain it we discover we really don't know what it is at all.

So, what *is* an economy? What are we talking about when we talk about the 'economy'? What do we mean when the economy 'grows' or 'declines'?

Here's the way I define an economy: an economy is how well off we make ourselves with what we have to work with. It's the total, aggregate well-being of individuals within a given circle of interest. It is our quality of life. That's an economy.

In economics, we like to note that everything has a cost – "There's no such thing as a free lunch," as Milton Friedman liked to say. Despite some ideological attempts to dispel this universality of costs, it remains true in its intended meaning. All improvements to our well-being come at some cost. They simply do not happen without our paying some price. The costs could be in the consuming of resources, in our time and effort, and so forth. And, often, someone else foots that bill. But the bill must always be paid.

Perhaps the best way to understand this cost is as the 'opportunity cost' foregone. When you've spent something – your time, money, resources, energy – you can't get that back. What *else* could you have done with it? What would you have done if you hadn't spent it on what you chose? That is the real cost of anything, the opportunity cost.

As a result, an economy is the production of well-being at the cost of the resources (including time and effort) required to make the production of satisfactions occur (and the opportunity costs that those resources imply). It's not just 'stuff' we make. An economy that produces tons of 'stuff' that makes no impact on our quality of life is a devastated economy. We can't live off of useless stuff.

When we say that an economy is growing or 'booming,' what that really means is that average quality of life is increasing – we're getting better off. We're doing more with what we have. Perhaps we're solving our problems better with new innovations. Perhaps we're producing the same satisfactions at a lower cost, doing more with less, which means that we have more left over. These savings can let us buy other things we couldn't previously afford, or take more vacations, or invest more. A declining economy, then, is one that is doing less with what we have – overall well-being is *decreasing*.

What's important to note, here, is that we're not talking about some abstract system or machine that has pulleys and levers that we can manipulate to keep it running smoothly. We're talking about *people*. The economy is *us*, it is our livelihoods. Even Robinson Crusoe (or, if you're a youngster, Chuck Noland [Tom Hanks] from the movie *Cast Away*), alone on his island, was an economy, producing and consuming as efficiently as he could muster.

Where does economic growth come from, then? Where do these increases in overall well-being derive from? The answer, I hope you can clearly see, is *entrepreneurship*. It's entrepreneurs who create, innovate, streamline, cut out the middleman, who do things a different way than has always been done and either succeed in making life better off for their customers – and, thereby, for themselves – or else fail trying. It's entrepreneurs who find new ways to make our lives even better with the scarce resources that we have at our disposal. It's entrepreneurs that drive economic change and growth.

But economists lost their way a little over a century ago as they lost sight of the *people* that are the economy – that 'thing' they study – and turned it into a machine. People became mere automatons, simple and predictable. This was all done in the name of science (which F.A. Hayek, Karl Popper, and others would call 'scientism'), reducing conscious beings into unconscious entities that could be studied in the same way as all the other natural sciences. Of course, we're each so different – we have different characteristics, we like different things, and we do different things if left to our own devices – so economists had to adopt the language and framework of statistics, presuming such individual differences to be essentially random and, thereby, casting them as normal 'variance,' which could be accounted for in statistical analyses.

Thus, the modern social scientific paradigm was born. The 'economy' was reduced to that 'system of exchanges' that my students are familiar with, replete with pulleys and levels that can be adjusted to 'fine-tune' the machine.

Ultimately, the entrepreneur was lost to economics. As several astute economists (yes, there are some!) have pointed out, modern economics' notion of *equilibrium* – a state of balance between supply and demand, which is supposed as the natural state of an economy (except for occasional shocks, which are instantly corrected) – has no entrepreneur. It already assumes economic efficiency, there is nothing for an entrepreneur to do. Thus, while some economists would pay lip service to the entrepreneur, the entrepreneurial function had no place in those economists' theories.

I point this out because most of what is taught in business school derives from this entrepreneur-less economic paradigm. What can an entrepreneur really learn from such a theoretical framework? The answer is *not much*. In fact, it's probably worse than nothing. What entrepreneurs learn from that economic paradigm is *wrong* and, thus, misleading.

Entrepreneurs today, for example, will often, like the economist, treat the market as an entity to be corralled, their customers as numbers of a statistical analysis. The era of Big Data promises the end of entrepreneurial error, where entrepreneurs can predict precisely what the market will do and cut out all inefficiencies.

But such entrepreneurial activity is all premised on a fundamental misunderstanding of the most central construct of all of economics: *value*.

Getting Back on Track

Here I'm going to argue for a 'counterhistorical' solution to this 'wrong turn.' Counterhistory refers to the method of retracing steps to find where we went awry, and turning instead onto the already-established paths that heterodox scholars had forged against the mainstream's tide.

While most economists misunderstood value and lost the entrepreneur, the so-called 'Austrian school' did not. To offer just a bit of background, the Austrian school – so named because its early founders and primary advocates (Carl Menger, Friedrich von Weiser, Eugen von Böhm-Bawerk, Joseph Schumpeter, Ludwig von Mises, and F.A. Hayek) were all from Austria – is a heterodox school of economics that began in the latter end of the 19th century with a unique approach to understanding economics as a science. To be excessively brief, the Austrian school argued, with other philosophers of the time, that *social sciences* are inherently distinctive from *natural sciences* and must be approached differently. We cannot study people the same way we would study rocks and electricity. People are conscious and have free will (as far as we can tell). So using the revered Scientific Method™ to study people is problematic. Rather than a *predictive* science, as are the natural sciences, social sciences, and economics specifically, can only be sciences of post hoc *understanding* – we cannot predict what people will do as if they were mindless automatons.

For about a half a century, the Austrian school was a dominant perspective in the field of economics. Its academic predominance was severely disrupted by the geopolitical turmoil in early 20th century Europe, with Austria at the center of two world wars. After World War II, the academic center of the world shifted to North America, which predominantly held the 'positivist' view that social sciences and natural sciences are essentially the same and can be studied in the same way. The Austrian school was marginalized and lost its purchase. But, at least in part because the entrepreneur was missing in the prevailing Chicago and Keynesian school theories, the Austrian school has maintained a loyal contingent of heterodox scholars that has been growing over time.

The Austrian school plays a large role in this book – I consider myself an Austrian school economist. To a large extent my arguments are an argument that we would do much better to go back to the days of Austrian school influence and go from there. But that's a simplification. The Austrian school has in fact advanced significantly since its heyday, and there are more 'Austrian' scholars now than ever before. So we don't need to go back, we just need to flip the switch, so to speak, to turn our perspective in the right direction.

The Purpose of This Book

In this book I'm going to take you deep into the philosophical and theoretical realm before resurfacing again at the practical level. You need to understand *what value really is* if you are going to escape the whims of luck on your entrepreneurial journey.

In the first section, I'm going to take on the economic theory of value head on. I will start by showing you where it went wrong, how it is *still* wrong, and why it matters. I will then lay out my own contemporary research on value. My work distinguishes the objective from the subjective, the physical experience from the mental experience, neither of which is captured in classical economics.

Once we understand the true nature of value, we can begin to unravel the errors that a mistaken value concept has evoked – ideas such as *value creation* and *value capture*. Entrepreneurs do not *create* value as if some valuable thing comes into existence with their innovative willing. As it turns out, entrepreneurs don't get to decide what's valuable or not. Value is determined by consumers, and not merely by what they say they want.

After laying bare the true nature of value, I will then take you on a journey through the process of its emergence. How do we learn what to value? How do we determine how much things are worth to us? Where does *new* value come from?

Finally, I will carefully extrapolate what entrepreneurs can learn from all of this. How can one learn what consumers will value? Many entrepreneurs have already discovered that such learning requires actually interacting with consumers to discover what they really need. But, although some have supposed that it's as simple as *asking* them what they want, it really isn't. Asking is certainly better than not asking. But it turns out that Steve Jobs was right – consumers quite often *don't know* what they want. You have to figure out what they *should* want and then convince them that they *do* want it. Not at all an easy task.

I will discuss in somewhat less depth what to do with the knowledge of what consumers need (i.e., their problems), which you will need to solve in a way that vastly outperforms the solutions those consumers already use to satisfy the need. I will teach you about your customers' uncertainty – we hear a lot about the entrepreneur's (your) uncertainty, but it turns out your customer will have to bear a significant amount of uncertainty also. If you want to succeed, you'll need to help your customer mitigate or bear that uncertainty.

In each of these chapters, my aim will be to teach you what I've learned from my research, to teach you what I believe to be true economic principles. I will augment this learning with implications, guidance, and tools that will help you put what you've learned into practice. My goal is to teach you how to truly understand your customers so that you can deliver something to them that they will value dearly, that will delight them, and that they will love you for.

You can do it. It's not a simple or easy process. Nearly all entrepreneurs do not take on such an endeavor, which is why I can make the bold claim that they've just gotten lucky. They don't really know what their customers really needed. They guess. They may guess right. It may be an educated guess. But it's a guess, nonetheless.

You don't have to guess. Even if you don't guess, you may still fail. It's a tough road. There will be competition. There will be unexpected challenges. You will likely deal with trials and heartache. And, in the end, you may not even be able to convince your prospective customers that what you have is right for them. But if you follow the program laid out here, you will at least have something truly benefi-cial to offer them, with a compelling sales pitch, whether they choose to want it or not. And that is really the best you can ever do.

Contents

Section 1: **What is Value?**

Chapter 1
A History of Value

This book is not a secret formula for success. It is not a scripted checklist for starting a business. There are plenty of books like that out there, and if that's what you're looking for, you've found the wrong book. But I think this book is much more important than those. The truth is, no recipe for success is universal. What worked for Jack Welch or Warren Buffett or some other random person that made it pretty big is not a recipe for everyone. It worked for a particular person in a particular context at a particular time. Welch, Buffett, and the other person might have learned some valuable lessons on the way. Those lessons might even be good or correct principles for everyone, to some extent. But unless you know *how* and *why* those principles work, you cannot know *if* or *when* they'll work for you.

That's what this book is about – understanding the foundational principles of entrepreneurial success. There are many thousands of ways you can go about your business. In fact, I highly recommend you find your own path rather than following the documented path that someone else blazed. If you merely follow others' footsteps, you will not find yourself ready and able to go off script when, inevitably, things don't go according to plan.

In this book I am going to teach you the economics of entrepreneurship that standard business schools don't yet understand (I'm working on it! Give me 10 more years, maybe I'll sway the academy by then). I'm going to teach you the core principles that you need to know to succeed. I won't make you successful – there are far too many variables (including yourself) to make such a silly promise. But I *can* put you on sound theoretic footing and provide you with key understanding and tools that will make you far less prone to failure.

There are no certainties in entrepreneurship. The essence of entrepreneurship is dealing with uncertainty. But some people are much better at navigating uncertainty than others. My research has been in understanding uncertainty and how entrepreneurs best navigate it. I'm not usually one to toot my own horn, but my work (with some excellent co-authors) is, I think, groundbreaking and will change the way you think of and understand your role as entrepreneur. I think you'll find this book full of insights that will change the way you think of and do business.

Are you ready?

This first section of the book is a deep(ish) dive into the weeds of economic value theory. If you're not really into the deep philosophical and academic stuff, you might just skip Section 1. But before you do, let me make a case for why you shouldn't.

A few years ago, I came across a blog by Samid Chakrabarti that observed, interestingly, that an abnormally high number of successful startups were headed by

https://doi.org/10.1515/9783110750805-001

philosophy majors.[1] The list was impressive, including Peter Thiel, Reid Hoffman, Patrick Byrne, and many other recognizable names. Chakrabarti wondered if there was some kind of connection there. It was an interesting enough question that I jotted it down in case I ever had enough time to collect some data on it and test the hypothesis (update: I haven't). But the logic is simple enough: entrepreneurs that have a deeper understanding of how the world works, of how *people* work, are at an advantage. This understanding provides a foundation for sound *judgment* – that key function that is at the heart of what makes entrepreneurship *entrepreneurial*. You can't teach entrepreneurial judgment. But if you understand better than others how the world works, your judgment will tend to be better.

It is for this reason that I have written Section 1 – I hope to provide you with an understanding of how the world works, and how economies work, at a deeper level than you've likely ever been shown. And at the very heart of such an understanding is this abstract concept that has been the center of academic debate from the beginning: *value*. Economists thought they figured it out a century and a half ago. In fact, they did make a huge step forward, but they stopped far too soon. Economists *don't* understand value as well as they think they do. And it is this misunderstanding that is at the heart of all the errors that academics have made since then with respect to entrepreneurship. So that's where we need to start.

Value before Adam Smith

Philosophers have theorized about *value* for millennia now. I don't have the time, space, or interest to do a deep dive into the philosophical history of value. My historical review will be superficial, but it will be accurate. I'll focus on the main developments that are relevant to where we are today and how we got here.

The first big development in the history of value theory, as far as modern thought goes, can be attributed to Aristotle. In his 4th century B.C. *Politics*, Aristotle made a key distinction between *use* value and *exchange* value. *Use* value is that value we get from *using* a particular good. *Exchange* value is the value we get back from that good in trade.

Every good has both use value *and* exchange value. An apple, for example, has a certain usefulness to me. If I eat it, it offers me nutrition and calories, as well as a certain pleasurable experience in its sweet taste. But instead of eating it, I could instead choose to *sell* or trade it. The value that I could get in exchange for the apple, say 50 cents, is the exchange value. So the value to me of the apple is, in

---

1 The link, now broken, was: http://blog.samidh.com/2010/03/08/why-philosophers-make-formidable-entrepreneurs.

fact, the *higher* of the use value or the exchange value. If I value the use value more, I will choose to eat it. If I'd rather have the 50 cents, I'll sell it.

But Aristotle was unable to unravel the underlying mysteries of these value concepts. Where did use and exchange value come from? Certainly, they are distinct, but also somehow connected. Aristotle was unable to solve this riddle.

Adam Smith and the Cost Theory of Value

Between Aristotle and Adam Smith, there are few developments worth discussing here (some thinkers that at least considered the notion of value include Thomas Aquinas [13th century], Ibn Khaldun [14th century], and William Petty [17th century]). But none had yet cracked Aristotle's riddle, which was again picked up by Adam Smith in the latter half of the 18th century. This is the problem that Smith tackles in his famous *An Inquiry into the Nature and Causes of the Wealth of Nations* (or, just *The Wealth of Nations*) in 1776, trying to explain where exchange value or *prices* come from. By solving this riddle (somewhat), Smith becomes the father of modern economics, spawning a flood of interest and further thinking on political economy.

Smith begins with Aristotle's distinction and explains the paradox:

> [T]he things which have the greatest value in use have frequently little or no value in exchange; and on the contrary, those which have the greatest value in exchange have frequently little or no value in use.[2]

For example, air and water are some of the most useful goods to us (high use value), yet they historically have zero or very little exchange value. On the other hand, a diamond is not exactly useful – it's pretty and all, but it's use value is merely in looking at it and showing it off. Yet the exchange value of a diamond is way higher than that of air or water.

This problem has become known as *the value (or water-diamond) paradox*. Thus, while some argued that *utility* or use value was the mechanism that explained exchange value (e.g., J.B. Say), Smith rejected this explanation on the grounds of this value paradox.

Smith's solution to the problem of exchange value is what we call the *cost theory* of value. In short, Smith proposed that exchange value is derived from the total *cost* of its production. Many actually confuse Smith's theory as a *labor theory* of value (i.e., that exchange value derives from the cost of labor to produce). But while Smith focuses mostly on labor in his work, it is only because labor constituted a large part of most production at the time, and his theory is, in fact, a cost theory.

---

2 Smith, A. 2007. *An Inquiry into the Nature and Causes of the Wealth of Nations*. Hamshire: Harriman House, p. 18.

The cost theory has a strong intuition to it. For one, empirical evidence at the time provided strong support for the theory. Virtually all prices at the time closely mirrored their costs of production. And, of course, no successful business person would sell *below* cost.

In short, Smith proposed that prices tended to the level of cost, including and especially the cost of labor to produce it, in conjunction with the quantity of money, and adjusted by the "haggling and bargaining of the market."

Karl Marx and the Labor Theory of Value

Building on and from Smith, Karl Marx observed that the cost of goods could ultimately be traced back to purely labor costs. For example, the cost of the apple is in the cost of the labor to grow and havest it. But what about the costs of the materials and machinery that are used, such as fertilizer and irrigation? Marx argued that the costs of those goods are also derived from the cost of their production – the fertilizer and water are priced in from the cost of labor to produce or collect those goods. All goods, for Marx, ultimately reduce to pure labor costs, going all the way back to the labor needed to extract raw materials.

This observation led Marx to a *pure labor theory* of value – value is equal to the labor inputs in its production. This labor theory of value is, actually, a centerpiece of his communist philosophy – because total labor value is captured in the exchange value (price), the capitalist exploits workers by paying them *less* than the total value that they output, thereby capturing a profit (thus, all profit is an exploitation of labor).

While interesting, Marx's theory is highly problematic and has been rejected by all but a very few radical economists (I can only assume ideology motivates them to overlook the very obvious problems). First is the "transformation problem" – how does labor value get 'transformed' into prices (or vice versa)? Paul Samuelson observed that Marx's labor theory "*by postulate* made prices average out to equality with values."[3] Marx has no explanatory mechanism for this other than the mere shifting of resources from one industry to another until a system of prices (and profits) reaches an equilibrium state. Scholars show that Marx ends up with a tautology.

One result of this tautology is that we cannot explain the value difference between an apple pie and a mud pie if they both took the same labor to produce. Marxists (including Marx's later work) tried to rescue the labor theory by explaining that value comes only from 'socially necessary labor' – a mud pie is not 'socially

---

3 Samuelson, P. A. 1971. Understanding the Marxian notion of exploitation: A summary of the so-called transformation problem between Marxian values and competitive prices. *Journal of Economic Literature*, 9(2): 399–431, p. 414.

necessary.' But this revision, then, defines labor's value in terms of its end utility, returning again to the tautology.

Another criticism of the labor theory of value is the problem of *time*. A value assessment at time *t* is (or may be) ignorant of whateven labor went into its production at *t-1*. If you found a ring on the beach, and had no idea what it originally cost (or correspondingly, how much labor went into its production), how would you value that ring? Labor theorists argue that it's not the labor that it *took* but the labor that it *would take* to create it (at time *t*) that determines value at *t*. But this is still problematic. The same labor can produce two identical goods that result in different values and prices sold just minutes apart. Or how would it explain the value difference between a 1-year-old and a 20-year-old bottle of wine?

A final criticism worth noting is that the labor theory cannot explain the value of unworked resources, such as land. If I had a 5-acre plot of land, I could probably fetch a pretty good price for it. But what if I told you neither I nor anyone else had ever stepped foot on that land? It doesn't matter much for its market value, but how could it be valuable at all, according to Marx?

The labor theory of value had a strong heyday in the latter half of the 19th century. It still remains popular among ideologues. But it was and is unworkable as a theory of value.

The Marginal Revolution

The value paradox was finally solved in 1871 by three different economists, individually (yes, all in the same year): William Stanley Jevons, Leon Walras, and Carl Menger. The solution was, as it turns out, not a rejection of utility but a modification of its theoretical connection between use value (utility) and exchange value (prices).

Let's take use value as given – an apple has a certain utility for me. The *price* or exchange value of that apple is derived from its *marginal* utility. How many apples are there in the market? How many people want them? For what reasons? What is the use value for those different reasons? These questions underlie the mechanics of marginal utility theory. Marginal utility theory states that the *price* of a good corresponds to the *least valued* use that its supply affords.

Let's say, as a simple example, that there are 10 apples in the market. Mary wants 3 to make apple pie, and one extra just to eat plain. She's willing to pay $2 each for apples in order to make apple pie, but only $0.50 for the extra apple. Jerry wants to make applesauce and needs 5 apples. He's willing to pay $1 each for those apples. Jessica just wants two apples to eat, for which she'd pay up to $0.75 each. Well, the first apples to go are the one's Mary wants for her apple pie, leaving 7 left on the market. Jerry scoops up the next 5 for his applesauce, leaving 2 left. Jessica takes those. This means that the extra apple that Mary wanted is unavailable. But here's the point. What price did Mary, Jerry, and Jessica pay for those apples? The answer, according to marginal utility theory, is *$0.75*. The price is set by the *lowest* use value (assessed as total willingness to pay) that a good's supply can meet. After all the higher-valued uses (for the apple pie and applesauce) are filled, the supply can still provide a couple more apples for the next use, which is just eating them plain. The highest bidder for that use was Jessica's. But note that if there was just one more apple on the market, the expected price would have been $0.50 instead.

This is a simple example and you're probably thinking that the apple seller wouldn't reduce the price an additional $0.25 each just to sell one more apple. Fair enough. This was just an illustration of what the mechanics of marginal utility theory say. There was no competition or uncertainty in this example. In the real world, sellers *don't know* what the total demand will be and what each buyer's individual use value rankings are. And buyers don't know what the total supply will be and, thus, what kind of deal they might be able to get. But competition drives prices downward, sellers conceding prices down to the lowest-valued uses that their supply affords so that they can sell as much as possible. Thus, when the market equilibrates, the price will generally hover around the price level of the *marginal utility*, or the utility *at the margin* between the use value that was last supplied and the use value that was left unfulfilled when supply ran out.

This intellectual innovation, that exchange values are determined by use values in conjunction with total supply, was a massive breakthrough – which is why it's known as the *marginal revolution*. It not only solved the value paradox (extremely valuable water and air are free because they are so abundant, diamonds are expensive because they are so rare), but it also gave economists a useful framework for theorizing on how economic actors would act given certain economic conditions.

Game Theory

Soon after the marginal revolution, Alfred Marshall suggested that *utility* could be treated as a unit of analysis, and that mathematical models could be derived to compute the maximization of a utility function – *expected utility theory*. This theory was later formalized further by John von Neumann and Oskar Morgenstern in a book that was entitled *Theory of Games and Economic Behavior*.[4] It was a look at how economic actors behaved in certain experimental situations – *games* – that laid the ground for modern behavioral science. Von Neumann and Morgenstern laid out four logical axioms that enabled expected utility to be widely modeled: completeness, transitivity, independence of irrelevant alternatives, and continuity. We don't need to go into details over these assumptions. For the most part, they

---

4 von Neumann, J., & Morgenstern, O. 1944. *Theory of Games and Economic Behavior*. Princeton: Princeton University Press.

make a lot of sense. Game theory is still widely used and studied in psychology and behavioral economics.

Subjective Utility Theory

A final development worth noting is Leonard Savage's[5] advancement of expected utility theory in response to advancements in statistics that observed that the probabilities that people act on are not objective or constant. Different people weigh the likelihood of different outcomes differently. Even when the probability of some outcome is easily calculable, it doesn't mean that an actor will act rationally in accordance with that calculation. You might 'hit' on 17 in a game of blackjack.

This recognition meant that we can't perfectly predict people's behavior from 'objective' outcome probability distributions. We have to use *their own* subjective probabilities if we are to understand how they act. Thus, expected utility or game theory was augmented with subjective probability theory, and became *subjective utility theory*. In short, where the economic actor does not know the real probabilities of an expected utility, we replace the objective probability with the subjective one – what the actor *thinks* is the probability. This leaves us with the same probability-theoretic logic, but lets us better see individual choices through their own lens of 'bounded rationality.'

Bounded rationality – a term coined by economist Herbert Simon – simply means that reality is perceived through a limited lens of perception. We can only see pieces of the whole of reality at a time. Thus, we make our decisions from a ranked utility set derived from what limited information we have so far perceived. This leads, behavioral economists argue, to all sorts of biases and cognitive errors, which they have endeavored to uncover and, ultimately, correct. If we know how and why our minds misperceive reality in a way that leads to an 'irrational' choice, we can find workarounds to correct our perception and make more rational choices.

The Problem with 'As If' Theorizing

Well, I've already given the climax of the story away – we took a wrong turn somewhere along the way. Since then, we've been trying to make subjective again the objective value that we have supposed. But we keep doing it with the same basic philosophical assumptions that produced the objective value concept in the first place. The result is a kind of subjective-objective mash-up value concept that kind

---

5 Savage, L. J. 1954. *Foundations of Statistics*. Oxford England: Wiley.

of seems plausible at first glance, but actually collapses into nonsense upon closer examination.

Let me see if I can explain how and why today's behavioral economics doesn't really work before trying to trace back where it went awry. The problem is, in essence, that the entire framework – subjective expected utility theory – is *not* how we *actually* make decisions. And what's perhaps worse is that behavioral scientists pretty much know it and don't really care.

Though the problem didn't start with Milton Friedman (we'll get back to where the problem started in a minute), it was Friedman that popularized what's called the 'positivist' approach to economics. Very briefly, this approach to social science treats social phenomena as real, objective entities capable of being measured and studied. In short, economists (and psychologists for that matter) adopted the assumptions and methods of the natural sciences (e.g., physics, chemistry, biology) to study human and social phenomena (like economies).

Of course, human actors aren't at all really like the unconscious things that are studied in the natural sciences – an important point that philosophers have pointed out for centuries now. But Friedman argued that, so long as humans act *as if* they follow clear and predictable decision patterns, then economic models can predict accurately enough how an economy will perform under certain circumstances. Thus, although human actors do not in fact make our decisions from a given set of options with real and objectve probabilities (even if unknown and, thus, subjectively assigned), we can see that, for the most part, humans pursuing their own subejctive well-being act very much like this purely rational economic actor – *homo economicus*, as it has come to be called.

Now, while there is significant appeal to this 'as if' theorizing and it has long dominated the economic mainstream, there are also a couple of big drawbacks to it. First, if our models are not accurate reflections of how humans really behave, if they are only simple and artificial 'as if' models that generally capture how we tend to behave, then we can't really say if or when someone will *not* behave that way. We just don't know. So we can never tell when we're going to get it wrong.

As it turns out, this is a pretty big problem for economists. For example, except for a handful of Austrian school economists, no one saw the 2007–2008 housing bubble collapse coming. Economists' models were built on various assumptions and predictors that were all still quite strong at the time. Almost everyone predicted continued growth for years to come. But, we know now how wrong they all were.

In fact, economists' track record in predicting economic phenomena is *horrible*. They almost never get it right. Sometimes they get it close enough to right that they'll claim a win, but just as often (or moreso), their predictions prove the opposite of what transpires. Some economists like to play both sides of the fence, making contradictory predictions so that they can point to the prediction that proved right and pat themselves on the back. And every time a prediction fails, they can always find a convenient excuse for why they got it wrong. But the fact remains –

we can't accurately predict economic actors because we don't really know *how* people make their decisions.

A second problem with 'as if' theorizing is that it is developed from how people *behaved* in the past. Basically, economists collect a bunch of data on how people behaved in a certain scenario, create an economic model with all the factors that they believe to have influenced the behavior, and run a statistical regession to 'fit' the data to the model. In other words, with the data they collected from past behaviors, they generate specific numbers that they can attach to the variables of their model and make claims like 'a 1.000% increase in marginal tax rate corresponds to a 2.732% increase in economic investment.' I made those numbers up, but I kid you not, that's the supposed level of scientific precision that they pretend to achieve.

Now, of course, the problem with this is that we *don't* always do the same things over and over again. We learn. We change our preferences. Sometimes we just get tired of doing the same old thing and want to try something new. Our culture evolves and we come to think differently about things over time. The idea that the past predicts the future is so fallacious that it's amazing that it holds so much weight still.

The fact is, the social sciences are in a crisis right now – it is called the reproducibility crisis. This crisis originated from an immense effort on the part of a large community of scholars to reproduce 100 of the most seminal research studies in psychology,[6] studies that really shaped how psychologists understand how we think and act. Only 40% replicated. A staggering 60% of the 'scientific effects' that scholars found years ago disappeared when tried on a new sample of participants. That's truly frightening. We scientists don't understand people nearly as well as we pretend to.

A third important problem is that, while economic models provide a semblance of scientific rigor, it is in fact merely *scientism* – the misuse of scientific methods on things science cannot study. A susceptible public – and scientific community for that matter – eats up economic studies as if they prove something. But what's funny is that most 'scientific' studies of economic phenomena are contradicted by other studies. For example, if you were interested in what economic effect the minimum wage has on businesses, you can pull up one of many studies that shows that an increase in the minumum wage has no effect on, say, unemployment or other plausible outcomes. But you could find even more studies that find the opposite, that it has a significant effect on employment. Which studies do you believe? They're all 'scientific' and peer reviewed. As it turns out, you can find a 'scientific' paper to 'prove' just about any ideological prior that you have.

---

6 Open Science Collaboration. 2015. Estimating the reproducibility of psychological science. *Science*, 349(6251): aac4716.

A big reason for this is that people act according to their own beliefs. If you study a certain group that believes ideology A, then you will find that their actions comport to the expectations that a research with that same ideology has, confirming their bias. But another researcher of ideology B could research a different group that believes differently and find the very opposite. Not all social phenomena are so subjective and contingent on beliefs. There are, in fact, actual scientific 'laws' in social science (like the law of supply and demand, the law of diminishing marginal utility, and so forth) but they are very few and far between. What an employer does if and when the minimum wage is increased – whether she simply increases her employees' wages or cuts back her workforce – may depend on whether she believes the law to be just or not.

In short, economics' use of 'as if' theorizing as a basis for forming expectations of what people will choose is incredibly fallacious and dangerous. And to think that a host of behavioral scientists advocate we get the government to use this faulty science to try to manipulate people into making better choices. What could go wrong?

A Wrong Turn

But again, the science didn't go wrong beginning with Friedman. It's pretty interesting because, while the field of psychology had grabbed onto the positivist philosophy very early on and has held fast to that paradigm throughout its history, the field of economics emerged as a more subjectivist field with some objectivist tendencies. It then turned predominantly subjectivist for nearly a half century before subjectivism lost the mainstream to positivism, which has held the predominant position since.

While there have been economic theorists for many centuries, most grant the title of the 'father' of economics to Adam Smith. In *The Wealth of Nations*, Smith theorized that national economies prospered through heightened productivity. He saw the most advanced economies as comprising economic actors that were free to 'divide' their labor, i.e., to specialize in various tasks and, thereby, increase productivity. The insight was brilliant, and spawned a small flood of new interest into how economies worked.

I already overviewed the history of value theory previously. While Marx's economic theory captured a large *political* audience, economic scholaship was largely dissatisfied with Marx's economic theory. It was, again, the marginal revolution that finally got the field of economics moving again.

But in this revolution there were some differences in opinion, most notably with regard to what *utility* really was. For Menger it was a subjective assessment. For Jevons it was a psychological state. Walras supposed it to be a need satisfaction. Most economists didn't take heed of the important, but somewhat subtle, differences between these distinct utility concepts.

In any case, Menger gained a fairly large and important following – the afore-mentioned Austrian school – which adopted and developed a wholly subjectivist science of economics. In other words, the Austrian school started with the premise that human actors were agents to themselves, that they could choose their own ends and form their own subjective preferences. Thus, we cannot really *predict* what they'll do, we can only explain it *ex post* based on what they chose to do. Economics is, thus, a science of explanation only, and not a predictive science.

Other economists, more of the positivist school of thought, took a different path. They adopted Jevons's utility concept (as psychological utility), which Alfred Marshall integrated into mathematical models of economic action. While this math-ematical approach was very attractive, economists of the time couldn't make it work as a scientific framework. They didn't have the necessary foundations of how people would act in a particular instance to aggregate into a valid predictive mathe-matical model. The Austrian school ruled the day.

That is, until John von Neumann and Oskar Morgenstern developed game the-ory in 1944. They laid the theory of rational action – expected utility theory – com-plete with basic axioms. It was the breakthrough the Marshallian positivists were searching for. Suddenly, positivism could work – economics *could* be a predictive science, just like physics.

The Austrian school's subjectivist theories, which had by then become quite profound and extensive, lost their attraction. The economics field flooded to the mathematical modelling approach, which was compellingly (enough) justified by Friedman to ignore futher objections from proponents of the Austrian school.

But the thing is, the Austrian subjectivists were right all along. You can't turn the economy into a math equation. People aren't (all) mindless, predictable autom-atons that follow a strict, prescripted path.

Perhaps most importantly, economists' adoption of equilibrium-based mathe-matical modelling completely precluded the entrepreneur! There is no entrepreneur in modern economic models. In fact, the only theories of entrepreneurship came from the Austrian school.

The turn away from the Austrian school in the 1940s meant that nearly all eco-nomic attention would turn to testable propositions. With very few exceptions, economists ignored the entrepreneur altogether. And most of those few exceptions generally treated the entrepreneur as just a small business.

Theorizing on how businesses got their start was delayed for decades. Today, we still suffer from those effects. Management scholarship developed largely as a branch of microeconomics, still holding to the tradition of positivism. But, of course, one of the largest looming questions for management scholarship was *how did the business come to be in the first place*? Early theories of entrepreneurship in the modern era were problematic, again equating the entrepreneur with a small business.

A breakthrough came in the late 1990s and early 2000s when Scott Shane and Sankaran Venkataraman rediscovered the Austrian school and its work on entrepreneurship.[7] But management scholarship didn't realize that the Austrian school adopted a totally different philosophical foundation. Entrepreneurship scholars cherry-picked Autrian insights and brought them into its still positivist (or 'realist') paradigm.

It didn't work very well. It just led to logical contradictions and confusion. And at the very heart of it all is a persistent, positivist misconception of what *value* is. Entrepreneurship scholars are still trying to figure it all out. I'm actively trying to help the field see that the solution is a turn back to true subjectivism. Whether or not I succeed doesn't matter. What matters is what this all means for *you*.

---

7 Shane, S., & Venkataraman, S. 2000. The promise of entrepreneurship as a field of research. *Academy of Management Review*: 217–226.

Chapter 2
Where Modern Entrepreneurship Theory Goes Awry

Now that you know the background of value theory and how we got where we are today with the marginal utility theory of value, we can now examine how modern entrepreneurship theorists see and understand the entrepreneurial phenomenon through this value-theoretic lens. The goal of this chapter is to show you why business schools aren't very good at teaching entrepreneurship – including or especially, perhaps paradoxically, the super high-cost (e.g., Ivy League) schools (at least for now – who knows, maybe one day one of those huge-endowment schools will hire me on and I'll have to change my tune).

Practitioner educators are only marginally better, if at all. These former (and sometimes active) entrepreneurs have experiences to share and practical lessons they've learned. But it is rare that one truly understands how the economy works. They're specialists that have learned a lot about a very narrow section of the economy. In fact, as I argue in the Preface, most of them don't even really know how or why they're winning. It's hard to teach someone to succeed when they've only gotten lucky – or worse, they turned to teaching because they didn't get lucky.

I don't really mean for this to be an instructor-bashing session. Honestly, I admire and appreciate many entrepreneurship instructors, most have some good, practical insights to share, and they almost all certainly mean well.

The problem is that almost all college entrepreneurship curricula are based in theories of entrepreneurship derived from marginal utility theory, and that means that they're faulty. But, as I'll explain in this chapter, it's worse than that. They're *misleading* in a way that spells doom for most entrepreneurs. That super high new venture failure rate? That's because entrepreneurs don't know what they're doing – even after learning about it in school or from mentors.

Modern Entrepreneurship Theory

What *is* entrepreneurship? What differentiates an entrepreneur from a non-entrepreneur? Is it small business ownership? New venturing? Innovation? Taking chances? What is the *essence* of entrepreneurship? Is there something different about entrepreneurs that makes them entrepreneurs?

Modern entrepreneurship scholarship has worked on these questions for over three decades and continues to come up with only more confusion. We are currently in a bloody (albeit quite cordial) battle of wits over the foundations of entrepreneurship theory. There seems no end in sight.

But there are (at least) *four* different theories in contention (not including my own, which I'm still developing): the Schumpeterian innovator, the Kirznerian opportunity

https://doi.org/10.1515/9783110750805-002

discoverer, the Penrosean opportunity creator, and the Knightian bearer of uncertainty (and risk).

Schumpeterian innovation

The first prominent theory of entrepreneurship was proposed by Joseph Schumpeter, an Austrian economist, in 1911.[8] In it, he described the entrepreneur as an *innovator*, which he defined very broadly. An innovator, for Schumpeter, is different from an *inventor*, who devises a new solution. The innovator is the person who brings something new to market, who *changes* a market.

Schumpeter's work comes during the heyday of the Austrian school. Schumpeter is a trained Austrian subjectivist, but his heart and mind get sort of turned to Walras's theory of marginal utility and general equilibrium theory toward the end of his career. General equilibrium, to remind the reader, is a basic economic assumption that an economy at any point in time is *balanced*, that supply and demand have cleared at a particular price. Certainly, there can be changes to these conditions, causing prices to shift, but these changes are 'exogenous,' i.e., caused by external forces. Whenever there is a change to some condition, the market immediately re-equilibrates to account for that change at a new price condition.

But there's a problem in Walras's account: equilibrium cannot account for growth. So where does the economic growth that has been quickly accelerating – ever since the Enlightenment and the liberalization of the world – come from?

Schumpeter solved this conundrum by introducing the entrepreneur. General equilibrium, he argued, is regularly disrupted by the innovator-entrepreneur, who creates 'new combinations' of resources that are valued more highly. This introduction of some higher-valued innovation alters the general equilibrium state to a new and higher-valued one, causing the economy to shift upwards in growth. An innovation, then, can comprise of a new product, a new and more efficient process, and other market changes that alter how industries compete and the total economic value that they generate.

Schumpeter's theory remains one of the most beloved. But it's hardly infallible. For example, Schumpeter turns away from his Austrian heritage to adopt a Walrasian concept of marginal utility. Thus, a higher-valued innovation and equilibrium state are *objective* and measurable, at least in principle.

Can you calculate the total economic value of a new innovation *a priori*? That sure would be nice, wouldn't it?

---

8 Schumpeter, J. A. 1911. *Theorie der wirtschaftlichen Entwicklung.* Leipzig: Duncker & Humbolt.

Kirznerian opportunity discovery

While Schumpeter's theory occupied theorists for a while, it clearly wasn't workable for a true and holistic theory of entrepreneurship. For starters, there is a lot of entrepreneurship that isn't innovation – many entrepreneurs are simply imitators or even arbitrageurs who can make a quick buck from buying low and selling high. So Schumpeter's innovator-entrepreneur was a good start, and had some promising features, but couldn't capture entrepreneurship *in toto*.

Enter Israel Kirzner, a South African who also trained in the Austrian school under Mises and Hayek. Mises in fact advanced a very important theory of entrepreneurship in his own work, which I'll come back to later. Kirzner[9] saw in Mises's theory of entrepreneurship the solution to one of economists' most glaring problems, which they had persistently just ignored for decades. Economists had almost all fully bought into general equilibrium theory (the one that omits the entrepreneur) as a framework for economic analysis. To reiterate from the previous chapter, this theory supposes the market to be perfectly efficient and at all times in a state of 'general equilibrium.' Equilibrium is that state where the market is fully cleared, where the supply curve intersects with the demand curve, and a stable price emerges from the intersect. Of course, supply, demand, and prices change over time, and so the equilibrium point of the market also changes. But, Kirzner recognized, economists couldn't explain *how* it shifted. Its persistence within general equilibrium was simply assumed. No one knew how a supposedly stable state of equilibrium, upon meeting some disruptive change to or in the market, would find its way back to equilibrium at the new point.

For Kirzner, the entrepreneur was the solution to this important problem. If we understand the market as an evolving *process*, and not always in some static state of equilibrium, we can see that there *is* a role for the entrepreneur, and that is to apply their unique knowledge and information of the new state of the market and 'correct' the disequilibrated state, thereby moving the market to the new optimal state.

A quick example might be helpful to illustrate Kirzner's argument. In 2021, the U.S. and much of the world faced a massive shortage of lumber, along with many other key supplies, due to the disruption of the supply chain caused by government lockdowns in the wake of the Covid-19 pandemic. Supply chains find an efficient equilibrium in the constant movement of ships around the world. This regular movement was stifled by government-imposed closures, which led to shipping barges congregating in certain nations, not returning as they normally would. As a result, supply chains were severely disrupted, and the problems were only exacerbated by mishaps such as the blocking of the Suez Canal when a cargo ship got stuck sideways.

---

9 Kirzner, I. M. 1973. *Competition and Entrepreneurship*. Chicago, IL: University of Chicago Press.

This disruption to the supply chain has caused massive shortages across the globe. Here, we find the former equilibrium state of the market, prior to the lockdowns and shortages, woefully unable to deal with these supply chain issues, and the market finds itself in a state of inefficient *disequilibrium*. Standard Walrasian theory doesn't really know where to go from here. Enter Kirzner's entrepreneur. The entrepreneur, 'alert' to these market inefficiencies and to specific market information, looks for a way to correct the inefficiencies, capturing a profit as reward. In this case, entrepreneurs might solve the issues in a few different ways. They might find new supply to fill the shortage.[10] They might develop workarounds to government policies that were inhibiting the logistical flow of the supply chain. Or they might find alternative solutions to consumers' needs that do not require use of the short supply. Whatever the solution, entrepreneurs find new ways to address consumers' needs within the new state of economic affairs, and create a new efficient state – a new equilibrium.

But Kirzner's conception of entrepreneurship, while an important step, is also problematic, and has been roundly criticized. It is true that exogenous shocks to the market can create market inefficiencies for entrepreneurs to correct. In a legitimate sense, we can call this the discovery of real entrepreneurial 'opportunities.' But a lot of times, entrepreneurs themselves creatively make these opportunities for themselves. The curious case of the Pet Rock is a helpful illustration. There was no market need for a rock to be sold as a pet. Nothing in the market changed that suddenly made rocks valuable to have – *except* for the clever marketing actions of the entrepreneur himself, Gary Dahl. Perhaps you could say that the opportunity didn't arise until Dahl had persuaded people to want a Pet Rock, but that seems disingenuous. In this case, there was no opportunity just waiting to be discovered. So this theory appears incomplete.

Penrosean opportunity creation

Although Edith Penrose did not produce a theory of entrepreneurship *per se*, her theory of firm growth[11] has been adapted modernly to explain the missing creative element of Kirzner's theory. Penrose was a student of Austrian school economist Fritz Machlup, from whom she developed an affinity toward Schumpeter's work. In Schumpeter's work she saw the solution to the yet unanswered question: how do

---

10 As a side note, this is why price-gouging laws are harmful, and not helpful. The entrepreneurial impetus to draw in new supply is generally the profit motive, which is curtailed by price-gouging laws. So, in shortages, price-gouging laws delay the re-supply by making it less profitable to do so. Also, price-gouging laws don't allow the price mechanism to allocate those resources optimally. First-comers get the supply and the late-comers get nothing, even if they need it more. Remember the toilet paper crisis of 2020?

11 Penrose, E. T. 1959. *The Theory of the Growth of the Firm*. Oxford: Blackwell.

firms grow? However, she departs from Schumpeter, and returns back to some of the original subjectivism of the Austrian school, in various ways.

Penrose saw the firm as a collection of resources. But her conception of resources was not the same as the neoclassical economists', who see resources as anything that has utility. Penrose was a subjectivist (per her Austrian school heritage), and so saw resources through the lens of subjectivism. Thus, for her, resources are not simply given utility, but are determined by the *services* to which they are employed. A pile of wood can become a crate, baseball bats, a fire, art, a table, etc. The *resource* that is the pile of wood depends on what use it is put to and how much that use or 'service' is valued. Wood for bats is a different resource than wood for fires – even if it is the same type of wood. We can't say the wood has x amount of utility, because utility depends on *how* it is used and the uses it can be put to are virtually endless.

It is in this conception of subjective resources that we can find the foundations for a theory of the creative entrepreneur, a theory that was mostly elaborated by Austrian school economist Ludwig Lachmann. Lachmann argued that resources, conceived this way, are characterized by *multiple specificity* – i.e., they can be put to (or specified toward) many possible uses. The key task of the entrepreneur, then, is to find new and better uses for the resources they have at their disposal. This entrepreneurial task is sometimes referred to as *bricolage*.

To elaborate somewhat on this principle, what a 'resource' is, actually, is just a concept. In many cases, there is real, physical matter that the resource concept refers to – a stockpile of iron, for example. But not all resources have physical referents. Knowledge and time, for example, are often considered resources, but do not have some physical existence – they only exist in our minds. But whatever the resource concept refers to, physical or cognitive, the concept itself is just an idea. This means that resource concepts can be altered or displaced by other concepts. That pile of iron does not have a single, specific and given use and, thus, given value – it actually has literally endless possible uses. Although most possible uses are low value and, so not worth producing, a creative entrepreneur might engineer a new use previously unimagined that is superior in value to its prevailing uses and, thus, create new economic value.

While this theoretical approach to entrepreneurship is highly promising, the modern version of this view is somewhat problematic. In the modern theory – the opportunity creation approach – its advocates have rescued Kirzner's opportunity concept as its centerpiece. However, in this formulation the corrigible market imperfections are innovatively created by the entrepreneur's own actions. By *causing* a shift in market demand, the market finds itself in manufactured disequilibrium, primed for entrepreneurial correction. Perhaps the clearest example is the fashion industry, where the demand for clothing styles does not preexist, but is engineered by fashion designers and popularized by trendsetters. In other words, fashion is *made* fashionable by its creators.

Again, while promising, this view falls short in some key ways. Most notably, the rescuing of the 'opportunity' concept in the modern presentation of Penrose's and Lachmann's ideas was, I think, a mistake. While a useful metaphor for normal social parlance, the opportunity concept, especially as a central explanatory variable for entrepreneurial science, is imprecise and misleading. It casts an implicit image of some real, objective thing that entrepreneurs either discover or create. But there is, actually, no such thing. It's just a simple (and simplistic) concept that we use as shorthand to explain people's actions. Why did the entrepreneur quit her job? "Because she saw an opportunity and took it" is easier than saying "Because she imagined an idea for a new consumer solution that she hoped and expected others would find sufficiently valuable that they would pay a price higher than the total cost of producing that new solution."

Knightian judgment

The last modern theory worth reviewing originates with Frank Knight, who elaborated on the critical role of uncertainty in the market process, which inhibits market efficiency.[12] Said somewhat differently, Knight in essence dismantled general equilibrium theory by simply observing that equilibrium cannot exist where there is uncertainty. And since uncertainty not only exists virtually everywhere in the real economy, but is pervasive in all of life, the idea and usefulness of general equilibrium is severely conscribed to a matter of curiosity at best. Anything beyond that would be overtly misleading.

Although Knight did not formally elaborate a theory of entrepreneurship in the book, he considered entrepreneurship the central mechanism for dealing with uncertainty. In essence, the entrepreneur bears uncertainty by making judgments. Good judgments, which prove to be correct, are rewarded with profits. Bad judgments are punished with losses. Thus, while general equilibrium theory essentially assumes away profits and losses, these are of course real outcomes that business people actively pursue. And it is from their *judgments* regarding the optimal use of resources, and the values and potential activities of others, that such profits are made or not. If there were no uncertainty, there would be no profits or losses.

As a quick note, let me remark on the radical nature of Knight's concept of uncertainty. Typically, economists understand uncertainty as a soft unpredictability – outcomes in the world are probabilistic, but we often have a hard time optimizing our actions in this probabilistic world because we don't always know the probabilities. And even if we did, there's no guarantee that the outcome we want will be the one that we get, since there's an element of chance. But Knight saw uncertainty as far more radical – and realistic. Why would we assume that all outcomes of the real world can have

---

12 Knight, F. H. 1921. *Risk, Uncertainty and Profit*. New York: Hart, Schaffner, and Marx.

probabilities assigned to them? In fact, this is almost never the case in the real world. What's the probability that I will go swimming today? You might intuitively understand that this question implies a [0,1] option set (don't swim or swim). Some might even take this to imply a 50–50 chance. But that's clearly wrong. The supposed probability depends on all kinds of factors: What's the weather like? Do I like swimming? Is there a pool nearby? Do I have time, etc.? But Knight (and others since him, including myself in my own research) makes a critical observation – ultimately, the decision is mine to make, and I haven't made it yet. There is no probability, because judgment and choice aren't random rolls of the dice or spins of the wheel. They are intentional. Whether you believe in free will or not, we are nowhere near able to predict people's behaviors, even probabilistically. To calculate the probability that I will swim today, you would have to know what all my options are and the comparative probabilities of each. But, as it turns out, the things I can possibly do are literally endless – it is an infinite set of possibilities. And this means that probabilities are essentially wrong and misleading when dealing with true uncertainty, such as that of human action. We can only make judgments in uncertainty – we cannot make probabilistic calculations.

In the modern version of Knight's entrepreneurial judgment theory as put forth by, e.g., Nicolai Foss and Peter Klein,[13] Knight's insights have been expanded to also include the insights of Mises, Penrose and Lachmann. In short, judgment over the allocation and use of resources under uncertainty, and the bearing of the risks associated with that uncertainty, is conceived as the essence of entrepreneurship. The entrepreneurial function is to put resources to new use and, since there is no guarantee that any such new use will pay off, the entrepreneur must risk those resources in the uncertainty of an unknown and unknowable future.

Interestingly, this framework makes the entrepreneur the capitalist, the owner of resources, who has ultimate say over how their owned resources are used. So, while we might call someone an entrepreneur who has a creative idea, if that person funds the venture with others' money, that person is not the one bearing the uncertainty. In fact, in this case, it is the investors, who put their own resources at risk, that are the real entrepreneurs. This interpretive fact has led to some criticisms of this framework, as it essentially redefines what an entrepreneur is such that there is no difference between entrepreneur and investor/capitalist, even if it was not their idea.

Modern Entrepreneurship Theory Applied

I hope you can see some of the merits of these modern theories of entrepreneurship. But despite their virtues, their application in the classroom has been challenging.

---

13 Foss, N. J., & Klein, P. G. 2012. *Organizing Entrepreneurial Judgment: A new approach to the firm.* Cambridge, UK: Cambridge University Press.

In fact, the academic field of entrepreneurship has been widely criticized as having one of the widest academic–practitioner divides. These modern entrepreneurship theories are rarely even taught in the classroom and, when they are, are taught as informational only. It is hard to see, as an entrepreneur, why I should care whether the essence of entrepreneurs is opportunity discovery or judgment.

Entrepreneurship textbooks do a decent job of bringing some of the basic theoretical ideas into practical terms, often with case studies as illustrations. The prevailing textbook approach is the opportunity discovery approach. Students are taught how to spot a valuable opportunity, how to business plan, how to assemble a team, collect resources, strategize, market, launch, and manage the venture. But this approach to entrepreneurial education is premised upon the mistaken assumptions of the opportunity discovery view – that the entrepreneur can discover an opportunity that is presumed *ex ante* valuable, and go from there. But value is radically uncertain, as Knight explained, yet to be determined. So the textbook approach to new venturing is very risky, advocating that the entrepreneur make huge bets on ideas that very often do not pan out.

And, perhaps worse, the case methodology can be useful for business strategizing and for capturing the benefits of experiential learning *sans* experience. But entrepreneurial journeys are always radically unique – different people doing different things in different places and different circumstances. The successful approach of one venture is virtually never exactly the right approach for any other venture. I sometimes see entrepreneurs very closely mimicking their entrepreneur heroes. Now-defunct Theranos's Elizabeth Holmes, who tried to follow in Steve Jobs's footsteps to such a tee that she would even dress like him, comes to mind. But Holmes was not Jobs, and Theranos was not Apple. Every entrepreneurial situation is different, and entrepreneurs cannot always or even often rely on others' situational experiences. They must make their own judgments and forge their own path.

Fortunately, most experienced entrepreneurs recognize these drawbacks of textbook entrepreneurship. And, since many university entrepreneurship classes are taught by experienced practitioners, many of the modern classes are no longer taught using the simple textbook approach. Often, entrepreneurship classes are instead taught using some standardized methodology, such as the Lean Startup method and/or the business model canvas. But although these are widely regarded for a reason – they have proven adequately successful, and are based in largely good and correct principles – they are also problematic in various ways. Lean Startup, for example, was devised experientially by entrepreneur Eric Ries,[14] who landed upon some key principles of success, such as learning from consumers and quick adaptation. But he also gets several things wrong, such as early launch. The

---

[14] Ries, E. 2011. *The Lean Startup: How today's entrepreneurs use continuous innovation to create radically successful businesses*. New York: Crown Business.

principle behind the early launch of the 'minimum viable product' – to instigate the learning–adaptation process as quickly as possible to minimize losses is good, but it doesn't sufficiently understand the value process and so runs into problems of building value perceptions. In fact, it almost guarantees that your first customers will be dissatisfied, which can be a big problem as I'll explain in Chapter 14.

Effectuation theory is also sometimes taught in the classroom as an alternative approach to the standard textbook method. Effectuation theory is not a theory of entrepreneurship *per se* (which is why I didn't introduce it in the prior section), but researchers have found that experienced entrepreneurs tend toward a more adaptive approach to entrepreneurship (like the Lean method) than most inexperienced entrepreneurs, and that the adaptive approach tends to be more successful without risking as much. Theorists have uncovered several standard principles to this 'effectuation method,' which include risking only what you're willing and able to lose and no more, selling yourself (and not necessarily a particular idea) to others to get their buy-in and resource contributions, and then searching for the most valuable things you can do with your pooled resources (rather than starting with a particular idea already in mind). This is again a more successful approach than the textbook approach, but it is slower, more complicated, and can be difficult for entrepreneurs, especially if they're new to new venturing or if they're not extroverted or self-confident.

In short, entrepreneurship is not easily taught. In fact, entrepreneurship education has historically been considered something of a joke, something to forget once you start getting your hands dirty. And I can't fault experienced entrepreneurs for this perception. But I also think those entrepreneurs are fooling themselves if they think that their own mentorship is vastly better in creating successful entrepreneurs. I see mentorships as regularly peddled, even in universities, but very rarely to success. In fact, they may do more harm than good, again because each entrepreneurial venture and situation is too unique for successful application of one entrepreneur's experience to another venture. This is not universally the case – serial entrepreneurs *do* get better at their craft over time, so experience does matter. But serial entrepreneurs exhibit these experiential benefits most clearly when they serially enter related industries, where such experience matters. This same principle applies to mentorship – mentors are largely only helpful when they are expressly familiar with your industry. But this means that the best possible mentors are your competitors, who aren't likely to want to coach you to success.

But the problems of entrepreneurial education, and the academic–practitioner divide, are relics of weak and incomplete theory, particularly based in classical utility theories of value. My thesis in this book is that, by getting value theory right, it provides a foundation for a *good* entrepreneurial education, one that is universally applicable and adaptable to any venture and entrepreneur.

Chapter 3
Value as a *Process*

Okay, so now I've told you what value *isn't*. But what *is* value and why has it been so difficult to pin down? I mean, I'm claiming that some of the best minds in the world have gotten the most central construct in economics wrong for centuries, are still getting it wrong (and don't know it), and that I've solved the mystery where no one else could. Well, not exactly. Actually, I'm building on a long economic tradition – the Austrian school – that has been generally neglected and dismissed for largely ephemeral and dubious reasons, as well as a new and growing academic movement in the marketing discipline. My contribution is mostly connecting these schools of thought, which have developed independently and ignorant of each other.

My main thesis is that each of these schools of thought – even marginal utility theory – has gotten a *part* of value theory right. Value is a *process*. And each of these theories captures a distinct part of that process. Individually, they are each enough to develop and make sense of socio-economic phenomena. But none is sufficiently complete to produce a fully coherent theory of entrepreneurship or to prevent theoretical errors.

Once the entire value process is grasped, the picture comes into focus, and we can finally see and understand the essential entrepreneurial challenge.

Is Value *Subjective* or *Objective*?

It is widely accepted that value is *subjective*, but what does that mean?

According to *Merriam-Webster*, the word 'subjective' means, first, "of, relating to, or constituting a subject," but also, secondly, "characteristic of or belonging to reality as perceived rather than as independent of mind." 'Objective,' correspondingly, can mean "expressing or dealing with facts or conditions as perceived without distortion by personal feelings, prejudices, or interpretations" or else "having reality independent of the mind." But note that the two definitions for both of these terms are hardly identical. In fact, although they're clearly related, it would be a bit of a stretch to even call them synonymous. But out of these two distinct meanings of the terms has arisen significant confusion and ambiguity about the real nature of value.

Generally, when an economist tells you that value is *subjective*, he or she means that it is *idiosyncratic* – that it is unique to each individual. This is because the usefulness of something depends on the idiosyncratic needs, situation, and preferences of each individual. The value you get out of an all-you-can-eat sushi buffet depends on how hungry you are, how much food your body generally needs, whether or not you have any allergy or sensitivity to any of the ingredients, and of course how much you like sushi. It also depends on time and circumstance, e.g.,

https://doi.org/10.1515/9783110750805-003

whether you have the time or money for such a meal. Thus, the total *utility* of that sushi dinner, priced at $29.95/person, is different for everyone. Most people, at any given time, value the sushi dinner *less* than the $30, which they keep, or instead they prefer some other thing to the sushi dinner and spend the money on that something else. So at any time, only a very small subset of the total population will actually be at the sushi restaurant.

In this formulation of value, it is *subjective* in the first sense of the term, but it is *objective* in the second – that is, although it is idiosyncratic, it is nonetheless *real*. The sushi dinner has *real*, albeit heterogeneous, utility for each of us.

But modern scholars have begun to push back on this formulation of value, as we discussed in Chapter 1. Let's say I ordered dinner at a sushi restaurant at a price tag of $30 for the all-you-can-eat option, but the restaurant is slammed and I wait for an hour for my first roll before deciding that it was taking far too long, and that I needed to get going if I was going to make the 9 p.m. movie showing that I already got tickets for. How much value was there in that sushi dinner? It would seem that the answer is *none*. In fact, you could argue that it was *negative*, that I was made worse off by taking up my night with only frustration and unsated hunger to show for it.

Now, you might say, "But Professor Packard, it's not that there was no value in the meal, it's just that you didn't *get* the meal." Okay, let's revise the example and say, then, that I got my first roll and the fish was rancid. After a single bite, I spit it out and nearly lose my lunch too. The other rolls I had ordered are the same. To make matters worse, the restaurant owner demands payment for the food I ordered, but didn't eat. Was there value in this scenario?

Real Value

What some scholars – Steven Vargo and Robert Lusch in particular – have concluded is that there is no value except and until a benefit is achieved (or a 'service' is provided). Note how 'benefit' is different from 'utility,' which is usefulness. *Usefulness* is imagined and expected, *benefit* is real and attained.

Brilliant 19th century French thinker Frédéric Bastiat explained: "the great economic law is this: Services are exchanged for services."[15] What he meant by this is that what people *really* want when they buy something is not the thing *per se*, but the service it provides, the benefit they expect to get from it. You don't buy a burger, a shirt, an iPhone just to have it but for what it does for you. You might argue that collectibles you buy just to have, but those also you buy for the fun, the status, the accomplishment that having them provides. Even when what that thing that you get in exchange is *money*, the reason why you want that money is ultimately

---

15 Bastiat, F. 1848. *Essays on Political Economy*: Kessinger Publishing, LLC, pp. 161–162.

the benefit that you can get from it – typically the things it can purchase, but sometimes even the status and prestige that just having the money affords.

But let's be careful here. Vargo and Lusch's *service-dominant logic* is still imprecise in in that it equates value with a service. But a service is the *purveyor* of a benefit, and not the benefit itself. In the service-dominant logic, it is assumed that what constitutes a service is that which provides a benefit. But this is a very narrow conception of 'service' – more typically and, I think, correctly, services are *attempts* at providing benefit. It is certainly conceivable that a service fails in doing so.

From this service concept, however, we finally arrive at our formal definition of value. *Real value* is a *change* in one's status from a state of lesser well-being to a state of greater well-being – it is *benefit*, an *increase in well-being*.

The implications of this definition are important. Remember that sushi buffet? How much value did I *really* get? The right answer is *less than zero* – I was *harmed* by the experience, my status went from higher to lower well-being, in a few different ways. First, it was disgusting and gave me a stomachache. Second, I'm out my time, time that I *could have* used to do something else, something more valuable (recall that this is what is called the 'opportunity cost'). And third, I never got the meal that I needed. I was left hungry. That sushi joint took my money, and I didn't get an ounce of benefit – I was left *worse off*.

Subjective Value

But this real benefit isn't the only thing that matters. In fact, I don't even know how much actual benefit I'll get from some product when I need to decide if I want to buy it. If value is real, objective benefit attained in consumption, how can I use that in my expected utility calculus to make economic decisions. Or, in more simple terms, if I can't know what value I'm going to get, how do I decide if I want to buy it?

The standard economic decision-making process is often given as a value-price-cost, or VPC, framework (see Fig. 3.1). In it, the total economic value created by a producer is given as the total value created minus the total cost of its production: gain minus loss.

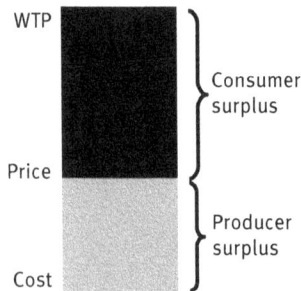

Fig. 3.1: The Traditional VPC Framework.

That total new value created is split between the producer and the consumer, depending on the price. The producer must sell at a price (P) higher than cost (C). The consumer will only buy at a price (P) lower than the expected value they'll get from it, assessed as maximum willingness to pay (WTP). So, depending on industry and market conditions, P will be somewhere between C and WTP. For example, under monopoly conditions, P is expected to be pegged up close to WTP, whereas in conditions of fierce industry competition, it would be expected to plummet close to C. The consumer captures a surplus from the exchange in that the total value he or she got was greater than the cost he or she had to give up, which was the price. The producer also captures a surplus in that the price gained from the consumer is greater than their all-in costs to produce it – their profit. In this way, and to the extent that there is no coercion or fraud, economic exchange is truly win-win.

Now, as we just realized a moment ago, we can't know at this stage what the value (i.e., benefit) will actually be, especially for some brand-new product that we've never tried before. But even with familiar products, we can't know for sure exactly what value we'll get from them – it depends on a lot of things. The value you get from your favorite foods depends a whole lot on how hungry you are (the quip 'hunger is the best seasoning' rings true for a reason). So, in a real sense, every value experience you have will be unique in some ways.

So this is where subjective value comes in. Economic decisions are made according to *subjective value*. The best and most accurate formulation of subjective value is developed by the Austrian school of economics, which I introduced in the preface. Carl Menger, the school's 'founder,' defines subjective value as "the importance that individual goods or quantities of goods attain for us because we are conscious of being dependent on command of them for the satisfaction of our needs."[16] That's a great definition, but let me put it a little differently. Something is subjectively valuable to us to the extent that we *value* it – that is, subjective value relates to the *verb* form of 'value.'

So WTP is a *subjective value*, and not *objective value*.

Value as a Process

What we can conclude here is that value is not *either* subjective *or* objective – it's not one or the other, *it's both*. There is *subjective value* in how people value things and a *real* or *objective value* in the real benefits achieved. These are, in fact, distinct.

This is an important insight, because it means that all of our theories, which have exclusively dealt with one or the other, are incomplete. Marginal utility theory,

---

16 Menger, C. 2007 [1871]. *Principles of Economics*. Auburn, A.L.: Ludwig von Mises Institute, p. 115.

on which virtually all of mainstream economic theory is constructed, is based in what philosophers call a 'reified' value concept, meaning that it is a subjective concept made objective. Utility is, to remind you, 'subjective' in the sense that it is idiosyncratic, but objective in the sense that it is presumed real and given. The service-dominant logic proposes a wholly objective value concept in the 'service' (i.e., benefit) that a good produces for its consumer. The Austrian school embraces a wholly subjective value concept, the value one ascribes to a good. All of these (including my strongly favored Austrian school) are capturing only part of the story.

This is where understanding value as a process comes in. What I've developed is a *process* theory of value, by which I mean that it considers value to be dynamic and evolutionary. In other words, how we value things over time keeps changing as we learn, as our needs and preferences evolve, and as new solutions are introduced to the market. As a result, the real value we know and have over time also evolves as we find and create for ourselves better experiences – we learn over time how to make our life better and better.

I'm going to really go into some depth into this idea for you and show you how it changes how we think about entrepreneurship. But before I can do this, we need to lay a little philosophical groundwork. It gets a little deep, and you might do just fine skipping this section. But this is the foundation for why subjective value and objective value are both valid and must be incorporated into the theory, and is going to give us some cognitive foundations for the chapters that are to follow.

Representationalism

Representationalism is the prevailing philosophical view of human perception. It says, basically, that we don't perceive reality *per se*. What we 'see' or 'hear' or 'feel,' etc., is a mental 'picture' that our minds create for ourselves out of sensory stimuli.

Have you seen the Warner Bros. movie *The Matrix*? It's a classic by now, so if you haven't seen it yet, I don't feel bad about spoiling it – that's on you. In the movie, the people of the world are plugged into a networked artificial simulation of reality (that is called 'the Matrix'). When the protagonist, Neo, gets 'unplugged' from this system and has difficulty grasping the new (and actually real) reality that he finds himself in, his mentor, Morpheus, plugs him back into a simple simulation to show him how what he thought was 'reality' was all just a simulation. The simple simulation was that of a lounge chair, and nothing else, not even a floor. Neo touches the chair and feels it.

"This isn't real?" he asks.

"What is *real*?" Morpheus replies. "How do you define *real*? If *real* is what you can feel, smell, taste, and see, then *real* is simply electrical signals interpreted by your brain."

This is the essence of representationalism. We don't consciously experience reality directly. Reality is consciously perceived through our sensory systems – electrical signals interpreted by our brains. In essence, your minds creates and plays a movie of reality for your consciousness to 'watch' or experience from the sensory signals it gets. We're nowhere close to understanding how this happens; it's really quite remarkable. In fact, philosopher David Chalmers calls this 'the hard problem' of philosophy, the task of explaining how and why *objective* experience is accompanied by conscious, *subjective* experience – why we even have experience. It's the 'hard problem' because it may be impossible to ever solve.

This is important because it is not at all uncommon for us to experience something *other than* reality *per se*. The obvious examples are illusions and hallucinations. But it's far more pervasive than just those obvious cases. In fact, cognitive psychologist Donald Hoffman believes (with compelling evidence) that our brains purposively *misrepresent* reality in certain ways that improve survivability. Neuroscientist Beau Lotto[17] similarly argues that our brains alter the perception of reality in fundamental ways that lead us to see the risks of reality not always as dangers but often as curiosities and challenges, which is why we laud the risk-takers – explorers and innovators – and not the careful rule-followers.

But what this means is that there are two sides to every experience: (1) an *objective* side and (2) a *subjective* side. The 'objective' side is the part of the experience that is *real*, the change that is actually happening in reality. When we eat a meal, there are physical and physiological processes going on, ambient processes, digestive processes, and neurological processes, for example. The 'subjective' side, on the other hand, is what happens in your mind, what is often called the 'sensory experience,' but I will call the *conscious experience*.

What you 'perceive' is the *conscious experience only*. You can't 'see' reality *per se*. You don't have access to it, except indirectly through your senses. Your senses get stimulated and send their corresponding signals to your brain, which creates a mental 'image' therefrom, which is your conscious experience.

Because of this, what you consciously experience can become disconnected in certain ways from reality in so-called illusory experiences. The passage of time is a common illusion, when it 'flies when you're having fun,' for example. It is, in fact, very common to experience mini-illusions throughout our day, where we perceive something in the background of our consciousness and presume its cause as part of our general conscious experience and its interpretation, when in reality it was caused by something else. Inside your new Ford Mustang, for example, you might smirk at the mechanical power exuded in the loud, low rumble of the engine – a sound that has, in fact, been artificially manufactured electronically since 2015.

---

17 Lotto, B. 2017. *Deviate: The science of seeing differently*. New York, NY: Hachette Books.

This is the essential explanation of the objective–subjective duality of experience. It is why value is both objective *and* subjective.

Mental Models

Another important philosophical foundation that will come into play in our journey toward understanding and learning value is what is often called one's *worldview*, i.e., how we see and understand reality. Because, per representationalism, we don't see reality directly, but represent or *simulate* that reality as a conscious experience, there is an interpretive layer that parses the inputs of perception and creates from them understanding and meaning.

For example, as I write this book, I am looking at a computer screen, I am hearing the air conditioner, I am feeling the soft office chair and the clothes on my back. But what I'm really experiencing are, of course, simply different colors, sound waves, and pressures that are stimulating my sensory nerves. I experience these *as* a computer screen, as the sound of the air conditioner, and the feel of an office chair and clothes because my mind interprets them as I experience them. I have in my mind categorical concepts (like computer screen, air conditioner, etc.) that my mind will insert into the representation that it creates for me.

The way it works, in a nutshell, is that our minds have an active and ever-growing mental model (some call it a mental map) of reality in our minds. We sometimes say that this mental model is the lens through which we perceive reality. This is, in a way, quite literal. This mental model is comprised of all the concepts that we have learned and all their causal linkages. When I say that I know that pressing my foot on the accelerator makes my car go, that claim is chock-full of implicit assumptions, meaningful concepts, and causal linkages that allow me to understand and navigate my reality.

The term *learning* means, essentially and most precisely, a revision to one's mental model. We learn when we add to or alter our mental model in some way. Altering the mental model is often described as 'changing one's mind,' which is an apt descriptor. Each layer of learning is constructed atop lower, fundamental assumptions about how the world works – we add to our mental model by interpreting new information in coherence and conformity to our more basic assumptions. So what we mean by 'worldview' is really the more foundational level of assumptions we have made about how the world works. All other causal assumptions are constructed atop those base assumptions. This is why changing our entire worldview is so difficult and is aptly described as a 'mental crisis.' It is also why the older we get the more stubborn or 'set in our ways' we also tend to get. It becomes too difficult for us to change how we view and understand the world because so much of our knowledge is premised upon those base assumptions. So when challenges to our worldview are presented, we tend to dismiss or ignore them or else stretch interpretation in order to keep our fundamental beliefs intact.

Mental representation is a process that employs our mental model actively as a *simulator*. With specific inputs, we put them through the causal interpretation machine of the mental model to play them out to their implication. What we think or expect is thus wholly dependent on the causal interpretations we have made in constructing our mental model of reality. What scientists have called 'rationality' would thus be an utter and perfect coherence of our mental model with the laws of nature. As a side note, the concept of 'rationality' as understood by social scientists is utter nonsense, but that's a topic for another day.

The Valuation Process

So now that we can see that there are two sides to the value experience, let's turn it into a cyclical process. We'll start with the objective value experience – the experience of some benefit in consuming some good, let's say pizza (I might be hungry as I write this).

What happens when I eat that first slice? This is my book, so I'm putting pepperoni, Italian sausage, and bacon on there. You can do what you want with your own mental example. The first bite comes at peak need – I am *hungry*. The magnitude of my need – a lack of caloric matter within my digestive system from which I can metabolize the energy I need to properly function physiologically – is accompanied by an experiential feeling of what Mises calls 'uneasiness,' in this case hunger pangs. So, when I take that first bite, the taste of the pizza, which is amazing, is severely augmented by the initial and powerful relief of that uneasiness. That bite feels *good*. It tingles my taste buds, it warms my insides, and my body immediately sets to its digestion. I already feel a little less hungry. There is both a physiological change *and* an accompanying experience of pleasure and satisfaction.

But that conscious experience is not *subjective value* as we have conceptualized it. Subjective value is, instead, an action – we *value* things. This happens *after* this pizza-eating experience. I *value* the pizza – I ascribe to it the pleasure and satisfaction that I just experienced. This is where subjective value derives.

Because the term 'value' has a noun and a verb form that are, in fact, distinct – the noun form is the benefit gained, while the verb form is the attribution of that noun-form value to something – let's better distinguish these by using the verb *valuate* instead of the verb *value*.

After I've eaten the pizza, I valuate the experience, which means that I assess the subjective experience and attribute it to what I perceive are its causes. In this case the experience is pretty straightforward – I ate a pizza slice and had an enjoyable taste sensation as well as relief of my hunger pangs. So I valuate the pizza for that experience.

But the valuation process is also a learning process – I am comparing the experience to what I expected it to be. In fact, there are *two* valuation processes – a *predictive* valuation and an *assessment* valuation. Before I purchase and consume the pizza, I form a predictive valuation of the experience that I expect the pizza will do for me – how good it will taste and how nice it will be to relieve those hunger pangs. After the experience, I compare my subjective experience with that expectation and revise what I know about that pizza for future reference. That pizza was awesome, I'm going to go back to that place from now on. My future predictive valuations will then be based on this new value knowledge.

So we can start to see that value is actually a cyclical process, constant and never-ending, as we remain aware of our continuous experiences and adjusting our value knowledge and expectations based on those experiences. I'll explain each of the stages of this process in the following chapters.

Revising the Economic Calculus

So let's talk about what this means. In the classic formulation, we would assess economic value creation in the VPC framework. As a quick reminder, value in this framework is assessed as customer willingness to pay (WTP), the total price that, when put to it, they'd be willing to pay if it was asked of them. A penny more, and they'd walk away and say, "No thanks, too pricey." P is the price charged by the producer. And C is the total cost of production, including both primary (e.g., materials, labor, marketing, etc.) and secondary (e.g., accounting, office space, janitorial services, etc.) costs.

What you end up with is an analysis that looks essentially like this. So long as consumers are willing to pay more than the selling price, they're happy. They get a 'consumer surplus' beyond what they were asked to give up. And, so long as the price charged is greater than the costs of production, the producer also gets a surplus, which we call *profit*.

Let's keep using that stupid sushi restaurant as an example. The price tag on the meal was $30. Clearly I was willing to pay at least that. Let's say I would have gone up to $40 for that meal – more than that, I would have gone somewhere else. And the restaurant makes the sushi for, on average, $10 per customer, all in. That is, considering all the costs – building rent and expenses, employees, food costs, etc. – the restaurant divides those costs across all their customers and it comes out to be $10 total per customer in costs. So, according to this analysis, the restaurant has created $30 in value. $30!! Great deal! I got $40 of expected benefit, and it cost $10 to produce that benefit. We call this total economic value created. I capture $10 of that created value, and the sushi restaurant pockets $20 of profit.

But hang on now, let's remember the whole story here. I didn't actually *get* $40 in value. I *actually* got *$0* in value. In fact, you could legitimately argue that I got *-$100* in value. That is, you would have to pay me $100 to be willing to go through that same awful experience again.

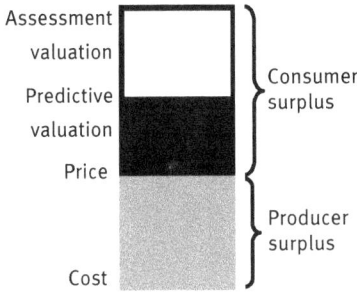

Fig. 3.2: Revised VPC Framework.

Well, that changes the whole analysis, doesn't it? In other words, you can't just stop at willingness to pay – that's only an *expectation* of value (what I will call a *predictive valuation*). It's not the value *per se*. In fact, our value expectations are wrong quite often.

In reality, we don't know what the *real* value is until we've actually experienced it. How much benefit did I *really* get? So it isn't correct to assess economic value with respect to WTP. Instead, WTP is just a prediction of value, and the *actual* consumer surplus is with respect to the benefits assessed *after* the experience (see Fig. 3.2). In this case, I assess the total value to be -$100.

What's the *true* economic value created? Well, I was harmed to the tune of $100 and had to pay $30 to get it. So, in total, I incur $130 in damages, while the restaurant still makes its $20 profit. The total economic value created in this scenario is actually -$110, since the restaurant used $10 of economic resources to hurt me $100-worth.

Now, it's true that the restaurant still walked away with a nice little profit. This is why economists and business scholars haven't really paid much attention to the *true* nature of value. From the business's perspective, who cares?

Well, you should, and here's why. What am I going to do now? Am I ever going back to that restaurant? Of course not. So that restaurant is down one customer. Oh, but I'm not done yet. I'm going to tell my friends about it. Down a few more prospective customers. And I'm going to leave a terrible, 1-star review online. Down a lot more customers. And I am fully justified in doing so. I was put out $130 in exchange for the restaurant's profit of $20. I am hurting, and I want to see that restaurant burn (well, not literally). Honestly, I'm a pretty mild-mannered guy, and it takes a lot to rile me up. But this restaurant crossed a line, and I'm going to make it my mission to protect others from them.

In other words, the restaurant didn't just walk away with a profit. You have to look further than that. This could be a business-ender for them if I have anything to say about it. This is why good businesses are relentless in ensuring that every customer experience is a positive one. Yes, it can be costly in the short term. But good businesses play the long game, building customer excitement and loyalty.

Let's extend our new analysis a little more. Consider the scenarios in Fig. 3.3:

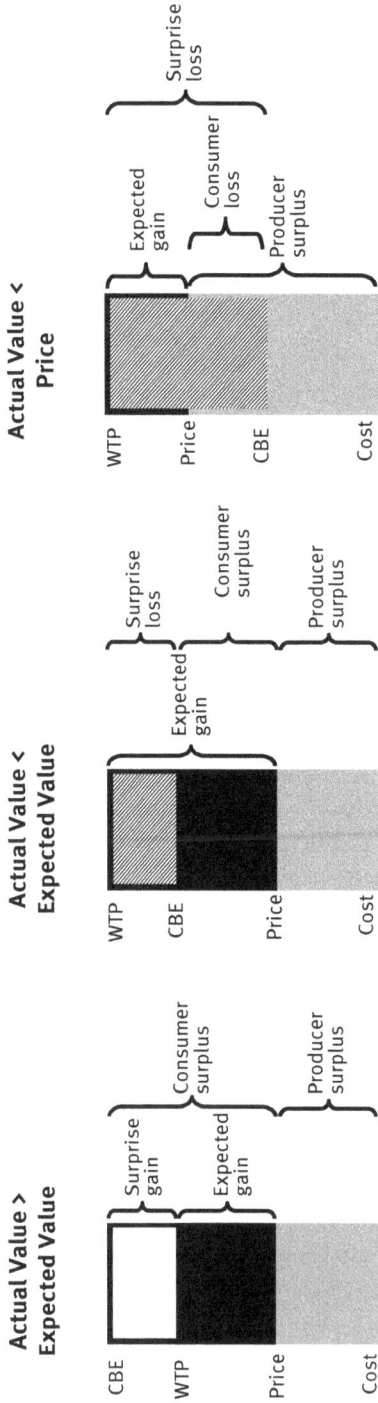

Fig. 3.3: VPC Scenarios.

In the first of these (far left), we have what I call *surprise gain*, where the consumer benefit experienced (CBE) was *greater* than even their total willingness to pay. That is, the customer expected so much value (WTP) and got even *more*, it was even *better than expected*. This is the money scenario. Let's say the sushi restaurant was amazing, one of the best dinner experiences I've ever had. The food was exceptional, the service was outstanding, and the atmosphere was top notch. It was Michelin-star worthy. I would pay $100 to have that experience again.

What's the outcome in this case? Well, now I'm a loyal and repeat customer, I'm coming back over and over again. I'm telling my friends about my new favorite restaurant. I'm leaving a five-star review with a detailed and glowing description of everything I love about the place. They've acquired me as a repeat customer and will get many others in the near future as a result of my surprisingly positive experience – I *want* them to succeed.

The last (far right) case is the bad experience example we already covered. It entails what I call a *surprise loss*, where the total experienced benefit (CBE) is *less* than expected, *and* an actual *consumer loss*, where the total benefit is less than what the consumer paid for it. In that case, the consumer is out, and there is an overall economic *loss*.

Note that my example where I got *negative* benefit (i.e., harm) is not exactly uncommon, but it's also far from common. The far more common is the example in the middle, where the actual benefit is overall positive, but not as much as expected. This happens all the time and is particularly common in entrepreneurship. This occurs when you have a very strong sales pitch, but lack a strong product or service to match. In other words, this happens when your product is mostly hype.

Hype products are always flashes in the pan. I will warn you now, and I will warn you again later – *do not overhype your product*. If anything, you need to *under-hype* your product (to achieve the leftmost case instead).

Let's illustrate the middle example. The sushi was worth $35 to me. There is a positive consumer surplus. *But* there is also a surprise loss. I expected $40 worth. What am I going to do now? Well, it's not very clear. Would I go back? Maybe. But I won't be itching to go back. I won't be telling my friends about it or leaving a positive review. Overall, my expectations were not met, and so my total experience was actually an *unsatisfying* one, despite the positive benefit. Psychologically, my experience is negative because my expectations were too high. And that is going to make a difference in my future behavior.

Summing Up

To summarize, understanding that value is a process – that there are value predictions, value experiences, and value assessments – is actually a big deal. As an entrepreneur you will need to be careful in how you create value (actually, the right word is *facilitate*, but I'll explain that later), how you manage your customer's expectations, and how and what you learn over time. The graphic here illustrates what I call the value learning cycle and will serve as a basic illustration for the next section.

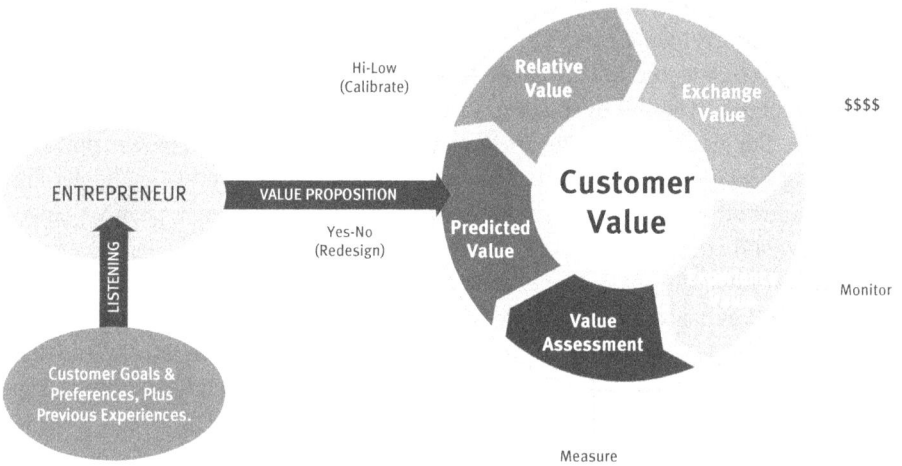

Fig. 3.4: The Value Learning Cycle.[18]

—————
18 This figure was created by the Mises Institute's Economics for Business program and used with its permission.

Section 2: **The Value Learning Cycle**

Chapter 4
Predictive Valuations

How much is something *worth* to you? We make this calculation all the time, but almost always intuitively. Have you ever *deliberated* on how much something was worth to you? If so, it was probably for something that was pretty expensive – something that you felt would be valuable to you, but you would certainly feel that price tag if you paid it. These fringe cases can draw our careful deliberation, but even then, scholars can't say a whole lot about how we make such judgments.

This claim would, of course, come as quite a surprise to behavioral economists and marketing scholars who have devoted their careers to understanding this decision process. I can't, and don't want to, turn this chapter into a drawn-out critique of behavioral economics. That wouldn't benefit you much. But because it is such a controversial claim, let me provide, in a *very* concise and incomplete way, a quick rationale for my dismissing decades of research. Well, 'dismiss' is not exactly the right word. What we've learned from behavioral economics is useful in some important ways. But the paradigm of behavioral economics is also altogether misguided in fundamental ways – ways that make what we learn from its experiments rather different than what behavioral economists think we learn.

If you asked a behavioral economist, he or she could likely rattle off various factoids about how the brain works, how we see reality through biased perception, and how our brains make all sorts of cognitive errors. My argument, which I briefly explained in Chapter 1 and which others have made before me, is that behavioral economics has started with a fundamentally flawed premise and has proceeded to unravel human cognition *as if* our brains worked that way. In reality, our brains deal with complexities and uncertainties that behavioral scientists don't ever get close to touching – in fact, they can't. You can't simulate real-world uncertainty in a lab.

Real-world uncertainty comes from the inherent unpredictability and indeterminism of the world, and of people in particular. We cannot know what people will discover or create, how they will change, or even what they will want. We don't even predict our own future preferences very well. Behavioral economics studies an artificial world, a world that doesn't really exist. We can learn things about ourselves from those artificial studies. But it is more than a stretch to believe that how we typically make decisions is through probabilistic calculus. I digress here, and it would take a much more thorough and academic argument to make my case (as an aside, I and several of my colleagues have been building this case in the academic journals), so let's get back to the topic *du jure*.

My aim in this chapter is not to get deep into the psychology of decision-making. Our interests here precede consumer choice. Choice is from given options with defined value expectations (i.e., marginal utility). But where do those value

https://doi.org/10.1515/9783110750805-004

expectations come from? Economists have neglected this question because they don't need to know – the value expectation is presumed by their marginal utility construct, which of course I've already rejected.

In reality, predicting how much value we'll get from something is very far from objective, and is in fact highly uncertain. Yet we find precisely this prediction at the very beginning of our valuation process (see Fig. 4.1). So let's try to unpack what it is and how we do it.

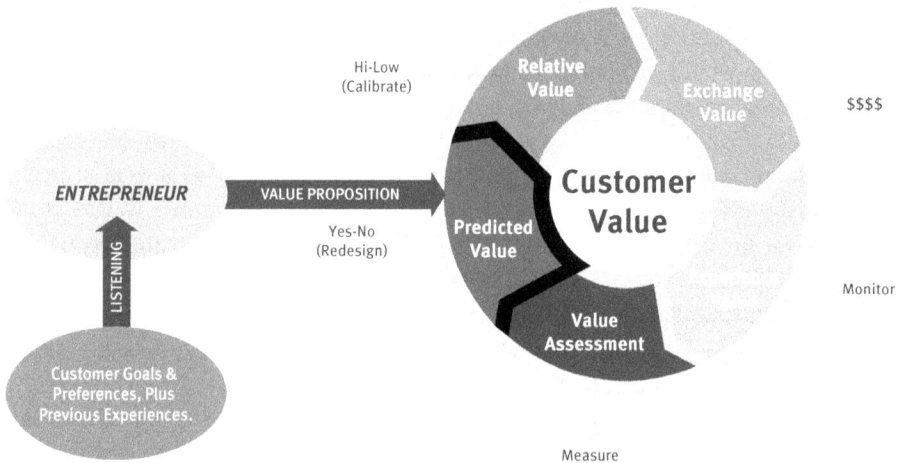

Fig. 4.1: Predictive Valuation in the Value Learning Cycle.

What is a Predictive Valuation?

The point of experiential learning is to facilitate action through prediction. Action is predictive – it is intentional, pursuing some preferred future state. The more we know about how the world works, the better we can act to manipulate the world to our advantage. But every action is a prediction based on our causal knowledge.

I know that pizza is food, so if I eat pizza, it will sate my hunger pangs. The logic of if (eat pizza) then (sate hunger) is learned through socialization and experience. I can now use that knowledge to my advantage. If I ever get hungry, I know of at least one way to address my uneasiness and achieve a higher-value state.

But the sating of hunger is a prediction based on my understanding of causality. What if the relief I always got from eating pizza was not satiety, but something else that felt good? As it turns out it was the carrot sticks that I always have with my pizza that actually filled me up. This knowledge error can lead me to make poor value predictions – I might decide not to have carrots this time. Then, eating the pizza doesn't sate me as I expected, and I'm left unsatisfied and dissatisfied.[19]

That's not a realistic example, but there are plenty of realistic ones also. If I bought a new sports car that attracted some new and welcome social attention, I might mislearn that buying expensive stuff wins me friends. In fact, we might quite accurately explain materialism, self-image problems (such as anorexia or bulimia), and other social anxiety problems as precisely mislearned value knowledge. When the predictions from such misunderstandings fail to sate the true social needs of the actors, they are left unsatisfied and unwell. I'll come back this mislearning in Chapter 7.

Predictive valuations are assessments of imagined value, which imaginations are constructed from our *value knowledge*. Value knowledge refers to one's knowledge of the potential value of things, as I'll elaborate shortly. Consumers predict a future valuation through an imaginative mental play-out of a future experience through this causal value knowledge.

Recall that, according to representationalism, our minds create a mental experience from the sensory data that it collects, in essence using the sensory input as a 'movie reel' that it plays in our minds of what is going on at the moment. We call this 'mental simulation.' Well, one of the most amazing things about our minds is that it doesn't have use sensory data as the reel. We can also use other things as inputs.

For instance, we can 'relive' memories, by playing (mentally simulating) those memories back through our minds to feel the experience again. This is generally how we form predictive valuations for things we're familiar with, value experiences we've have before. I go to the same pizza place because it's my favorite. Predicting the value that I'll get from that pizza is primarily a mental task of value reliving, although the prediction may need to be adjusted for the present context.

But memory simulations of relived value experiences are only useful for familiar value propositions. What about *new* and innovative value propositions?

We can also put in *counterfactual imaginations* as the movie reel that our mind simulates. We can imagine what the world would look like if the sky were red instead of blue. We can foresee the look in our spouse's eyes when we surprise them for their birthday. And we can envision what a consumption experience would be like. Your mouth might water in anticipation of that menu item that sounds so good. You might get giddy with anticipation in the days (and sometimes months!) leading up to Christmas morning. You can just feel the ocean breeze of that Caribbean cruise you have planned for next month.

---

19 Although 'unsatisfaction' and 'dissatisfaction' are often used interchangeably, they are distinct concepts in the value-as-a-process framework. *Unsatisfaction* refers to a failure to sate a need, a failure to achieve value. *Dissatisfaction* refers to an assessment valuation – who you blame for the failure – which will be explained in Chapter 7.

We can play out all kinds of possible and expected future scenarios in our mental simulator, previewing just what that experience will be like and what value we'd expect to get from it. In this way, we can not only predict familiar value, but unfamiliar value also.

But, of course, just how accurate your predictive valuations are hinges on how accurate your value knowledge is.

Value Knowledge

Value knowledge is an individual's understanding of their own subjective needs, wants, and preferences. In particular, it is causal knowledge of what, how, and why certain solutions improve well-being. This entails what is causing the uneasiness, i.e., what the unmet need is, how it is addressed, what solutions work best, and why.

Let me here, for clarity's sake, offer a few definitions. A *need* is a basic requirement for human functioning. Needs are objective – they are given by our state of being, the necessities that our bodies, minds, and spirits require to be well. A *want*, in contrast, is subjective, a *belief* that something would satisfy an unmet need. A *preference* is, specifically, wanting one thing *instead of* another, i.e., between two things that we believe to address the same need. Finally, *demand* is what we're actually willing to pay for. We can want something, prefer it even, but not have the resources to procure it. I may not be able to afford that exotic sports car (yet!), but I can still want it!

Needs Knowledge

Needs are directly and explicitly tied to *well-being*. If I am not perfectly well, it is because some need remains imperfectly sated – it could be better satisfied. Generally speaking, none of our needs are *perfectly* satisfied. All needs could be better satisfied. Needs (and their satisfactions) have two dimensions, a quantitative and a qualitative dimension. While most of our needs have some quantitative optimum where we are fully sated – and going past that point can even be harmful (e.g., overeating) – there is no boundary to qualitative dimension except perfect euphoria. No matter how good your favorite restaurant is, it is always possible that you could have an even better eating experience.

I cannot go into too much depth here in the theory of motivation, which is the theory of human needs. But I will proffer a surface-level introduction here, and go further in Chapter 6. It's a little difficult to discuss human needs theory because there are several competing theories. Many have heard of Maslow's hierarchy, but social psychologists have long moved on from that theory – there are parts of it that are at least partially true, but others that are not.

Part of the reason I don't want to go too far into these weeds is because I have a unique theory of human needs of my own – it is similar to others, but still distinctive. Human motivation isn't exactly my field, so I've left it alone for now, but it is a pretty important piece of the puzzle we're trying to solve here. So let me summarize some of my thinking on this topic.

Scholars have often confused needs and wants. What we *want* is what we act on. Well, more specifically, we act on demands, i.e., those things we (believe we) can afford to do. But these wants (and demands) are subjective derivatives of our learning process. Their aim is to satisfy needs, but they are not always adept at that. We often mistake our needs, as I've already explained.

Needs, and not wants *per se*, are directly tied to well-being. We don't act on our needs, we act on our wants. In fact, we don't really know what our needs are! Needs are *latent*. We aren't born with an innate and perfect sense of what exactly our bodies, minds, or spirits are trying to tell us. All we have is a general feeling of discomfort, often localized, that offers some clue that something is wrong. We learn what these discomforts – or 'uneasiness,' as Ludwig von Mises calls it – are with experience. If I feel a discomfort in my stomach area, I am familiar enough with that sensation to recognize it as a hunger pang, that my body wants food. If I feel a pain in my arm, I may not immediately know what the source of the pain is. I will examine the spot of pain to see what caused it – perhaps a scrape from a nearby bush that I didn't see.

Broadly speaking, we have at least two categories of needs: physiological and psychological. I believe there is also a third, which we might call spiritual. Each of these has subcategories that I won't spend time here unpacking.

Our physiological needs are the necessities for proper and optimal bodily functioning and feeling. We have various such needs, broadly falling into categories of aliment, hydration, warmth, and safety. When things go wrong, we have additional medical needs to try to fix them.

Psychological needs pertain to mental health. We are still learning about these basic psychological needs. They include, for example, self-esteem, healthy social relationships, and intellectual stimulation. We can likely add several others, such as security and, perhaps, even excitement. Satisfactions of these various psychological needs are needed for a healthy and happy mind.

I also include spiritual needs as a primary category, and I think this is supported by research. You might, if you choose, throw these factors in with psychological needs, but I think there is, or may be, more to it than just mental needs. These needs include a need for purpose and meaning and for hope – which have all been shown to be highly correlated to subjective well-being. I would also throw into this category charity – helping others, even anonymously, also correlates significantly with increased well-being.

Again, these various needs are latent and we don't exactly know how they manifest in each of us. We can't even tell to what extent they manifest the same in each of us, although it is certainly the case that they manifest similarly. But I don't need the same amount or type of nutrition as does my wife for optimal bodily performance. Our needs are different. We can, safely I think, assume that all our various needs vary across persons. Learning what our various and unique needs are is the ultimate purpose and aim of the human experience.

Wants Knowledge

Wants are the subjective expressions of one's interpreted needs knowledge in the form of what state of consumption would attain their optimal well-being given the current state of the market. These wants can be expressed and articulated, as they take the form of specific solutions that may or may not actually satisfy underlying needs – there's no guarantee that we want what is actually best for us. Some wants are derived directly, albeit imperfectly, from the needs that the consumer experiences. Others are more socially derived, and may have little to do with underlying needs, except in terms of the need for relatedness to other social actors. For example, I might seek out a product solely due to its brand popularity with an in-group.

Wants, and not needs, are the basic human motivation that drives action. As a result, individuals (consumers) often fail to properly address their needs, leaving them perpetually unsatisfied and unwell. A kid with a sweet tooth would, if he could, eat ice cream instead of the nutritious meal he should eat. The hunger pangs inform him of his need for nutrition, but his want drives the action. By feeding the ice cream craving, the want is satisfied, but the innate need of proper nutrition is left largely unsatisfied, leaving him relatively unwell. It's only when wants become congruous with needs that optimal well-being is achieved.

So value knowledge is, really, our *wants knowledge*. It is the sum total of expectations of what solutions are or may be best at addressing the needs mechanisms and improving well-being. We want what we think will best satisfy our various and preferential needs.

These wants are hierarchically ranked, from immediate and pressing wants to long term goals to aspirations. We (re)organize our wants dynamically, toggling from want to want over time and replacing less effective wants with new and more effective wants as we navigate our changing needs experiences and as we learn of various possible solutions to those needs.

Demand Knowledge

Demand and action are two sides of the same coin. We demand something if it is more efficient for us to pay someone else to do or provide it for us. We act – do something for ourselves – when it's better for us if we do it ourselves. A lot of things *could* be provided for us, but it's not worth paying someone to do it for us – driving us around, making our beds, even bathing and dressing. Other things are too complex or difficult to do ourselves, and so we turn to specialists to do them for us – cooking a fancy meal, dry cleaning a suit, or building a car, for example.

Determining what to do or to demand is a momentary judgment. At every moment we assess our most pressing needs and determine specific, realistic wants for those needs, and from those needs choose a specific option to take. We dynamically revisit those judgments with changes in circumstance. For example, at a particular moment, I may want and demand a hamburger to satisfy my hunger pangs. But, after getting to the burger joint, I realize that my more pressing need is bladder relief. My immediate, action-driving intentions are diverted from the ordering line to the restroom – the burger can wait.

Mental Models of Value

Like all knowledge, value knowledge is integrated into our mental model of reality. This is, in essence, the totality and culmination of all our causal understanding of the world – how the world works. The aspects of a mental model pertaining to value include our scientific causal or technical knowledge (i.e., what things (can) do) and our needs knowledge (what must be done to be well). Mental models of value contain the memories of past value experiences, our attributions of those value experiences to their causes, and our familiarity with the various solutions – value experience generators – that are available to us. It is this value knowledge that is what we know about what we can want to solve perceived needs.

Forming Predictive Valuations

Value knowledge is the culmination of firsthand learning from past consumption experiences as well as information gleaned from other sources, such as marketing information or observations of other consumers' experiences (including endorsements and reviews). We generally trust our own firsthand experience over all other sources of value knowledge.

But you have to have tried a product to have such an experience. What about the many products you've never tried before? You clearly *can* make value predictions for products and services that you have never before experienced (otherwise you would never try anything new!). But how?

Recall that a predictive valuation is an assessed *imagination*, a mental simulation of a future experience. In fact, it's an imagination regardless of whether it is based on your own past experience or if it's something totally new to you. The difference here is whether you use a memory as the simulation reel or else a new reel constructed from other factors.

When using memories as the simulation reel, we may perceive contextual differences between the remembered experience and the future experience. For example, if I had pizza last night when it was hot and I was starving, I may look at the leftover slice of cold pizza for breakfast. We can mentally account for these perceived differences in altering the simulation reel. I can imagine what the cold pizza would feel and taste like, given my more moderate level of hunger this morning. Of course, we can only make this corrective to the simulation reel to the extent that we can predict the contextual differences – when we know when and where we will experience the consumption again. Where these are unknown, we tend to just use the memory reel unaltered for our mental simulation.

When constructing a new simulation reel, we pull whatever information we can glean from various sources, depending on their perceived trustworthiness. We use advertisements, testimonials and endorsements, reviews, and our third-person observations of other's consumption experiences as evidence. But some of these may matter more in our reel construction process – you probably don't trust the salesman's pitch as much as your neighbor's recommendation.

Also, what is called 'consumer human capital' is accounted for – how well can you consume the thing you're considering? Some things need skilled consumption to provide greater value. Computers, for example, are much more valuable when you know how to use them effectively. If you need some consumer human capital to capture value, how much do you have? If you don't feel like you can consume it effectively, that will be accounted for in your simulation reel.

Once a reel is constructed, the predictive valuation is generated from running the mental simulation and then assessing the simulated experience for its value. How much do I like the cold pizza that I'm imagining eating for breakfast?

Now, it might be tempting to say that we form from our predictive valuations a price we would be willing to pay, but we don't have quite enough information just yet.

Chapter 5
Exchange Value

There's one more key process before we can determine whether or not to buy a value proposition or not, and that is to take what we know and understand about its potential value and to translate that expected value into a number price, a price we are willing to pay (see Fig. 5.1). As it turns out, translating imagined value into a price tag isn't as simple as some might make it. But again, our marvelous brains do it regularly, seemingly without effort.

We honestly don't know much about how our minds do this. Oh, we've discovered a few things, some which are actually quite interesting and helpful. But most of what we know is still superficial. We're a long way from really understanding how we make sense of subjective experiences and turn them into specific preferences and valuations.

More often than is perhaps understood, we don't know what price we should or shouldn't be willing to pay. We often use socio-economic cues – if everyone else is willing to buy pizza at $15, I probably should too. But it's a complex and imperfect science, one that is certainly part of our value learning cycle.

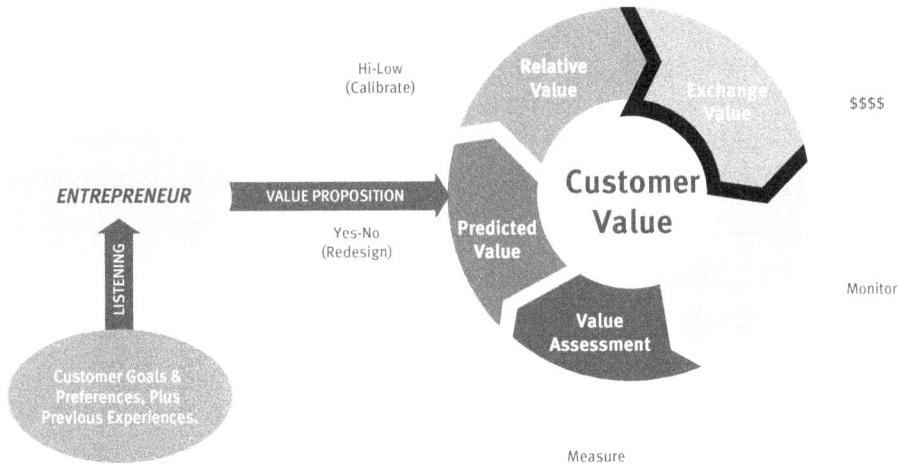

Fig. 5.1: Exchange Value in the Value Learning Cycle.

Exchange Value

Before delving into the *how* of exchange value, let's quickly review the *what*. As I reviewed in Chapter 1, economists have, since at least Adam Smith (and likely

https://doi.org/10.1515/9783110750805-005

before), distinguished between *use* value and *exchange* value. Use value is meant to be essentially what I've been touting as real/actual value – it is what something is worth to us in its use, the benefit that we expect to get. Exchange value is what something is worth in exchange, the price that we would be willing and able to part with it for.

If I had an apple, that apple would have a certain use value to me. But if I knew Mary also likes apples, then the apple would also have certain exchange value to me – I could sell or trade the apple to Mary. The value that I could get in return is the apple's exchange value. The keep or sell decision – think the TV show 'Love It or List It' – hinges on whether the use value is more than the exchange value or *vice versa*.

Economists have, again since Adam Smith, been particularly interested in trying to make sense of exchange value. Use value is intuitive, obvious, and subjective (in the limited sense). But where do *prices* come from? This was the question that occupied Smith, Ricardo, Marx, the marginal revolutionaries, and many economists since then.

But they made a fundamental error in understanding and treating these as unique value types. The Austrian school, beginning with Menger, argued correctly that exchange value *is* use value – it's *another's* use value. There is no exchange value for me unless Mary is willing and able to trade. Mary's willingness to pay is based on her own perceived use value. In essence, then, exchange is an exchange of use values. If I trade her my apple for her sandwich, we have exchanged based on our subjective use values – the use value of the apple is, to me, smaller than the use value of the sandwich, while for Mary it is the opposite. By exchanging, we both end up with higher use values and are mutually benefitted.

But what if I exchange for money – what if I *sell* the apple to Mary? Clearly I have no intention of *using* the money. What would I do with it? Well, the answer is obvious – what I would do with it is buy something else that I *can* use. I exchange the apple for the exchange value of money, which represents *future* use value. In other words, exchange is *always* among use values, immediate or future. We use mediums of exchange – money – as a store of value that is capable of easily facilitating future exchanges for use value.

Provided we are freely allowed to trade, then, it does not significantly matter whether we have things of high use value or of high exchange value. Ultimately, things that are valued higher in exchange (e.g., money) will be traded away for things that we value in use. It is use value, and not exchange value, that underpins our theory.

Value Uncertainty

Let's now turn to the process of determining exchange values – how do we determine how much we are willing to pay for something? The foremost principle to understand here is that value is *uncertain*. By 'uncertain' I mean something specific – I don't mean that the value proposition has this mystical cloud obscuring it, I just mean that we feel uncertain about it. When we think of something's valuation, when we predict a value experience, we know quite clearly in many cases that what we think we're getting isn't necessarily what we're actually going to get. There's a decent chance that it's going to be different than we expect.

Certainly, there are a lot of things businesses can do to reduce this uncertainty for customers. If you've already tried the value and experienced it, the only uncertainty you have is how consistent that value will be in future experiences. For products of high and known quality, consumers have high confidence in the product's future value – and they value that certainty. Entrepreneurs can reduce consumer's value uncertainty with samples, guarantees, testimonials and endorsements, etc. The most effective type of uncertainty mitigation tool will depend on the type of value and its solution.

Value uncertainty is one of the biggest inhibitors to willingness to pay – we are willing to pay far less where the value is uncertain. This is why the first-mover advantage is, or can be, such an advantage. Later comers' value is more uncertain to consumers than the first-mover's, whose value is already established, which those later industry entrants must then overcome. Often second movers are able to overcome the first-mover advantage only if they are already reputable brands.

Relative Value

Generally speaking, we need some help figuring out what price tag is appropriate for the predictive valuation that we imagine by comparing it to other, often more familiar, price tags. That is, how we value things is not only subjective, it is also *relative* (see Fig. 5.2). We don't make predictive valuations in a vacuum. We contextualize how we would value things in relation to all other things. In economics, this concept of relativizing value is reflected in the concept of the 'opportunity cost.'

Opportunity Costs

An opportunity cost is defined as the value foregone in any choice. Typically, this is framed in terms of purchase decisions – if I buy this, I can't buy that. But the opportunity cost concept is much broader than that.

There is an opportunity cost in everything we do. If I take the time to write this book, then I cannot spend this time doing something else. I have foregone those other things I could have done in order to take the time to explain to you the concept of opportunity costs. Was it a good tradeoff? Time will tell (or maybe not, it's

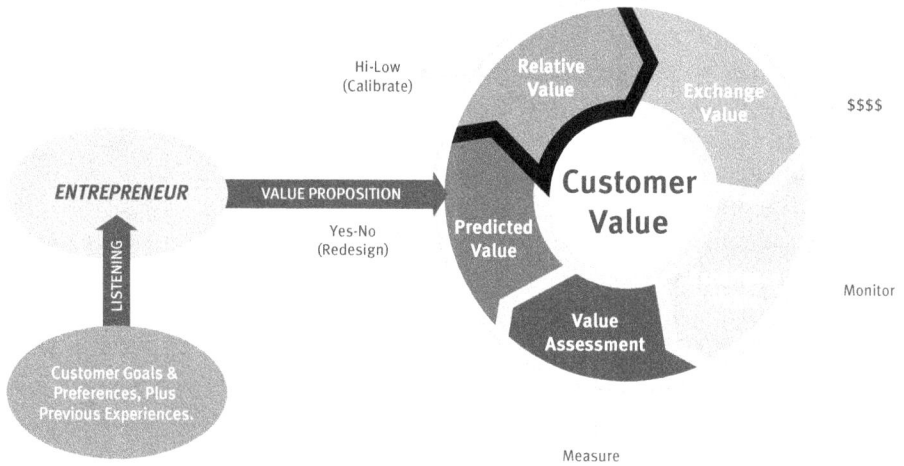

Fig. 5.2: Relative Value in the Value Learning Cycle.

often hard to know if something was really worth it since the counterfactual is always uncertain).

In economics they discuss opportunity costs as the *next best* thing that is foregone, the next highest-valued (or greatest utility) option that was lost by taking the preferred action. But this is pretty limited thinking. What was really given up is *all* of the other value opportunities that could have been taken instead. If I choose to make a sandwich for lunch, I have not only given up the tacos and burger that I could have had instead, but also the 15 minutes that it takes (and everything that time could have been used for). I even gave up anything else that bread, peanut butter, and jelly could have been used for. There are always endless opportunities forgone in each action taken.

We don't always think of or care about the opportunity costs of our decisions. Often, we have one intention in mind at a time and don't consider alternatives that we may be giving up. This is because we already have an 'optimum' value knowledge of the ways we best satisfy our various needs. So we cycle through those solutions to keep our needs optimally satisfied, sparing little thought to what else we could be doing, or what we could be doing differently. But this doesn't make the opportunity cost any less real.

Let me make one more point that will become relevant later on in this chapter. Again, economists will typically define the opportunity cost as the next best thing that is foregone. That is more or less right, but take care about what this means. If I pay $15 for the pizza, that doesn't necessarily mean I can't buy something else for $15. Let's say I have $4,000 in my bank account when I buy that pizza. I still have $3,985 left to do with as I see fit. The $15 foregone does not prohibit me from purchasing and consuming other things that I value. In fact, I can consume a whole lot of stuff before I run out and actually feel the foregone $15. But again, we need to be careful, that $3,985 may need to carry me for a few weeks. So it's not necessarily the case that the $15 is inconsequential. By the end of the month, I may really feel that missing $15 as I wait for my paycheck on the 1st of the next month. The point is that opportunity costs are in fact hard to quantify or predict. In some cases, it may be marginally insignificant, while others end up being severe. But what matters, at least for now, is that opportunity costs are real and important factors in consumer decisions.

The Infinite Opportunity Cost

Let me tell you about one particular opportunity cost that economists have struggled to see because of their general equilibrium theory-caused myopia: the *infinite* opportunity cost. The infinite opportunity cost reflects the fact that the *best* thing that can be done with our time and resources at any time is *yet to be discovered*. For every decision that you make, every solution you choose over others, one solution that you don't choose is the *better one* that you might innovate.

Pause for a moment and reflect on some of your typical daily activities and solutions to your various needs. Is brushing really the *best* way possible to clean your teeth? Or could some other method or technology do it quicker, better, easier? Is an automobile the best way to get to work each day? Or could there be a faster or easier way to get there? Is a computer the most effective way to do my work? Or would a newly engineered workstation may my work easier?

The assumption that 'this is the best way to do it' is always wrong. There is *always a better way*.

We accept the infinite opportunity cost in almost all cases because we do not yet know what that better way might be or the time and cost of it. But a great many entrepreneurial ideas have come from rejecting the infinite opportunity cost, of refusing to just accept the status quo, and admitting that "there's got to be a better way!"

Immediate Opportunity Costs

Getting back to the valuation process, the opportunity costs that are most pressing and relevant to the value learning process are what we might call *immediate* opportunity costs. These are the costs of the most immediately relevant alternatives to the value proposition being considered. Typically, this is the valuation of the solution that you *now* use to solve the need that the new value proposition is purporting to address, and adjust that for perceived value differences.

There's a new pizza joint around the corner. How much would I pay for one of their pizzas? My baseline is how much I pay for pizza now – let's say $15 for a large. Then I would adjust that price up or down based on whether I think the value would be more or less than my go-to. Of course, at around $15, my opportunity cost is pretty small, so I may be willing to pay that just to find out if it's better or not. Then I wouldn't have to guess. But for something pricier, where the opportunity costs are high, I'm not going to be as willing to just eat the cost if it isn't as good.

Benchmarking New Value

Let's complicate the example with something that doesn't have an easy comparison. Let's say that an entrepreneur has come up with a new device to clean hair. You put it on your head and, in 2 minutes, remove it to find a clean head of hair. How much would this device be worth to you? $50? $200? $3,000?

Well, certainly you value clean hair (I hope). But it's difficult to put a price tag on something totally new. There is significant value uncertainty here. To predictively assess the value of this device, you need to compare it to something.

What we normally compare new products to is how we typically solve the problem being addressed. How do I normally clean my hair? How much do I now pay in money, time and effort, and other costs to get the same value as promised by this new device? Currently, I clean my hair by shampooing every morning. It takes 10 minutes of shower time, I style it while wet, and it usually takes about an hour to dry if I don't blow dry it. My costs, then, are the product (shampoo), time and effort (10 minutes), and other inconveniences (e.g., having to wait for hair to dry or blow dry). How much do I value those things?

Of course, these aren't very easy calculations. In terms of the latter, the inconveniences, my assessment of them has almost entirely to do with how much frustration they give me. Shampoo is relatively cheap, but over time those costs add up. But if the device saves me time drying my hair, it also makes it more difficult to style, which is easier when wet.

So the value expectations of new things are hard to relativize.

The Williams and Sonoma bread maker case is illustrative. Williams and Sonoma introduced an automatic bread maker to the market in the 1990s with a price tag of $275, a price they determined after a lot of market research. But sales were unimpressive. Customers didn't know how to value the new technology because they didn't have a good benchmark. What's more, few people had spent the time learning to make bread at home to have a strong preference for homemade over store bought. But, with a little consulting advice, they decided to introduce a second bread maker – a larger and somewhat more advanced version – to market at twice the price. Sales of the original version soared. With something else to relativize the value technology, it was easier for customers to decide it was worth it.

Now, don't let this mislead you. Getting customers to value your product highly isn't just a matter of clever pricing. If your product doesn't deliver the value of its price tag, customers aren't going to be happy and your product is going to flatline. But the example illustrates the importance of using other things to relativize value.

When you don't have any benchmark to use, the value uncertainty can be prohibitive. For new value propositions, then, you may need to help your customer relativize the value.

One way to do this is to paint a clear picture of how much they currently spend solving the problem the traditional way. How much money they spend on shampoo, water, and time, for example. This is a common sales tactic, but it's effective – provided you don't overdo it – for this reason. If you overdo it, your pitch suddenly loses credibility and you've lost the prospective customer.

A second way to do it is to offer multiple price points. Even though customers are just as unfamiliar with the other products that you price, it still offers them a way to relativize the value. It's cheating in a way, because you can relativize to whatever level you want. But be careful when using this approach. You will be tempted to pump up your price above its market value, which will result in dissatisfied customers, a sullied reputation, and eventually a failed product.

Finally, if you want to bootstrap the production process, it may be possible to first introduce to the market a 'high-end' product at a luxury price point. The early sales, although likely meager, will then build a high-end brand and can fund the development and production of a less-advanced version that can then be introduced at a more affordable price. The 'anchoring' of a high-price initial product sets up the more affordable option nicely. You see this strategy effectively employed by a lot of companies who build their brand with niche premium options, then leverage that high-end brand to successfully enter broad markets. The brand is diluted by this, of course, but sales skyrocket.

Value Constraints

You also need to recognize and be aware that how one values your value proposition my hinge on various constraints. The two most common are *money* and *time*, but there may be others. When translating expected, relative value into willingness to pay, that willingness to pay may be small or even zero, even if their expected valuation is large. This happens when the opportunity cost exceeds their value constraints.

Financial Constraints

Most consumers have financial constraints – the opportunity cost is real and valuable. Wealthy consumers may not have a real opportunity cost – at the margin, they have everything they really want which money can buy. But most of us are not so wealthy. The financial cost of a product has a real cost to it – we must sacrifice something that we want when the money runs out.

The size of this opportunity cost, in real terms or in terms of felt sacrifice, matters a lot when determining how much one is, in fact, willing to pay for something. High predictive valuations with too-high opportunity costs are wishful thinking or pipe dreams. They are things that would be amazing to experience, but simply cannot be afforded.

To put this in more basic terms, consumers who have limited financial wherewithal must allocate those funds to their most necessary uses. Food, housing, and such are almost always first. After those basics, what funds remain are allocated to other value propositions of great comparative value. If your value proposition is not among the most valued, it must be one of the many that are valued but foregone.

Time Constraints

Similarly, time can constrain in such a way as to become prohibitive. If and to the extent that the purchase and/or consumption of your value proposition takes time, such time may have a high time opportunity cost. Where it is too high, given the temporal priorities of the consumer, the value proposition must be foregone.

Willingness to Pay

The end of this process of forming predictive valuations and relativizing them is generally understood to be in determining some ultimate price one would be willing to pay. Of course, this is more theoretical than realistic – we don't in fact mentally calculate a number that is the maximum price we would pay. This is classical 'as-if' theorizing that I talked about in Chapter 1. When we look at a price tag, we simply determine *at that time* whether that price is worth paying. We rarely have a specific maximum number in mind. We just have a ballpark sense of predictive value and what sort of price that predictive value might be reflected as.

In the end, this may mean that we are surprised by the price, either positively or negatively. You might see a piece of art that you find quite appealing at a gallery, have a glance at the price tag, and be shocked at how much it costs. You might find a brand-name shirt that you love on the sales rack and be astounded at the bargain price. These reactions may be partially influenced by our own ignorance of the market and the standard valuation process, or it may simply be that you do not value the product very closely to its price (up or down).

The short of it is that valuation is a momentary process – we make predictive valuations when we need to. We don't walk around with a mental catalog of all the maximum prices we're willing to pay for all things. Really, we don't often know what that maximum willingness to pay is until we're pressed into it. Economists like to do little scientific tricks to figure it out – auction-style bidding experiments for example. In a bidding war, you're pressed by others into deciding how high you're actually willing to bid. But auctions are rarely how we actually buy things. In fact, most prices in our modern economy are non-negotiable. We simply make spot judgments over whether that price is worth paying or not.

Because it is momentary, it is not fixed or even stable. Instead, it can be easily influenced by other momentary factors – how much money we have on hand at the moment, for example. Persuasion techniques by clever salespeople can augment willingness to pay in a particular moment. It is influenced by social pressures, by one's emotional state, or by momentary hankerings.

This volatility of valuation is primarily a byproduct of that value uncertainty that I mentioned earlier. Because we don't know how valuable a product actually is, it is easy for our guesses of that value to be influenced. Once we have a solid, experience-based knowledge of how valuable something is to us, those other factors have far less influence on our value predictions. Have you ever had a salesman try to sell you on something that you had already tried and knew you didn't like? How easy was it to walk away with a polite "no thanks"?

To conclude this chapter, let us do a quick review of the main points. Exchange value is essentially the use value of others (i.e., customers). They determine their exchange value, and from it their willingness to pay, based on their predictive valuation of the use value of the good or service you offer them. This is a momentary judgment, imprecise and unspecific, and can be influenced by other factors. Really, customers don't have a predetermined or specific price they're willing to pay – instead they make yes/no judgments as they shop based on an abstract and imprecise sense of whether the good or service is worth the posted price. But this is no easy task, especially where value is uncertain. To make this judgment, then, customers relativize the good or service to similar goods and services with which they are more familiar. But this is a faulty process. We often guess wrong, which leaves us unsatisfied and dissatisfied. But it is through such experiences that we better learn what to want, as I will explain further next.

Chapter 6
The Value Experience

So far we have been discussing the *predictive valuation* process, the process of forming imaginative expectations of potential value. After we form and relativize predictive valuations and determine a price we would be willing to pay, we then act upon those predictions to make value exchanges.

The value exchange process is sufficiently straightforward and familiar to us all that I will not spend any time on it. Perhaps this is a mistake – the transaction cost framework is worth knowing. If you can find ways to mitigate transaction costs, you can create huge advantages for yourself. But transaction costs are tangential to the topic at hand, so I'm going to skip over them. Let's skip to the having and the consuming of a value proposition, the next stage of the value learning cycle.

This is the *action* step of the process. Action is, as we know, always accompanied by its consequent, including and especially the *experience* that the action entails. In this case, the value action is *consumption*. Let's unpack the consumption or value experience (see Fig. 6.1).

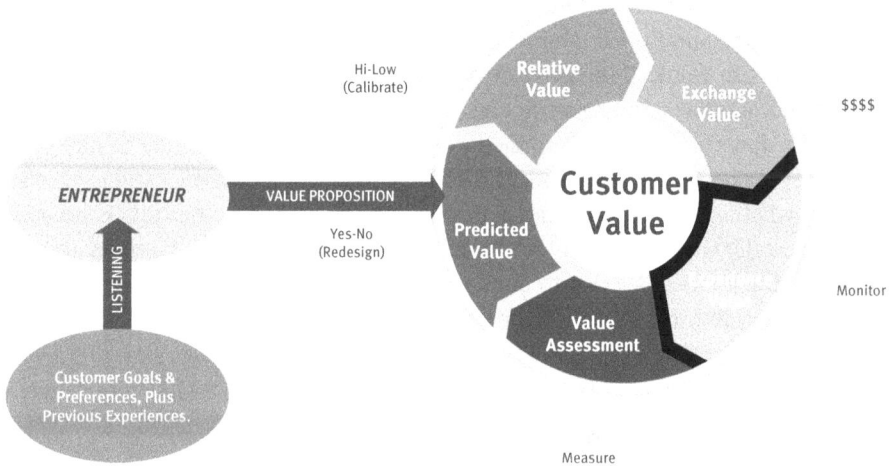

Fig. 6.1: The Value Experience in the Value Learning Cycle.

The Two Sides of Experienced Value

'Value,' as I explained in Chapter 3, is an experience – the experience of *benefit*. Because it is an experience, we can characterize it, using our representationalist foundations, as two-sided – having an objective component and a subjective component.

https://doi.org/10.1515/9783110750805-006

The 'objective' side is the *real benefit gained* – the improvement in well-being that actually occurred. Let's call this the *benefit experience*. A benefit experience is a process of physical, mental, and/or spiritual change that results in a state of higher satisfaction and well-being. Presuming I actually got my sushi dinner, the 'objective' value would be the total satiety and nutrition I received, as well as whatever other (e.g., psychological) benefits I might have gotten. Such benefit is often difficult to measure, but it is quantifiable – at least in principle – in terms of positive (negative) benefits (harms) or increases (decreases) in objective well-being.

A *subjective value experience*, on the other hand, is the conscious experience of that objective benefit, which will correspond, but not perfectly, to the objective experience. Let's call this second side of the value experience the *satisfaction experience*. Typically, when we receive a real benefit, we also experience with it a sense or feeling of satisfaction – the 'felt uneasiness' that Ludwig von Mises references is relieved. Such satisfaction experiences, when positive, may entail a feeling of relief, of pleasure, or enjoyment. When negative, the satisfaction experience might take the form of sadness, anger or frustration, irritation or annoyance, or other forms of discontentment. There are any number of forms this satisfaction experience can take. In fact, finite language is often a barrier to understanding the vastness of the range of satisfaction experiences that are possible. Satisfaction experiences are mental or conscious experiences alone, directly – but again not perfectly – tied to the benefit experience.

Let's go into a bit more depth into these distinct sides of the value experience.

Needs and Benefit Experiences

The *real* or objective value experience entails some real change in the world that alters the functioning of the human body, mind, or soul. Perhaps this is some physiological change, like the introduction of calories into the digestive system. It might be some situational change that induces a healthier mental or spiritual state. Whatever is the change, a value experience induces a positive change to one's *need state* or, in other words, it satisfies a real need to move the consumer to a higher state of objective well-being. To understand value, then, we need to understand the nature of needs.

Understanding Needs

There have been many theories of human needs over the last century or so. Generally, psychologists have been interested in needs as motives – what causes people to act as they do. No such theory gained as much status and recognition as Maslow's hierarchy.[20] In Maslow's theory, he defined needs as essentially a perceived disconnect between an individual's current status and a desired end-state. He depicted five universal needs as ranked in a hierarchical pyramid, with basic physiological needs at the most fundamental level, then safety and security, belongingness and love, psychological esteem, and then, finally, self-actualization, which is the attainment of that ultimate desired end-state. The hierarchical pattern of needs is, according to Maslow, a natural one of priority – you don't care about safety or security if you're starving, and will be willing to take risks that you otherwise wouldn't dare. Once your physiological needs are met, intimate social relationships take a back seat until you can secure your physiological well-being over time, and so forth.

The intuition of Maslow's hierarchy is strong, which is why it is still so widely taught. But there's one problem – it's wrong. Or, at least, it lacks empirical support. Studies have tested Maslow's hierarchy and found only partial evidence of its supposed ranking of needs priorities. Few academic psychologists today subscribe to Maslow's theory.

More recently, alternative theories have arisen to explain human needs and motives to act. One is McClelland's motive disposition theory, in which needs are action-driving toward their amelioration. Even more popular is Deci and Ryan's self-determination theory, which describes needs as "innate organismic necessities"[21] that must be sated to achieve well-being. Kennon Sheldon[22] developed a 'two process model' of needs that integrates these two approaches. That is, we have 'needs-as-requirements' that we experience as what Mises called 'uneasiness' when such needs are unmet. We also have 'needs-as-motives' that impel ameliorative action. In our framework I use the language of 'needs' for the former and 'wants' for the latter.

But why do we have needs? Ulrich Witt explains that needs arise "from a state of deprivation of an organism."[23] A body, mind, or soul requires regular nourishment with those particulars that they each require for proper and optimal functioning. Over time, those key necessities are expended, requiring replenishment. Also, needs can change over time, both slowly and suddenly.

One of the most important things for us to understand here is that *needs are latent*. That is, we are not born with an innate sense of what we need. Instead, when a need is unmet, the person experiences only some general feeling of 'uneasiness.' Our goal and motivation, then, is to figure out what is causing that uneasiness and figure out how to ameliorate it.

---

20 Maslow, A. H. 1954. *Motivation and Personality*. Oxford, England: Harpers.

21 Deci, E. L., & Ryan, R. M. 2000. The "what" and "why" of goal pursuits: Human needs and the self-determination of behavior. *Psychological Inquiry*, 11(4), p. 229.

22 Sheldon, K. M. 2011. Integrating behavioral-motive and experiential-requirement perspectives on psychological needs: A two process model. *Psychological Review*, 118(4): 552.

23 Witt, U. 2001. Learning to consume–A theory of wants and the growth of demand. *Journal of Evolutionary Economics*, 11(1), p. 26.

In some cases, the problem is obvious to us, either because we have already learned the need's uneasiness or else because the uneasiness is local to an obvious problem. An example of the former are hunger pangs, which we learn very early in life how they feel, what they mean, and how they're satisfied. An example of the latter might be a cut finger – the uneasiness is a sharp pain at the point of the cut, and the blood is a dead give-away.

But many more of our needs are far more difficult to disentangle. This is particularly the case with mental and spiritual needs, which manifest as various degrees of sadness, anxiety, fear, loneliness, despair, and so forth. Often, these feelings are convoluted, and it becomes difficult to pin down their source. Even physiological problems, in our advanced state of medical knowledge, can be very difficult to accurately diagnose.

Over time, we have learned, individually and collectively, various best-known practices for addressing prevalent needs as we understand them. We have learned about our psychological needs, such as autonomy, relatedness, and competence (per self-determination theory). We have learned what foods are better and worse to eat, although dietetics appears to be in something of a critical juncture in transition to a new paradigm of understanding how to better feed our bodies (i.e., the traditional food pyramid appears to be wrong). These solutions, however, come with only partial and incomplete understanding of most of our needs. Progress in satisfactions come, often, from advancements in our understanding of particular needs.

Benefit

Now that we understand needs a bit better, let's turn back to the value experience. One experiences *real value*, that is *benefit*, when he or she successfully satisfies an unmet need. To put that a different way, when one of their innate requirements for proper and optimal functioning is replenished after having fallen deficient, their well-being increases. Their body, mind, or spirit, whichever the case may be, advances or returns to a higher functional state and operates at a higher level of performance. They have become healthier in body, mind, or spirit.

Benefit experiences are, of course, common. You are likely experiencing several in this very moment, even if you are not aware of any. One, for example, is that your body needs to regularly replenish oxygen in the bloodstream, which it obtains from the air you breathe. Assuming you've been breathing as you read this book, you have been having repeated benefit experiences. Blinking, also, is a benefit experience that repeatedly relieves the discomforts of drying eyes. If you're inside, a heater or air conditioner may have kicked on as you read, returning the room to some optimal temperature for your comfort and health. Even something as simple as adjusting in your chair is a benefit experience that moves you from a state of comparative discomfort to a new state of greater comfort.

Of course, most of the benefit experiences entrepreneurs are concerned about are those produced by products and services. But it is important to get the baseline right. The goal is not to build a better mousetrap *per se*. The goal is to better address consumers' actual needs, to produce for them superior benefit experiences. Perhaps that entails building a better mousetrap. But once the entrepreneur gets to the bottom of the need – is the consumer worried about diseases that mice can spread, nervous about the spoilage of foods that mice might cause, concerned about the potential damage to their house, or simply afraid of mice? – a better solution to the real need can perhaps take different shapes.

Harm

Of course, not all value experiences are beneficial. Some simply do nothing for us, offering no real benefit. But some expected benefit experiences end up being *harmful*, creating or exacerbating needs rather than mitigating them away. Harm entails a decrease in well-being in some way. This can be in the form of creating a new need, exacerbating existing needs, or in inhibiting one's ability to ameliorate other existing needs.

First, some experiences may cause new harm to one's person – that is, they might inflict physiological, psychological, or spiritual damage to a person, decreasing their overall well-being. Pharmaceuticals can be an obvious example in the cases of severe reactions or side effects. But other harms can be somewhat more obscure and perhaps insidious. The benefits of social media, for example, are very often accompanied by psychological harms, distorting social reality and causing envy and other social ails.

Second, some experiences can exacerbate existing problems rather than resolve them. Political solutions are the quintessential example of this type of harm (and yet we keep turning to politicians for help). For example, often military interventions purportedly intended to keep us safer tend to instead drive the people of those nations to turn against us and lend their support to insurgents, rendering us less safe. Economic policies designed to help the poor have, let's just say, a very bad track record.

Finally, some value experiences may produce a positive benefit while also inducing negative side effects that are worse than the benefit gained, resulting in an overall loss. A common trope within the recent Covid-19 pandemic was that the cure shouldn't be worse than the disease. But, in reality, such tradeoffs can be difficult to predict, and politicians aren't always motivated to choose as we would for ourselves.

Regarding the last one, some products might cause material damage to the person's property – a poorly-designed Christmas tree lighting system may set fire to the tree and house, costing the owner severely. More commonly, this is the opportunity cost problem – if a purchased product is merely unsatisfactory, if it doesn't satisfy as much as expected, then there is very likely harm caused by the fact that the opportunity cost was foregone for that unsatisfactory experience. The consumer has foregone the opportunity for some other value experience for the unsatisfactory one. If the unsatisfactory experience is lower in benefit than the foregone one, he or she is harmed in net.

Satisfaction Experiences

Let's now turn to the subjective or conscious side of the value experience. When some change happens, especially when it happens *to us*, we perceive that change consciously or experientially. In fact, generally speaking, the word 'experience' connotes this subjective side of experience – we *experience* things consciously.

It is, of course, possible that a change occurs to us that we do not experience. This is, of course, related to that age-old philosophical quandary over what happens when a tree falls in the forest. If you define 'sound' as the objective sound waves that the falling tree would of course make, then the answer is yes, it makes a sound. But if you define 'sound' as an auditory experience, then the answer is no. Experiences are connected to and derived from changes in the real world, but remember that they are mediated by their perception. If you do not *perceive* the change, you cannot experience it.

When you eat a meal, what you experience are the tastes, textures, and temperatures of the food you put in your mouth. You also experience a growing sense of relief as your body moves from a state of hunger (deficiency) to a state of satiety. But what you *don't* experience is the digestive processes that bring nutrition to the various parts of your body. What this means is that we will often enjoy a food *despite* what real nutritional value it may or may not have – in fact, many of the foods we enjoy the most are some of the least nutritious.

This subjective experience of value is typically called the *satisfaction experience*. Like real benefit experiences, the valence of subjective experiences of value – satisfaction experiences – is also positive or negative. But whether it is positive or negative does not map directly onto the valence of the objective benefit experience. Whereas the objective experience is valenced positively or negatively by whether it increases or decreases well-being, the satisfaction experience is valenced by the extent to which it *feels good*.

The Experience of Satisfaction

Satisfaction is, in essence, an experience of pleasure, relief, joy, happiness, peace, etc. that leaves one feeling more 'satisfied' or contented with their situation. Said a little differently, it is a lack of desire for change, a sense of fulfillment. Thus, the impetus for action in one who is satisfied is ameliorated.

A perfectly satisfied person would not act, except in the specific sense in which 'sitting' or 'resting' are actions – there is no activity pursuant toward a higher value state. I have termed this state of perfect satisfaction the 'Nirvana state of rest.'[24] Well, for it to be a true 'state of rest,' it would have to be a perduring state of satisfaction. So the Nirvana state of rest is one of perfect *and persistent* satisfaction. But the point is that a satisfied actor is in a state of repose, the impetus for action absent.

What we typically mean by a *satisfaction experience* is a change in status from a state of *dissatisfaction* to one of *satisfaction*. Importantly, this state of dissatisfaction versus satisfaction is a *subjective* one.

Defined as such, it would strictly be possible to create a satisfaction experience by simply changing one's mindset. In fact, many of the world's religions and philosophies teach precisely this as a tactic to attain satisfaction *despite* a lack of satisfaction experiences. By *contenting* one's self with their situation, they can achieve a state of subjective satisfaction despite a state of objective well-being that is less than perfect.

However, while such endogenous change is important and good, a change in subjective mindset is *not* what is meant by 'experience,' which connotes an *exogenously* caused change in situation. When we say that we did something, the intentional act *per se* does not constitute an experience. Instead, experience is what happens outside of intentionality, what happens *to* someone rather than *by* someone. So action is *accompanied* by experience, but does not constitute experience in itself.

So let's define a satisfaction experience as an experienced change that is accompanied by a shift from a state of higher intentionality to a state of lower intentionality. By intentionality, of course, I mean the desire for change, the impetus for action. When satisfaction is experienced, the satisfied actor is less inclined to pursue further actions, at least in the direction of needs just satisfied.

The Tenuous Correlation between Benefit and Satisfaction

Because the satisfaction experience is a *subjective* one, whereas the benefit experience is an *objective* one, the correlation between benefit and satisfaction is not always perfect. To be sure, there is a strong connection. When we are made better off, objectively, we also tend to *feel* better, more satisfied. But it is not uncommon for one to *feel* more or less satisfied than the objective benefit actually attained.

I already gave you food digestion as an example. But a lot of products and services are particularly valuable because of the *subjective* satisfaction experience they provide. Entertainment, for example, produces an objective (psychological) benefit,

---

24 Packard, M. D. 2019. Entrepreneurship: Toward the Nirvana state of rest. *Mises Journal*, 7(3): 523–543.

but it is rather small. What we really pay for is the subjective experience, the joy and pleasure we get from laughing at a comedy, the exhilaration of a thriller, or the suspense of a drama.

In fact, it is only this satisfaction experience that we have cognitive access to at the time of the experience. We can, perhaps, learn of what objective change occurred from the experience, but generally speaking, the mental experience is all there is as far as we are concerned or know.

Scientists believe that there is a divergent, exponential relationship between benefit and satisfaction.[25,26] The greater the benefit, the exponentially greater the satisfaction. This is, of course, difficult to know for sure since satisfaction is subjective and thus, as I will explain in a minute, difficult to communicate. But there is plausible evidence to support this supposition.

Moreover, the experience of satisfaction is, in fact, largely shaped by expectations and the experience's conformity to those expectations. A consumption experience that meets high expectations is satisfying to be sure. But if it produces a strong benefit and yet *fails* to meet those high expectations, the experience may be one of unsatisfaction or dissatisfaction, despite the benefit.

This disconnect between the objective benefit experience and the subjective satisfaction experience, both in terms of valence (positive or negative) and magnitude, matters a great deal, as I will explain in subsequent chapters. To preview those arguments, it is *really* difficult to figure out what people's objective needs are when all they have access to is their subjective satisfaction experiences. They of course want to learn from those experiences what their real needs are so that they can better address them in their continuous efforts to optimize their well-being. But the learning process is problematic, as satisfactions do not always appropriately indicate the real benefits accrued from value experiences in consumption.

---

25 Ilgen, D. R. 1971. Satisfaction with performance as a function of the initial level of expected performance and the deviation from expectations. *Organizational Behavior and Human Performance*, 6(3): 345–361.
26 Weaver, D., & Brickman, P. 1974. Expectancy, feedback, and disconfirmation as independent factors in outcome satisfaction. *Journal of Personality and Social Psychology*, 30(3): 420.

Chapter 7
Assessment Valuations

The value learning cycle concludes, before beginning anew, with the consumer gleaning what new value knowledge they can from their recent experience (see Fig. 7.1). In other words, one's valuation of a product or service is updated based on their assessment of the actual experience. This occurs in two stages. First, there is a value assessment stage, where the value experienced is compared to the predictive valuation that was anticipated. Second, there is a knowledge updating process where experienced differences from expected value are integrated into the consumer's value knowledge, and preferences are updated. Let's get further into these processes.

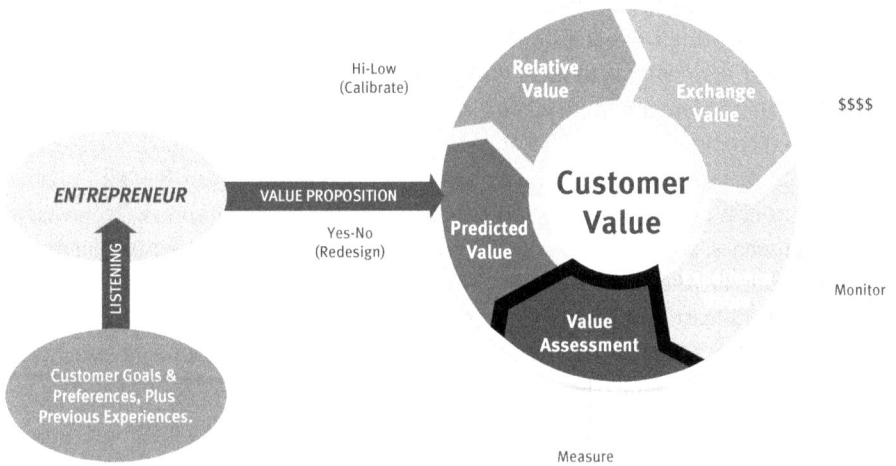

Fig. 7.1: Assessment Valuation in the Value Learning Cycle.

The Assessment of Value Experiences

Within and after a value experience, the experiencer – the consumer – *reassesses* their valuation relative to expectations. Said differently, they compare their satisfaction level with the anticipated value that they expected based on their predictive valuation.

Recall that only the *subjective* side of the value experience, the *satisfaction experience*, can be assessed in this way as only that conscious experience is immediately available to the mind. Objective change can be assessed to the extent that it can be and is observed. For example, we might assess cleaning products not by the subjective experience that using them evokes (not often an enjoyable experience),

https://doi.org/10.1515/9783110750805-007

but by the objective changes that the product makes in the observable state of the environment – which changes then affect our satisfaction level. In other words, cleaning products produce *indirect* value experiences. I'll discuss this more in the next section.

But for the most part, value is experienced directly, and we do not pay close attention to the objective changes in a value experience, but rather to the subjective experience of that value. Here the distinction between objective benefit and subjective satisfaction becomes vital to our understanding of the value learning cycle. We only assess the *subjective* experience, with little (indirect) heed to what objective benefit we might have gained. Our satisfaction with and, thus, valuation of some product is based, to a very large extent, on how that product *made us feel*.

Although this shouldn't come as much of a surprise to those who have some business experience, it shatters any remaining illusion that business is or can be purely 'scientific,' that value is objective, or that your success (or failure) is your own creation. Instead, value is, to a very important extent, emotional. This point will come up again in later chapters.

The Assessment of Satisfactions

As we experience value, we instinctively compare that experience to the one we imaginatively pre-experienced in the predictive valuation process. In fact, in some cases where our consciousness is fully and actively engaged with the experience, we may go through an experience with continued anticipation of each next step. For example, upon boarding a rollercoaster ride, the thrill-seeker will often experience the ride with ready and unfolding anticipation based on what they'd seen of the ride before reaching the front of the line. They are well aware and anticipative of the long climb, the steep initial drop, the loops and corkscrew, and many of the twists and turns before they occur. What the rider could not have predicted, however, are the intense feelings that accompany the near free-fall (and that feeling of their stomach lurching upward), the incredible speed of the ride, the g-forces of those sharp turns, and the surprise jerking of other twists and turns that were hidden and could not be observed prior to the ride. In other words, much of the immense felt value and satisfaction of rollercoasters is very often in the *surprise* exhilaration that one experiences from not having fully anticipated all experiential aspects of the intense ride.

What this example unlocks for us is the *comparative* nature of value assessments. A ride that goes exactly as expected is satisfactory and nothing more. The value that is assessed is equivalent to that which was anticipated. For a thrill ride, the expectation is surprise. As a quick side note, expecting surprise sounds like a logical impossibility, and I've seen scholars argue precisely that – if you expect to be surprised, then you wouldn't be surprised when the 'surprise' comes. But in fact we expect to be surprised quite often. We expect to be surprised on our birthdays, for example, not knowing what activities and gifts await us. We expect to be surprised when watching thriller movies. We expect to be surprised because we know that we don't know what is coming. In fact, I will argue in later chapters, Chapter 16 in particular, that you should always be expecting to be surprised throughout your entrepreneurial journey, very aware of your lack of knowledge.

Back to the point at hand, if your experience goes exactly as anticipated, your assessment of the value experience will perfectly reflect the predictive valuation. This type of experience falls into what Woodruff and colleagues call the "zone of indifference."[27] However, to the extent that the value experience *surprises* us, to the extent that it is *different* from what was anticipated, that surprise creates a heightened reaction, positive or negative depending on the valence of the surprise.

If a particular ride is surprisingly uninventive, if it is slow, has gentle twists and turns and is just predictable, the expectation of surprise and thrill is disappointed, the surprise is in the failure to surprise, and the rider feels *dissatisfied*. If, instead, the ride delivered on the expectation of surprise, the rider is *satisfied*. And if the ride delivered a thrill *beyond* expectation, they are *delighted*.[28]

This framework, of course, applies just as well to all other value experiences. If I dine at a fancy restaurant, my expectation for the food will be rather greater than the food I can get from chain restaurants. If the food compares more or less equally to that food, I am disappointed, of course. If that food is truly superior, I am satisfied and glad for my purchase. If that meal is absolutely divine, I will be talking about it for weeks.

The point is that an *assessment valuation* is made within or immediately after the value experience *relative to* one's predictive valuation. Indeed, the satisfaction experience itself hinges on expectations produced from the predictive valuation. The nature and magnitude of the satisfaction experience then informs the consumer of the achieved value, causing them to update their valuation of the consumed product in what we would call value learning.

Value Learning

Once value is assessed, we learn what we can from our assessment. Of course, as I've just explained, there is only new information to learn from if and to the extent that our expectations were *disconfirmed*. If the experience was exactly as expected, we learn nothing new – our expectations are not updated – at most, those prior

---

27 Woodruff, R. B., Cadotte, E. R., & Jenkins, R. L. 1983. Modeling consumer satisfaction processes using experience-based norms. *Journal of Marketing Research*, 20(3): 296–304.

28 Oliver, R. L. 2010. *Satisfaction: A behavioral perspective on the customer*. New York: M.E. Sharpe.

beliefs are only confirmed and strengthened. But if the experience is disconfirmatory, if it was somehow different than expected, then that experience provides new insights into what we should value and why.

Where there is new value information, the experiencer of the value is motivated to update their value knowledge, discussed in Chapter 4. Scholars are divided on whether learning is an intentional process or just an instinctive one. The position I will take is that it is intentional – we learn *because* we benefit from learning. There exists a clear motive for consumers to update their value knowledge, as this value knowledge forms the basis for future predictive valuations. Better value knowledge will thus ensure better satisfactions in the future, leading to better well-being over time.

But let's unpack this value learning process a bit. One of the more challenging aspects of the process, which is very often overlooked by scholars and business practitioners, are the processes of value attribution and imputation. That is, the things we value are *attributed* value that is ultimately *imputed* from the value experience. It is these attributions that are, in fact, *learned*.

Value Attribution

One of the core insights from Austrian economics, beginning with Carl Menger, is that *valuation* is something that we *do* – we attribute a valuation to the causes of a value experience. This is important, because it is not always clear what caused the experience or how.

Here, again, our representationalist foundations are critical. Remember that we only 'see,' and can thus learn from, the *subjective* side of the experience. We don't have direct access to the physical realm, where biological processes work to keep our bodies and minds operating smoothly. We don't always see what actually happens when those processes break down or are inhibited. We only have the subjective experience of feeling something wrong.

Social and cognitive psychologists have found that it is extremely common to *misattribute* our 'arousal'[29] or experienced feelings. In other words, when we experience something, it's not always obvious *how* or *why* we felt as we did. In fact, when you think about it, we *never* know exactly how or why we experience something just as we do. You'd have to simultaneously be a biologist, psychologist, a physician, and a neuroscientist to even get anywhere close to a 'correct' explanation, and even then we're just way too far away from having a sufficient scientific understanding of these

---

29 Schachter, S., & Singer, J. 1962. Cognitive, social, and physiological determinants of emotional state. *Psychological Review*, 69(5): 379.

processes to fully explain sensory experiences. There are a host of variables that play into how we feel in any particular experience. Pinning an experience onto one single cause is always wrong, although it is often fair to attribute it to a *primary* source. But even then, that 'source' is always reducible to sub-factors. The deliciousness of a bite of cookies and cream ice cream is a combination of several different flavors, textures, and even temperatures that interact into a strange and wonderful complexity of sensations that form a single, joyous experience.

Because we can only perceive a subset of possible causal factors (if any at all), it is very common to *mistake* the causes of our experiences. That's the misattribution of arousal – we pin our experiences on sources that had far less influence on the actual experience than we expect, sometimes none at all.

What is often called 'materialism' is one of the most frequent examples of this. Materialism is the misattribution of *social* benefits to *material* causes – if I buy this expensive sports car, I will have more friends or attract a mate. Real social relationships – those that in fact satisfy one's real social needs – are, in fact, never derived from physical goods. These are, of course, signals of status and wealth, of identity and personality. They have a clear and real effect. But it is never *because* of the car that you form a new a relationship. The relationship is altogether social and formed only socially. If you are socially inept, it doesn't matter how expensive your car is, you cannot form a meaningful relationship. The truism 'money can't buy you love' is true in an absolute sense. You can get another's interest and attention with such signals, but the formation of a love bond between two persons is a social process that involves sharing intimate knowledge, feelings, and experiences with and about each other. What can happen, though, is that a person misattributes an intimate relationship to the car itself and learns that money can buy love. When the current fling fizzles, more money is thrown at signaling wealth and status to buy more love, which simply isn't an effective way of getting what is really wanted.

The fact is, we don't really understand our basic needs very well, as we don't have an innate sense of what those needs are. We merely have a general sense of uneasiness or unwellness that we try to pin down.

Let me try to explain and illustrate this difficulty of getting to our *real needs*. Have you ever snapped at a friend or your spouse for something they said? How did you feel in that moment? Why did you snap? You probably felt a burst of anger, which is a secondary emotion caused by a more primary emotion, e.g., hurt, frustration, or perceived unfairness. But why did you feel that primary emotion – let's say 'hurt'? Was it really what they said? Or did you (mis)interpret what they said in a hurtful way? Did they really mean to hurt you? Probably not, so why did it feel hurtful then? Why did you interpret it to be hurtful? The answer is going to be impossible to disentangle – a host of factors are all at work. You might have been tired after a poor night's sleep and/or a long day. There might have been things that happened during the day that put you into a dark and pessimistic mindset – goals for the day missed, social interactions that didn't go well, events that happened that didn't go your way (like a stubbed toe, a sick child, or lost keys). Perhaps you were worried and anxious about things impending. But beyond these psychological factors, there are also physiological facts that come into play. Maybe you were hungry (being 'hangry' is a real thing). Maybe you were sore from earlier exercising. Or perhaps you were feeling sick. You might have been low in certain nutrients or 'chemically imbalanced' in some way. There are a ton of factors that may have combined to put you in a particular state of mind when those words were uttered that prompted you to interpret the words in such an unfavorable light that they invoked a visceral negative emotional response.

Despite this, most likely, you believed (at least in the moment) that the other person *made* you angry, they *made* you snap – this is the misattribution of arousal. We don't really know the causes of a particular experience, positive or negative, but our minds look for a likely cause to attribute it to. When we make a mistake in this process, we learn wrong things.

In short, because we learn from only a highly conscribed *subjective* experience, through sensory stimulation, we can perceive very little real information about what caused the experience, which can cause us to mistakenly attribute the wrong causes to our experiences. What we learn from this, then, tends to be fallacious. Over time, however, we correct our mistakes and improve our value knowledge.

Value Imputation

Let's elaborate on this value attribution process a bit more. So far we've only determined that we subjectively attribute (or misattribute) value experiences to its causes. But *how* we do this is called the process of value *imputation*. That is, value is 'imputed' from the value to those factors that cause the experience to determine the valuations of those various causes.

Recall that value only really emerges in a value experience – value is *experienced*. So if value is determined in and by the value experience as the total *benefit* attained within that experience, how do we value the individual components that led to the experience? If I am enjoying that bowl of ice cream, how much value do I ascribe to the cookies versus the cream? If I'm the producer, the ice cream maker, is my valuation of the cookies versus the cream different? How would I then value each of the individual ingredients – the cream, sugar, flavorings, etc.? Said differently, how do we know how much each component of the so-called 'value chain' is worth prior to that value experience? If I'm an entrepreneur and need to determine how much I'm willing to pay for each component of my designed consumer solution, how do I do that when value isn't determined until *afterward*?

The answer is, simply, I can't. Not formally, anyway. This is why entrepreneurship is said to be 'uncertain,' a point I'll come back to throughout Section 3 and again and in more depth in Chapter 13. That valuation process is, as I've explained in Chapter 4, a *predictive valuation* process.

The value that the entrepreneur predicted in their imagined solution is imputed to the components of that solution. If I think that I can sell a gallon of my ice cream for $10, I can then impute values to the ingredients and processes needed to make the ice cream. I will need the ingredients, of course, but also a facility and equipment to make the ice cream. I'll also need to hire workers to work the machines, and so forth. All of these costs are valued *by* the $10 gallons that I expect to sell. If I do not expect to sell enough of the ice cream to pay for all of those costs, then the imputed value of my product is not sufficient to warrant the costs of making it. This leads to what some call 'judgment failure' – a term I find a bit misleading since it's not really a failure of judgment but a judgment to do something else. Of course, if the imputed predictive valuation *is* sufficient, I will proceed with my plans.

But let's now say that the value *has* been experienced, that the ice cream was purchased and consumed. That value experience then *validates* or not the predictive value imputations that the entrepreneur made.

As I discussed in Chapter 3, traditional analysis says that it is the *sale* that validates the entrepreneur's predictive valuation and its imputations. But hopefully I've fully dispelled that mistake. It's not just one sale that needs to happen – I need many thousands of sales to cover my costs and turn a profit. I'm not going to get those sales if my first sales don't lead to a positive value experience.

If the value process is validated, then so too are the inputs to the value process. That is, the value of each of the factors that the ice cream maker had to invest in to create, market, and sell their product is also validated. The cream seller, the cookie baker, the machinery maker, and so forth, are all validated in their value *to the extent that* they contributed to the final value experience. And because they are validated, so too are the inputs to *their* products.

The total contribution of each factor to the final value experience is, of course, a subjective judgment. It is very difficult, perhaps impossible, to know precisely which factor created how much and which aspects of a complex value experience. So we do our best based on what we know and why.

Updating Value Knowledge

Once we have assessed a value experience, we then update our value knowledge – our mental models of value – based on the extent to which we believe the new value experience is representative. That last qualifier is important. If I think that a bad value experience was just a one-off mishap, then we might discount the experience altogether and leave our value knowledge intact. However, to the extent that we think the value experience reflects on the producer, we update our beliefs about that producer and, specifically, our value knowledge.

The cognitive processes that are involved in knowledge updating are beyond the purview of this book, and it's probably for the best. We don't in fact know a whole lot about how the mind learns. Yes, there is a lot of research into learning, much of it quite good. But it is still mostly superficial. We know some specific things, but we don't understand how it all works, i.e., how the mind changes itself. So I wouldn't feel very confident in what I might tell you. But this is neither here nor there.

What matters is that we subjectively update our understanding of what is valuable and why.

Because our value experiences can be distinctive according to the different circumstances and conditions in which they were experienced, that experiential variety can provide insights into what is truly at the heart of the benefit experience. To give a simple example, if I were to get a chicken sandwich that was to die for, only to be let down the next time I had that same sandwich, I might notice that the chicken was not crispy the second time and, therefore, attribute the much higher value to the texture and crispiness of the chicken. My value knowledge is thus updated and that will affect what I want and how I want it in the future.

Value knowledge updating includes knowledge about what needs I have, what the experience of the need is like, why I experience that need, how I experience the need (under different circumstances), what solutions exist for a particular need, how those various solutions work, whether they work, why they work, what those value solutions *feel like*, how well they work (how much benefit they impart), when they work, how to use them most effectively, when and where to use them most effectively, and so on.

It is amazing to think about how many products we know intimately about, having used so many throughout our lives. Our value knowledge is vast, and grows ever larger every day.

Updating Wants and Preferences

Let me conclude this chapter by briefly explaining the essential mechanics of how *wants* and *preferences* are formed and updated. That is, how do we choose what to want, including when there are multiple solutions that can sate the same need? We've already covered forming predictive valuations in Chapter 4. But what I mean by wants and preferences are not specific value predictions, but a *ranking* of value propositions and solutions to one's various needs, the wanting of specific things *instead of* others.

First of all, let me say something about the current state of economics on this question. Economics has, for many decades now, generally assumed that preferences are stable over time. In fact, this is a critical assumption of *homo economicus*, the rational economic actor. If the economist can't know your preferences consistently, he can't include you in his predictive models. I'm being a bit unfairly snide, as economists certainly know this, and many try to include preference updating to, in my opinion, very limited success.

Of course, preferences are *not* stable over time. They are *momentary* – what I prefer at time A can very easily switch by time B for many possible reasons, including the simple and very common desire to try something different. But more than that, every time we consume something, there's a good chance that we'll *learn* something and, thereby, change our knowledge and update our preferences.

Wants and preferences are essentially the latest manifestation of our most up-to-date value knowledge applied very circumstantially to a particular situational need. Wants include all those things that we believe would sate our various existing needs at any moment in time.

We can want a host of things at once. Each thing that we want at a time is wanted toward a distinct need. Thus, all of our wants at one time are intended to cover all of our present needs at that moment.

But if we're being careful and precise, we will recognize that what we really want are *specific satisfactions* to our understood needs. Because of this, we don't generally want more than one solution to a need at any given time. If I'm hungry, I choose *between* foods. I do not want more than one meal. I might say that I want two different menu items, but what I really mean by that is that both would be somewhat equally satisfying, and not that I want to eat both.

Because of this, we also have to form *preferences* between different solutions to our various needs. What we will actually demand is our *preferred* solution (given resource constraints) at that moment. Our preferences are based in subjective, often experiential details that have made the quality of one satisfaction more appealing than another. The qualities that drive preferences can be, more or less, stable over time in some cases, or they can hinge profoundly on the circumstances of the need. For example, tastes in clothing will often be fairly stable over time because we use our clothing style to signal things about ourselves and our identity to others. But food preferences can vary widely day-to-day or even meal to meal.

Again, as I said, this quality of satisfaction can include newness or different-ness, which includes in the experience a sense of mystery and intrigue, and will certainly prompt new value learning. Thus, preferences are *not* stable. We are always learning and updating our preferences. If my favorite pizza place, under new management, drops off in quality, it will not stay my favorite – I will update my preferences. But even if I don't, I might choose a different pizza joint every now and then anyway, just to mix it up.

Dynamic Value Learning

Hopefully, you can by now see the cyclical nature of the value process. In fact, life is essentially a continuous and endless value learning process. At every moment, we are seeking a higher-value state, a better quality of life. But it is worthwhile to understand the dynamics of this process somewhat more before we move on to the more practical applications of this value-as-a-process view in the next section.

At each moment we can only choose to do one thing, to pursue one value, to satisfy one need. Well, some actions can satisfy more than one need simultaneously. And some of us are able multi-taskers, but if we're being very precise, even multi-tasking is just a dynamic shifting of one's attention between different tasks. Our intentions are, generally speaking, directed at one need at a time.

What this means is that we manage our needs dynamically, shifting our attention from one need to another. We also shift from longer-term efforts to short-term and immediate needs. For example, you may need to take a break from your prototype development, which you expect will really improve your financial well-being in a year or two, to get lunch, which will satisfy your immediate hunger.

Generally, our immediate needs take precedence, but if we can address those immediate needs efficiently, the time that is left over can be turned to other wants and goals. These can range from immediate satisfactions, such as watching a show or catching up on sleep, to long-term goal pursuits, such as retirement planning or writing a will. We prioritize those things that we think will bring us the most satisfaction, accounting for uncertainty and what Mises calls our time preference (i.e., how long we're willing to delay gratification).

How and where we aim our actions across time will tend to be adjusted with the value learning we gain throughout the process. And the more value learning we can do, the better off we will be in the long run.

Section 3: **Learning from your Customers**

Chapter 8
Entrepreneurial Empathy

Apple founder Steve Jobs famously remarked:

> Some people say, 'Give customers what they want.' But that's not my approach. Our job is to figure out what they're going to want before they do. I think Henry Ford once said, 'If I'd asked customers what they wanted, they would have told me, "A faster horse!"' People don't know what they want until you show it to them. That's why I never rely on market research. Our task is to read things that are not yet on the page.[30]

In Section 2 I showed you how consumers decide what to want – how they learn what is valuable to them and decide through that process what they want to do and buy. But the goal of explaining this process has been so that you can learn what they want or, more importantly, *should* or *will* want so that you can deliver it to them. That is, in order to create (or, more precisely, *facilitate*) new value you will need to be able to "read things that are not yet on the page."

Here, in Section 3, I turn to *your own* learning process, i.e., how you can learn what your customers will want. When you're dealing with learning customers, most of them, as Steve Jobs famously noted, don't yet know what they want. You have to show it to them first. But how do you do this?

The key to this task is truly understanding your customer, to see what it is that they really *need*, even when they themselves cannot see it. The key to success, the primary skill required of successful entrepreneurs, is what we call *entrepreneurial empathy*.

Your task, as entrepreneur, is to get into the mind and soul of your customer, to truly understand them at a profound level. You have to be able to feel what they feel, to understand why they feel that way, and to innovate a better way of doing what they do so that they feel better doing it.

As it turns out, most entrepreneurs don't even bother. They *guess* at what they think people want or *should* want. If you ask me, that's not smart business – and it can be very costly if you guess wrong. How much time, effort, and money have you dropped into your venture? Are you really going to put that all on the line on a *guess*?

Of course, they don't think they're guessing. Companies will often spend huge amounts of money on compelling market research. This gives them the false impression of scientific knowledge – *scientism*, as Friedrich Hayek called it – where in fact that research is premised upon speculation and guesses (by consumers and others).

---

30 La Bella, L. 2016. *Steve Jobs and Steve Wozniak.* New York: The Rosen Publishing Group, Inc., p. 79. Where this quote came from is a bit of a mystery, and it may be apocryphal. But if it is not a perfectly accurate quotation, it is at the very least stitched together from quotations that he did in fact say.

https://doi.org/10.1515/9783110750805-008

To give an example, Kimberly Clark did extensive market research on flushable moist toilet tissue before launching it in 2001 as Cottonelle Fresh Rollwipes. The new product was the result of extensive market research, which revealed that regular toilet paper was simply not very good at doing its job, and that ~60% of adults had previously attempted some ad hoc moist wipe, such as a baby wipe, a washcloth, or sprinkled water on regular toilet paper. Kimberly Clark invested over $100 million in R&D and manufacturing and an additional $40 million in marketing, justified by projections of $150 million in sales in the first year and $500 million in year six. The product was touted as "the most significant category innovation since toilet paper first appeared in roll form in 1890." Proctor & Gamble (P&G) also quickly jumped into the market with their Charmin Freshmates later that same year.

Two years later, P&G scrapped the line completely, and Kimberly Clark's line of products was confined to the few markets where they were basically breaking even. Why were these products such flops? Barry Bayus recounts:

> The Fresh Rollwipes product was designed to be conveniently dispensed via a refillable plastic container that clipped to the standard toilet paper holder. Careful attention was paid to developing a dispenser that blended in with the consumer's bathroom. Both companies, however, underestimated the role of consumer embarrassment associated with toileting. Although many consumers already used some sort of makeshift wet cleaning method in the bathroom, they didn't like others knowing about it. The extra dispenser attached to the holder was right out in the open, possibly causing guests to wonder if something was wrong with household members because they were using these 'alternative' wipes.[31]

Of course, since this spectacular failure the toiletry companies have more recently 'fixed' the design issue and have instead packaged the moist flushable wipes in a flatter and more portable fashion much in the same design as baby wipes, which consumers have found more tenable. The idea was good – there was a real consumer need that they wanted solved – but the design of the initial solution failed to capture *all* of their needs, including their social needs.

Research shows that, despite decades of research and advancements in market research techniques, most entrepreneurs and managers still don't really know their customers nearly as much as they think they do. They're still working off of guesses and getting it wrong way too often. For example, a very good and important 2017 study by Tomas Hult and colleagues concludes:

> The results of our study reveal several important gaps between managers' beliefs about their customers and the actual perceptions and intentions of those customers. Among the most significant disconnects that we observe is that managers overestimate their customers' satisfaction, their ratings of some of its key drivers (expectations and perceptions of value), and the future loyalty intention expressed by their customers, while also underestimating their customers'

---

31 Bayus, B. L. 2008. Understanding customer needs. In S. Shane (Ed.), *Handbook of Technology and Innovation Management*: 115–141. West Sussex, England: John Wiley & Sons, p. 116.

propensity to complain. Taken together, this pattern of overestimation of their own firms' customer performance could lead managers to fail to take needed steps to improve drivers of satisfaction, satisfaction and loyalty, potentially damaging future financial performance and market share. What is more, our results show that managers also misunderstand the attributes that most strongly influence their customers' perceptions, underestimating (for instance) the importance of quality in driving satisfaction, and of satisfaction in driving both loyalty and complaint behavior. Taken together, these perceptual gaps (along with others considered below) provide strong evidence against both the depth and the breadth of managerial knowledge of their own firms' customers.[32]

You can do better – *much* better.

In this section I'm going to teach you why market research can fail so spectacularly, and what you can do to avoid such failure. Ultimately, however, there is no silver bullet, no cheat code that can guarantee you success. You will have to make your best judgment. But I will guide you through what you *can* do to ensure you are as close to the consumer's own mind and experience as possible when you make that judgment.

To start, in this chapter I'm going to walk you through my theory of empathy – simulated empathy theory – and show you how you can use it to vastly improve how well you understand your customers. And that is going to put you in a much better spot to succeed.

What is Empathy?

What is empathy? We're all familiar with the word. But the dictionary quickly reveals the complexities that the word entails. Merriam-Webster's dictionary defines it as:

> the action of understanding, being aware of, being sensitive to, and vicariously experiencing the feelings, thoughts, and experience of another of either the past or present without having the feelings, thoughts, and experience fully communicated in an objectively explicit manner.[33]

As it turns out, empathy researchers are, perhaps, more confused on the meaning of the term than any. Recently, several reviews of the academic literature on empathy have revealed a vast array of different definitions. Most of these recent reviews have tried to reconcile that array of definitions into a coherent single definition. But each of those attempts has come up with something different. We just haven't really figured empathy out yet.

The word 'empathy,' coined by psychologist Edward Titchner, is an English adaptation of the German word *Einfühlung*, which was developed decades earlier by

---

32 Hult, G. T. M., Morgeson, F. V., Morgan, N. A., Mithas, S., & Fornell, C. 2017. Do managers know what their customers think and why? *Journal of the Academy of Marketing Science*, 45(1): 37–54, pp. 38–39.

33 https://www.merriam-webster.com/dictionary/empathy.

Vishner, Lipps, and Prandtl. It means, literally, 'in feeling' or 'feeling into.' It was introduced and developed to represent the internalization of others' feelings (Vishner was a scholar of aesthetics, and tried to explain art enthusiasts' internalization of an artist's feelings as depicted in their art).

Today, the standard definition of empathy is an *emotional contagion* process – the internalizing of another's emotional state such that you feel the same as they do. There are several theorized mechanisms for such emotion mirroring, which include the natural imitative response of 'mirror neurons,' which are stimulated by observed actions.

But this definition of empathy isn't very useful to us for several reasons. First, feeling the same way as another is not *empathizing*. You're not feeling the same way for the same reasons. Feeling sad because you see another person feeling sad is no more the same sadness than feeling excited at watching a stunt pilot is the same experience as being in that airplane. It's not the same. So, on these grounds, emotional contagion doesn't even fit a satisfactory concept of empathy.

But secondly, and perhaps more importantly, merely feeling the same way as another does nothing for you as an entrepreneur. If you observe someone feeling sad and it makes you feel sad for that person, all it's done is made your day a little worse. You've learned nothing.

Empathy is more than this.

Some have added to this a second component of empathy: perspective taking. So it's not enough to just feel the way another feels, you also have to see it from their perspective. This gets us closer to where we want to be, but still not quite there. Adding the perspective-taking component is a huge advance. In fact, some entrepreneurship scholars have run with it, adopting perspective taking as the principle concern for entrepreneurs – figuring out what consumers want involves walking in their shoes and seeing things from their perspective.

The problem with perspective taking is that it gets us only as far as what *I* would do if I were in *their* situation. Walking a mile in another's shoes isn't the same as *being them*. Philosopher Amy Coplan[34] calls this 'pseudo-empathy' because it uses empathic imagination, but takes the first-person perspective. So you don't really get what *they* are experiencing. You only get what you'd be experiencing if you were them. But empathy is still more than this.

Empathy is what philosopher Edith Stein called "the experience of foreign consciousness."[35] Or, in Professor Coplan's words, it is "a process through which an observer simulates another's situated psychological states, while maintaining clear

---

34 Coplan, A. 2011. Will the real empathy please stand up? A case for a narrow conceptualization. *The Southern Journal of Philosophy*, 49: 40–65.
35 Stein, E. 1989. *On the Problem of Empathy* (W. J. Stein, Trans.). Washington DC: ICS Publications, p. 11.

self-other differentiation."[36] In other words, it's the simulated firsthand experience of *another's* firsthand experience *as if you were them* (while recognizing that you're not).

This definition is the basis of my work on a *theory of simulated empathy* or *simulated empathy theory*.

Mental Simulation

Empathy is a *simulated* firsthand experience of *another's* firsthand experience. It is a *counterfactual* representation of what *I* would experience if I were *them*. This isn't the same as what I would feel if I were in their situation, which is perspective taking. *If I were them* – with their body, their mind, all of their life experiences, their circumstances, their knowledge, values, desires, and so forth, if that person were me – *what would be my experience*?

Let me elaborate a bit on my introduction to mental representations from Chapter 3. Recall that all conscious experience is a mental representation. Let me use the word *simulation* here – our experience is a mental *simulation*. Our minds are effectively simulators that create a complex simulation for our consciousness to 'watch' or, more accurately, experience. You can think of it as a full-experience movie that our minds are constantly playing for our consciousness. We don't really understand at all how this happens – even the notion of consciousness continues to be hotly debated, and there appears no end to the debate as it seems to be almost entirely beyond observation and, thus, scientific study. But the scientific evidence from cognitive psychology and related neuroscientific fields is absolutely overwhelming that this mental simulation process is what, in essence, happens.

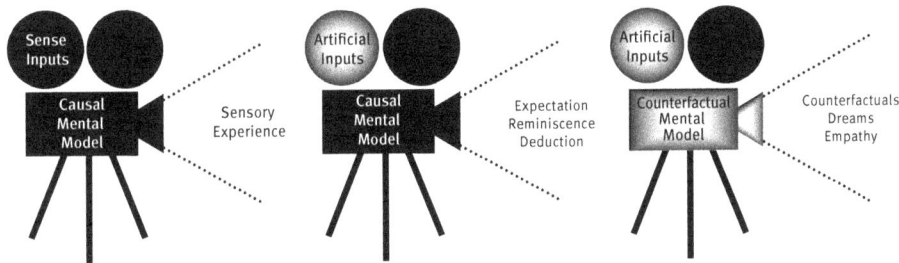

Fig. 8.1: Types of Mental Simulation.

---

36 Coplan, A. 2011. Will the real empathy please stand up? A case for a narrow conceptualization. *The Southern Journal of Philosophy*, 49: 40–65, p. 44.

There are three general types of representations or simulations, as illustrated in Fig. 8.1, categorized by the input to the simulation and the mental model used as the simulator. Let's use the metaphor of a movie that our minds play for our consciousness to experience. The input to the mental simulator is like the movie reel or script. The three simulation types are *sensory*, *logical*, and *counterfactual*.

Simulated experience is *sensory* if its main inputs are sense stimuli, intended to represent *what is really happening* in that moment. Your brain takes sensory stimuli – light hitting your optic nerves, the feel of pressure on your body from the things you're touching, the sound waves reverberating on your ear drums, etc. – and simulates from them a mental representation that is a holistic, conscious experience of what's going on around you. This means that your experience of reality, as we discussed in Chapter 3 and through Section 2, is *indirect*, mediated by mental simulation. Of course, this isn't to say (as some philosophers have) that there isn't a reality out there causing the experience. *Something* is impinging on your senses. But the way our brains interpret and thus simulate these sense stimuli doesn't always comport with reality as it really is, which is why we sometimes get fooled by our brains. As a child, I remember regularly seeing some 'bad guy' in my closet at night that was, of course, just hanging clothes that I just couldn't see clearly.

The second type is *logical* simulation, which occurs when we simulate an *artificial* input, provided by the mind itself, to its conclusion by playing it through our mental model of reality. We can run our mental simulators with all kinds of inputs: sensory, of course, but also inputs provided by the brain itself, such as memories and 'what ifs.' Think back, for a moment, to what you did when you woke up this morning. How did you feel when you woke up? What was the first thing you did? This memory experience I'm talking you through is another mental simulation. You are replaying in your mind a past experience, mentally simulating it and, in a very real sense, reliving it again. Such reminiscent simulation can, as a result, evoke strong emotions, sometimes the same emotions as experienced at the time (e.g., the excitement of a Christmas memory) or new emotions altered by changes in life circumstance (e.g., a fond memory of a recently passed loved one's annoying habits).

Logical deduction or reasoning is also a logical mental simulation with logical assumptions as the reel. When we 'think through' or 'reason out' some line of thought, what in fact happens is that logical assumption inputs are played out in simulation through the causal structure of our mental models, as we have constructed them over our lifetimes, to some mentally simulated outcome. We literally play the logic out in our minds.

Logical or 'will be' expectation is another type of logical mental simulation, a *predictive* simulation of what *will* happen given perceived present conditions as the simulator inputs. We play out reality in our minds from the current state of the present to some future state and what it will be like at that point in time, given what we know about and how we understand reality.

Third and finally, simulated experience is *counterfactual* if the inputs to the simulator are artificial and the mental simulator is a counterfactual mental model. A counterfactual mental model is a modified version of our mental model of reality that is designed *not* to represent reality as it is. Instead, it's a 'what if' scenario, reality from a 'what could be' perspective. What if the sky were red? What would it be like in the year 2400 A.D.? What if I were a foot taller? And so forth. We can simulate what these artificial realities would be like using the counterfactual as a mental simulator.

Creative imagination is perhaps the most obvious type of a counterfactual mental simulation. When an author makes up a fictional story, she creates a fictional world and simulates a storyline through that artificial mental model of the counterfactual world. When we wonder 'what if?', we simulate a counterfactual model of reality that replaces our true understanding of the world with a new assumption and simulate reality *as if* that assumption were true to derive some conclusion. When we look to the future, as we are very good at doing, the future is often another counterfactual reality. When we form 'could be' expectations in our mind, what really happens is we play out the future as a counterfactual with particular inputs (namely, a particular choice of actions) to its expected conclusion.

Simulated Empathy Theory

Empathy is a type of *counterfactual* mental simulation. It is a mental simulation of a *sensory* experience through a counterfactual model that is *intended to represent another's situational mental model*. Of course, because the sense inputs are not directly perceived, they have to be imagined artificially. The mental model used to simulate the experience is what you understand another to believe, experience, understand, and know in some particular scenario. Thus, if you do it well, your empathic experience is *essentially the same as theirs*. You get to experience what they experienced firsthand – not as if you were them but *as you think they experienced it*.

Let me go into some details of how this works.

The Knowledge Foundations of Empathy

First, let's talk about how we create a counterfactual mental model of *another's* worldview. Let's call this an *empathic mental model*, or, more simply the *empathic simulator*. So how do we do it?

It's perhaps not surprising to learn that we are much more capable of empathizing with close friends and family members. We're also better at empathizing with strangers that are very similar to ourselves than we are with dissimilar strangers. This is intuitive, but what does it tell us?

It tells us that empathy is *knowledge*-based. The counterfactual model that we create to represent another's situational worldview is based in what we know about that other person and the experience that we're interested in. But let us unpack this some more.

There are two key types of knowledge that an empathizer needs for an empathic experience: (1) knowledge about the other person and (2) knowledge about the experience. The first knowledge type is the makeup of the empathic mental model that simulates the empathic experience. The second knowledge type is the script or reel that is simulated through the empathic mental model.

First, we have to create our empathic simulator, a counterfactual mental model that represents the other's mental model of reality. This mental model is comprised of both *factual knowledge* of information about things (the *who, what, when, where, why*, and *how*), but also and more importantly, experiential or *phenomenal knowledge* of what various experiences were like. The fact is, you can't really know exactly what something is like for another person. Whereas factual knowledge is 'explicit' or communicable, phenomenal knowledge is 'tacit' or impossible to communicate, which I'll discuss in much more depth in the next chapter. We gain phenomenal knowledge – what a particular experience (phenomenon) is like – firsthand. Because you can't have the other's firsthand experience, what you do is copy your own mental model of firsthand phenomenal knowledge and, then, adjust the various aspects of it to reflect what you believe to be different in the other person's mental model.

A husband empathizing with his wife knows that there are large differences in their life experiences due, for example, to the fact that he is male and she is female. But he would have a hard time getting those differences right, having never experienced femaleness firsthand before. What he does is assume her experience is generally like his, but adjust that assumption based on what he knows about her and general female biological, cognitive, and other phenomenological (e.g., sociocultural) differences. As perhaps a tangential note, this copying of our own mental model as the baseline for an empathic model is arguably the reason for the so-called assumed similarity bias, where we assume the most others are like us – more like us than they really are.

Factual knowledge about the person having the experience is also critical to empathy as it is how we make the proper adjustments to the empathic simulator. These details entail, for example, information about the person's upbringing and life experiences, their views on a multitude of things, their values and preferences, their personal circumstances, their hopes and fears, and so forth. This is information that they can share about themselves. The empathic simulator is adapted with this factual knowledge. How the empathizer believes the world to work is adjusted for the learned differences. The man empathizing with his wife adjusts his empathic simulator to account for everything he knows and understands about his wife – her distinct preferences and opinions, her background and ideology, and so forth. The result of these adjustments is the empathic simulator that is then used for empathic simulation.

The input to this empathic simulator, the movie reel that is played, is what the empathizer knows about the *experience* itself, specifically the other's experience,

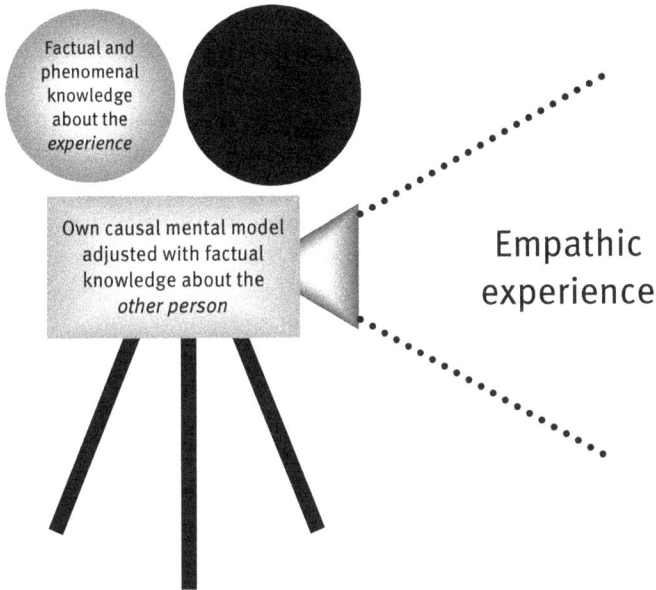

Fig. 8.2: Empathic Simulation.

which I will call the *empathic script*. Again, this knowledge is derived from both phenomenal and factual knowledge about the experience. Specifically, one first generates this script with their own firsthand experience of it, if they can. If they can't, if they don't have firsthand experience, they would first perform a predictive simulation act, such as I described in Chapter 4. Next, as before, this phenomenal knowledge script is then adjusted with factual knowledge about the other's unique experiential circumstances. When and where did the experience occur? Under what conditions? In what state was the other person when the experience happened? And so forth. Whereas the phenomenal knowledge provides the essential *how* it happened that cannot easily be conveyed, the contextual nuances of who, what, when, where, and perhaps even why it happened are added to the script through factual inquiry.

The empathic experience, then, is a mental simulation of another's experience, as captured in an *empathic script* through a counterfactual *empathic simulator* to produce a firsthand simulated experience of what an experience was like for the other (see Fig. 8.2).

The accuracy of this empathic simulation, of course, depends on the accuracy of the knowledge components that comprised both the empathic simulator and the empathic script. We can, in fact, empathize with anyone, but if I were to empathize with someone that I didn't know at all or share any common ground or background experience, my empathic imagination would almost necessarily be wildly inaccurate.

Coming back to the fact that we empathize better with family, friends, and other like people, this is the reason why. Our *phenomenal knowledge*, our experience-generated worldviews, are far more similar to those of people with whom we *shared* many of the experiences that made up those worldviews. Thus, our empathic simulators of our close friends and family members are far more accurate. Add to this the fact that we likely know a whole lot more factual knowledge *about* them and their experiences, such as the context in which they occurred (e.g., a known and familiar place), our empathic simulations of those close to us tends to be far more accurate. Yet, as husbands across the globe can attest, no matter how close he is to his wife, empathizing with her is limited and difficult.

The Temporal Unboundedness of Empathy

As a quick note about empathy, because it is a counterfactual mental simulation, it is unbounded by time. You can empathize with *past*, *present*, and *future* experiences that others did have, are having, or will or even might have. This is going to matter when it comes to figuring out what value proposition to develop.

Empathy and Entrepreneurship

So how does this theory help you? Why do you need to know how empathy works? Let's start, first, with why empathy matters to entrepreneurship, and then we can dig into how simulated empathy theory provides key insights into how to improve your idea and, thus, your chances at success.

What is the role of empathy in entrepreneurship? Entrepreneurship is a strong case of what scholars call 'epistemic interdependence' – the success of the entrepreneur's actions depend on a prediction of what others, particularly consumers, think, want, and will do. This epistemic interdependence puts the entrepreneur in a highly precarious spot.

It is well-known that entrepreneurs face uncertainty. But this is an uncertainty unlike any other economic uncertainty. Managers also face uncertainty, but their job is to manage the uncertainty – to deal responsively to market and other changes to reproduce and even, perhaps, incrementally improve some established value proposition, their product, for an existing market base over time. Employees face uncertainty, but their uncertainty concerns their employment and responsibilities; most of the more severe economic uncertainties are borne by their employer.[37]

---

37 This is why employees get paid less than they're 'worth' – they willingly forego the excess profits of their valuable labor in exchange for the security of the employment contract, a steady paycheck and

Entrepreneurs, however, take on the full brunt of economic uncertainty. No demand exists yet for whatever value proposition they might conjure or, at least, such demand is not yet established and routinized. The value uncertainty is absolute. Consumers don't yet know if they should want the value proposition, and so entrepreneurs cannot know if they will want it. This value uncertainty produces a severe economic uncertainty – will it be worth the cost of its development and production? In other words, *will it sell* at a price above cost?

So how do entrepreneurs, in the face of this radical value uncertainty, answer this question? The answer, as you undoubtedly guessed, is through *empathic imagination*. The entrepreneur can only form expectations of economic value by empathically imagining consumers' future value experiences and, therefrom, estimating total economic value.

It clearly follows from this that the more accurate the entrepreneur's empathic imagination, the better their entrepreneurial judgment and the more likely he or she is to succeed. *Empathic accuracy* refers to the extent to which your empathized experience accurately reflects the actual, firsthand experience of the other person, in this case your customer, that you empathize with. How closely does your empathically simulated experience truly capture the needs and/or value experiences of your (future) customer?

If your empathic simulation is poor, if you know little about your customer, then your simulated empathic experience is likely to mislead you to conclusions and expectations that are faulty. Such empathic errors may be small, leading you to generate a value proposition that is less effective than it could be, or very large, such as misunderstanding what your customer wants or needs altogether. Even a small misunderstanding can spell failure where the incumbent value proposition – the one your customers now use to solve their unmet need – is already 'good enough.' Arguably, virtually all entrepreneurial failures are empathic failures, where the entrepreneur did not understand their customers as much as they needed to.

So let's see what we can do to build better empathic simulators and scripts that will minimize empathic error.

Increasing your Empathic Accuracy

Recall that empathy is *knowledge*-based. It is, particularly, based in tacit, phenomenal (experiential) knowledge and augmented by explicit factual knowledge. Thus, the key to empathic accuracy is getting to know your customer at a profound level.

---

benefits. The uncertainties are shouldered by the investors, who capture a return on their investment if things go well, but if things go poorly, they incur the losses.

The next three chapters will guide you through the theory of learning from others and provide strategies for doing so effectively.

Chapter 9 will discuss the theory of communication and how you can talk to consumers more effectively. It would probably not surprise any experienced businesspeople reading this that it can be very easy to misunderstand your customers. It's easy enough to misunderstand the people you know best (as every married person can attest). If you can minimize miscommunication, you'll end up with more accurate factual knowledge about your customers, which will improve your empathy.

Chapter 10 will help you learn to increase your tacit knowledge about your customer through *experiential observation.* By immersing yourself in your customer's world, you learn firsthand a lot of what it's like to be them, their phenomenal knowledge. You can never fully know what that's like, but the more shared experience you can muster, the better.

Chapter 11 offers perhaps the easiest, and often the most successful strategy: targeting customers that you already understand well because *you're one of them.* This doesn't mean you can get away without learning and empathy, as I'll explain. But you have a distinctive advantage because you already speak their language and understand their pains at a level that others might not. But this strategy can limit your target market, so it may not be as profitable or compelling (especially if you're a dullard!).

The goal, then, is to give yourself the right and the most accurate and relevant knowledge to generate as accurate an empathic mental model (that counterfactual mental model that represents your customer's worldview) as possible so that you can experience firsthand the needs that your customers experience and the value of the solutions they now use.

One other thing you can do to facilitate accurate empathy is to put yourself in the same situation that you want to empathically experience to the best extent possible. Don't just imagine the other person's need, put yourself in that self-same situation in which they typically experience the need, if you can. This will vastly increase understanding and provide a better sense of how a solution might work for them. But, for it to be effective, it needs to reflect the customers' real experiences as carefully and correctly as possible.

Inferential Accuracy

Once you've empathized with your customer, you're not done yet. Empathy is the mere *experiencing* of another's experience, which, if done well, can let you experience your customer's needs for yourself (as though you were them). But to devise a new value proposition for them, you have to understand *how* and *why* they experience the need as they do. In other words, you have to *infer* from the empathized experience correct interpretations of what they're feeling and why.

The trouble is, two people can have the exact same experience and walk away with different interpretations of it. For example, if you and your customer come to different conclusions about *why* they experience a particular need, you'll have a hard time selling whatever value proposition you come up with to address it. They'll see your solution and think, 'that won't fix my problem.'

Now, this doesn't mean that you have to agree with their interpretation of their own need. This is a pitfall that market researchers can fall into. Remember that your customer is on an endless value learning journey, as I explained in Section 2. They don't know their needs perfectly already. So don't just assume that they're right about what they've concluded is the problem, or the solution.

But there's also the possibility that *you're* wrong about its causes, about what the real problem is. After all, not only could you have inferred inaccurately, you might have empathized inaccurately in the first place.

Tab. 8.1: Inferential Outcomes of Entrepreneurial Empathy.

		Entrepreneur	
		Misattribution	Accurate inference
Consumer	Misattribution	Short-term opportunity or failure	Failure
	Accurate inference	Failure	Long-term opportunity

Table 8.1 helps illustrate how and why this matters. To get a sale, you and your customer have to be on the same page – you have to both see the problem in the same way. If you do, then any solution you come up with, if better than what they already have, should appeal to them. But to *satisfy* your customer, you have to get it *right* – or, at least, right enough that what you produce is better than what they now have. To put it into the terminology of our value-as-a-process theory in Section 2, consumers will decide whether to buy based on their *predictive valuation*, which is based on their present understanding of their needs. But their satisfaction is based on the *value experience* when a real need is resolved.

If you want sustained success, and not just a one-off sale, you need to get it right. But how do you know if you got it right?

The honest answer is that you can't, at least not until they try it. But you can do some things to increase your chances.

The idea here is to use the two perspectives – yours and your customer's – to your advantage. If you both initially come to the same conclusion, then chances are you're onto something. You may not have it *exactly* right, but you almost certainly have it *more* right than previous solutions. Run with it. You can keep learning and improving your understanding over time with experience.

But if you and your customer come to different inferences, then you can use that also to improve your chances of getting it right. This means an extended back-and-forth to figure out who got it right or, perhaps, whether neither of you got it right and the answer is something else entirely.

Begin this process by explaining – in as much detail as you can muster – how you understand the experienced need *feels like*. Confirm with your customer, first, that your empathic experience is accurate. Of course, this experiential understanding is tacit, so this is going to be difficult. But if you've empathized accurately, if you have in fact shared the same experience, then a mutual understanding becomes possible. If you can't seem to communicate it, it may be because you misunderstood the experience.

After confirming, to the extent possible, that you understood what the experienced need is really like, go back and forth with your customer on *how* and *why* it feels that way. Let the more persuasive argument win. Be careful not to be too convinced you're right.

Eventually, you will need to come to a consensus, or else there can be no sale. If you're convinced that your customer is wrong and that you are right, you have a decision to make. Do you concede your customer's view and take the (more or less) sure sale? Or do you develop your own solution and likely lose this customer in the hopes of gaining more customers because your solution is good? The latter may seem the obviously better (albeit riskier) choice, but remember that it's possible that your customer is right and you are wrong. The customer's solution might prove to be the better one. There are no good rules of thumb here. You'll simply have to make your best judgment.

Chapter 9
Learning through Communication

Given the importance of knowing *about* consumers for empathy and understanding those consumers' needs, where and how do you learn that information? There are many methods for learning, ranging from scientific observation and experimentation to logical deduction. But here we're trying to learn about *other people* and, specifically, what's going on within themselves. What's their experience like? What needs to they have? What are their desires and preferences? What do they want and why?

When learning about others, especially about what's going on *within* themselves, one of the most common and useful mechanisms is learning *from* those others, especially through direct communication. Said differently, we merely need to *ask them.*

It is interesting to me that quite a few business scholars, thinkers, and consultants have arrived at this simple and basic insight over the past decade or so – if you want to know what your customers want, *ask them.* They're very willing to tell you. Entire books have been written on this very simple insight.

But here's the thing – just asking isn't as simple as they make it seem. And the answers you get are often not the answers you really need. As it turns out, despite how good many of us are at it, communication is not simple or straightforward process. It is especially problematic for consumer needs discovery, for reasons that I'll explain in this chapter.

Don't just ask. It's a recipe for disaster. Asking is of course helpful, but only insofar as you recognize and understand just how untrustworthy the answers you get can be. If you don't learn and recognize the pitfalls of communication, you're bound to be misled by your customers. Let's get into why.

What is Communication?

Let's start with the basics and define what communication really is. It seems like communication should be a straightforward concept, easy to define. As it turns out, it's not. After reviewing the communications research literature, I found all kinds of definitions that were claiming somewhat different things, reflecting different levels of analysis. I thought several definitions were reasonable, but I didn't find any that I felt fully and perfectly captured it.

There were two definitions in particular that, when taken together, I thought captured the essence of communication quite well. The first is from a 1964 book by Bernard Berelson and Gary Steiner, who define it as "the transmission of information, ideas, emotions, skills, etc., by the use of symbols – words, pictures, figures,

https://doi.org/10.1515/9783110750805-009

graphs, etc."[38] The second is from a 1966 paper by Gerald Miller, who explains that communication occurs when a communicator "transmits a message to a receiver(s) with conscious intent to affect the latter's behaviors."[39] Taken together, and adding the receiver to the equation, we arrive at a definition that I think is apt:

> Communication is a two-way intentional process wherein a communicator transmits a message (information, ideas, emotions, skills, etc.) via symbols (words, pictures, body movements, etc.) to a receiver with the intent of affecting the receiver's behaviors, and the receiver observes and interprets the message with the intention of learning from it.

This definition captures the intentionality and purpose of communication as well as its process and the variety of ways in which it can be accomplished. But let's unpack the complexities of this process some more, as it's not nearly as simple as we intelligent beings seem to make it.

Notice that there is a significant and complex two-sided interpretive process in communication. First, let's talk about the message that the communicator conveys. What does this message contain? What is the *content* of the message? Well, certainly it can contain virtually anything, ranging from specific statements of fact to opinions to expressions of feeling and emotion to imaginations of various types. The point of the expression or message is intentional, i.e., it is meant to affect the receiver in some way, whether to affect their emotional state or to convey information and knowledge, or to affect and alter their own intentions. In the case of consumer research, the message is what the consumer *wants* or *needs* with the intention that the receiver, the market researcher, learn how to better satisfy those wants and/or needs.

But in order to express this message, the communicator has to first translate that message into expressible symbology. What words are the best ones to convey the information I wish to share and that will produce the understanding that I intend? Will visual depiction help? Or body language? What should my face show when I state the message?

Most of these choices in how to make an appropriate expression we make instinctively, having learned them to the extent that they are second nature to us. But it should be very clear to us now that this is not nearly so simple a process as we make it seem. As a simple illustration, have you ever been stuck mid-sentence searching for the right word? Our language is immense and nuanced, and we often have many words that essentially mean the same thing, but which each convey a bit of distinct nuance that can be important. And sometimes it is difficult to recall all of those words, or to pull precisely the correct one to signify exactly what is meant.

---

38 Berelson, B., & Steiner, G. A. 1964. *Human Behavior: An inventory of scientific findings*. Oxford, England: Harcourt, Brace & World, p. 254.

39 Miller, G. R. 1966. On defining communication: Another stab. *Journal of Communication*, 16(2): 88–98, p. 92.

This same translation process is also a severe challenge on the receiver's side. Each expressed symbol must be observed (heard, seen, etc.) and internalized through a similar interpretive process. The meaning of each symbol must be understood as intended, which is aggregated into the general meaning of the message. Where the message is unclear, other contextual cues (such as the way in which it was expressed) may provide additional clues. Moreover, the *intent* of the message is interpreted – because communication is (as we've defined it) meant to affect the receiver's behaviors, the receiver assesses the intent of the communicator and whether they are aligned with it. If the receiver perceives deceit, manipulation, or other impetus underpinned by more malicious or disagreeable motives, the receiver is likely to dismiss the communication.

What Can and Can't be Communicated

I have already introduced you to the distinction between *tacit* and *explicit* knowledge, but here is where understanding that distinction comes to especial fruition. To review, tacit knowledge is that which cannot be communicated. This type of knowledge is distinguished from *explicit* knowledge, which can be. But let's really dig down into *why* some knowledge can and can't be communicated, a problem deeply examined by philosopher Michael Polanyi.

Have you ever tried to teach someone to ride a bike? Or, perhaps, you can recall your own experience being taught to ride one. How do you teach it? Certainly, you would explain the mechanics of it: the peddling, the steering, the balancing. But once you understand all of the mechanics of riding a bike, do you then know *how* to ride a bike? Of course not, because riding a bike can only be learned by *doing* it, by experiencing firsthand what it's like to ride a bike, how it feels, what it really means to balance, peddle, and steer. This type of knowledge, only attainable through firsthand experience, is *tacit* knowledge.

A fun thought experiment, proposed by Mark Jackson, called *Mary's room* illustrates this point. Mary, a scientist, was born, strangely, with virtually no pigment to herself and into a completely monochrome (black-and-white) room with no windows, where she's been locked away her whole life. All of her food is black and white. Her clothes are also. She's never seen another person, she's never been or even seen outside her room. Her computer, which gives her some access to the outside world, of course, also has a monochrome monitor. She has never before experienced color. There's nothing wrong with her eyes, she's just never seen it.

Of course, she's fascinated by this concept of color that she's never seen. In fact, she's so intrigued by it that she has become the world's foremost expert on color (especially red, her favorite). She knows the nature of light, the exact wavelengths that comprise the visible spectrum and each specific color. She knows the biology of the optic sensory organs, how our eyes perceive it, and everything else there is to know. She knows the color red, scientifically, to such an extent that there is nothing more she could possibly know.

The question Jackson poses is this: suppose Mary finally is let out of her monochrome world. Does she learn anything new when she *sees* the color red for the first time? I think the answer is, of course, *yes*. Whatever that new knowledge is – what red actually looks like – is *phenomenal knowledge*, which I introduced in the previous chapter, which is knowledge of what it is like to experience something.

Now, what's important to understand now, for this chapter, is that this phenomenal knowledge is *tacit* knowledge.

Tacit Versus Explicit Knowledge

Tacit knowledge, as I've said before, is typically understood as incommunicable knowledge. As it turns out, there are many things in life that can only be learned by *doing*. This is sometimes called 'experiential knowledge,' which I have called *phenomenal knowledge* in the previous chapter. Like Mary, we can know all about the factual knowledge of things, what things are, how things are done, and why. You don't have to have experience with a hammer to know all about how to hammer a nail. It's easy enough to see how it's done. *But*, pick up that hammer for the first time to pound on a nail and you will very quickly realize that those skilled woodworkers only make it *look* easy. After a few misses of the nail and perhaps a smashed thumb, you'd quickly realize that there is more to the knowledge of how to use a hammer than could be explained or even observed. Often, we refer to this experiential knowledge as *skill*, that knowledge that we acquire by performing specific tasks, and the more we perform the task the greater our skill.

But phenomenal knowledge includes more than just skill. There is a more profound type or aspect of phenomenal knowledge that goes beyond what we call skill, and need not entail any skill at all. Like Mary's experience of red for the first time, philosophers have called this *what-it's-like* knowledge or 'qualia', or knowledge of what it's like to have that experience. This specific type of knowledge is what I've been calling phenomenal knowledge.

Let's use the taste of salt as an example.[40] Think to yourself what salt tastes like. It is quite easy to imagine, I suppose. We've all tasted it many times. But now imagine someone who has not tasted it. Try to explain the taste of salt to that person. No, you can't use the word 'salty' to explain it, someone who hasn't tasted salt won't know what that means. You can't do it, can you? But why not?

---

40 I credit this example to Boyd K. Packer: https://www.churchofjesuschrist.org/study/ensign/1983/01/the-candle-of-the-lord

Polanyi explained that this phenomenal knowledge is born only of experience. Once two people have had the experience, those people could communicate *about* it and have some meaningful understanding. But they cannot communicate the experience itself to someone who did not have it. As the common quip goes, 'you had to be there.'

For this reason, Polanyi describes this phenomenal knowledge or 'know-how' as *tacit*, meaning that it is incommunicable, it cannot be expressed or shared. As I just mentioned, two people with shared experience can speak *about* it. One person can *describe* the experience in whatever detail can be mustered. But the phenomenal knowledge itself cannot be expressed.

In contrast, *explicit* knowledge is what we might call 'know-what,' the explicable facts and information *about* things. In the previous chapter I called this *factual knowledge*. This type of knowledge is comprised of specific characteristics of things, for which we have devised our complex language to describe. We have a tome's worth of adjectives and adverbs at our disposal to precisely characterize the nature of things – objects, ideas, events, people, actions.

Because tacit knowledge is innately incommunicable and explicit knowledge is communicable in principle, some scholars have placed tacit versus explicit on a continuum, where some knowledge is more tacit (difficult to communicate) than other knowledge. But this is a mistake, I think. Tacit knowledge is of an entirely different type. Any know-what is communicable in principle, even if difficult. The reason you might not be able to explain the process of nuclear fission to me is not because it is *tacit* (i.e., experience-based), but because you or I may not have the necessary wherewithal to share such knowledge. To communicate requires that both parties have a certain level of mutual understanding of words and concepts such that shared information can be properly interpreted. It's not that the knowledge of fission is incommunicable, it's that I don't have sufficient knowledge of nuclear physics to accurately ascribe the appropriate meaning to all of the necessary symbols (words) you would have to convey to explain it.

In other words, knowledge is not tacit just because it's hard to communicate. Communication is hard, period. We have a shared language, but that doesn't mean that we always choose the right words or correctly interpret how the other is using them. I'll get more into this in a second.

But phenomenal knowledge is tacit. It *can't* be communicated at all. The only way to get at another's experience is by sharing the experience or else through empathic mental simulation.

This matters a great deal because, as I've gone to great lengths to explain up to this point, entrepreneurship is all about *other's value experiences*, which are *tacit*! This is why understanding empathy is so vital to entrepreneurship, as I explained in the previous chapter.

Communicating Factual Knowledge

Empathy, as I explained, is a knowledge-based counterfactual simulation. You can empathize better the more you know about the other and their experience. The figure here illustrates the general theoretical framework. Each of the terms in Fig. 9.1

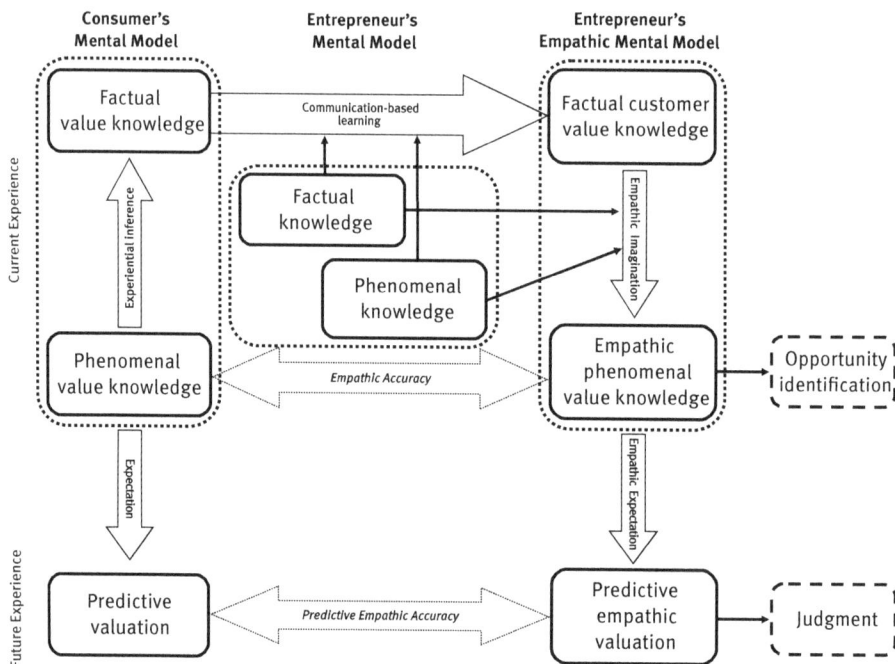

Fig. 9.1: The Role of Communication in Entrepreneurial Empathy.

should by now be familiar. The ultimate aim of entrepreneurship and its primary key to success is in the entrepreneur's empathic accuracy and, more specifically, their *predictive* empathic accuracy. One key thing you can do to improve your customer empathy is to communicate with them about the factual aspects of themselves and their experience, illustrated as the top arrow from consumer (on the left) to entrepreneur (on the right).

But, again, communication is hard. You know this already. We've all tried to communicate with someone in a way they we or they just weren't getting what we were trying to say. Or we've been the one's struggling to comprehend. We've all experienced the frustrations of another person misunderstanding us, perhaps in a way that put us in a bad light. Even the people who know us the most and the best will occasionally misconstrue our communications.

So let's now go into *how* we communicate so that, perhaps, we can see where the pitfalls are. Knowing these pitfalls, we can guard against them when getting it right, and understanding what they really mean, is of utmost importance. In entre-preneurship, miscommunication with your customer can ultimately spell disaster.

Figure 9.2 represents the two-sided communication process from consumer to entrepreneur, as well as the propensity for what I will can *interpretive loss*, meaning a loss in factual understanding. In the case of entrepreneurship, interpretive loss most often manifests as misunderstanding, specifically of what the consumer really

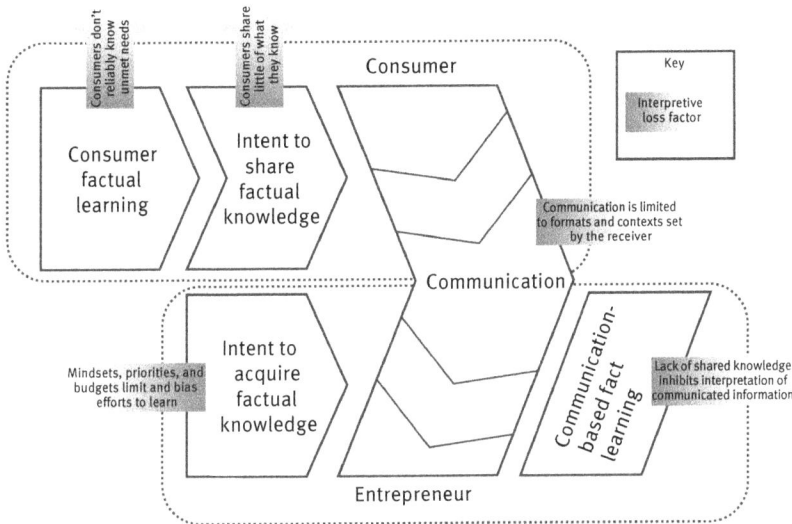

Fig. 9.2: The Communication Process and its Pitfalls.

needs. But this misunderstanding is not merely on the entrepreneur's side. As Section 2 makes clear, consumers misunderstand their own needs also.

Let's examine this interpretive communication process in some more depth. As Fig. 9.2 illustrates, there are five stages to the communication process. Let's unpack each stage further.

Consumer Learning

Consumers are innately motivated to learn their own needs – to increase their factual knowledge of them – as, by so doing, they can better resolve their need and, thereby, improve their subjective well-being. To briefly reiterate what was discussed in depth in Section 2, this knowledge is learned first experientially as phenomenal knowledge of felt uneasiness. Additional phenomenal knowledge can be learned experientially through consumption. From these unique experiences of uneasiness, along with the necessarily unique context within which the dissolution of that uneasiness occurs through consumption, the consumer then individually infers an interpretation of what their personal needs are, how to satisfy them, and why. This inference is *factual knowledge*. Thus, it can be communicated.

But this inferential process from phenomenal experience, as I have discussed in some depth in Chapter 7, is highly fallible and misattributions are common. I will not rehash those arguments here.

However, one thing worth adding is that learning from consumption comes only via existing solutions, limiting the discovery of the not-already-understood nature of needs. In other words, the value learning cycle is a discovery process *through* experience, which experience is given by existing solutions. Consumers can learn new things by trying them, but those new things exist because some intrepid entrepreneur already envisioned it. So their new knowledge tends to be limited to that which has already been discovered by others. Their new knowledge is quite limited.

Because entrepreneurs' factual knowledge about consumers and, thus, their empathic phenomenal knowledge is derived, in large part, from consumers' communicated factual knowledge (as I'll elaborate further shortly), one common source of interpretive loss occurs as a result of the imperfect consumer value learning process, which leaves the consumer's factual value knowledge always and necessarily imprecise and incomplete.

Marketing research[41] strongly suggests that consumers are poor predictors of their own future demand due, arguably, to misattributed causal value knowledge. A consumer who believes that she prefers to purchase environmentally conscientious products but never, in fact, actually derives enough satisfaction from that supposed preference at the point of purchase to actually buy them, will tend to convey to entrepreneurs misleading factual value knowledge. Equivocation of experiential causes of value is likely to mislead predictive empathy such that entrepreneurs mistake what their customers will really value in the future, which results in poorer entrepreneurial judgment.

Consumers' learned value knowledge and preferences are often ill-defined and susceptible to influence. Ambiguous or uncertain factual knowledge, especially with regard to the causes of the consumer's needs and satisfaction experiences, undermines its clear communication and, hence, any hope of accurate customer value knowledge (and, thus, empathic accuracy) on the part of the entrepreneur. In short, what consumers think they need and want is often uncertain, short-sighted, or even mistaken, which can mislead entrepreneurs, both in their real-time understanding of consumers' experiences (opportunity recognition) and in their prediction of future consumer experiences (value judgment).

---

41 For example: Kalwani, M. U., & Silk, A. J. 1982. On the reliability and predictive validity of purchase intention measures. *Marketing Science*, 1(3): 243–286.

Morwitz, V. 1997. Why consumers don't always accurately predict their own future behavior. *Marketing Letters*, 8(1): 57–70.

To avoid this pitfall, entrepreneurs ought to focus their communicative efforts on those consumers least likely to have misunderstood their needs experiences and derived therefrom false factual value knowledge. Who are these consumers with the best value knowledge? Eric von Hippel calls them *lead users*. These are consumers who are always at the cutting edge of a market because they are the ones with the highest needs. I'll talk more about these key customers in Chapter 14.

Consumer Intent to Share Knowledge

In a 2008 article, Zaki, Bolger, and Ochsner[42] argued that empathic accuracy not only requires effort on the empathizer's part, but it also requires the efforts of those being empathized with, in this case consumers. This is because a significant amount of the important factual knowledge needed for the empathy process has to be expressed in order for the empathizer to receive and internalize it. And communication is, in large part, on the communicator to express the communication effectively.

Misinterpretation commonly occurs as a result of unclear and ambiguous communications, which can happen when the communicator – the consumer in this case – puts little effort into being clear. The reasons for such a lack of effort are, of course, generally relating to a lack of incentive. Of course, there is, or should be, an obvious incentive for consumers to communicate their value knowledge – they want to be better satisfied! But providing feedback, as Hoyer and colleagues note in a 2010 research article, involves "monetary and nonmonetary costs of time, resources, [and] physical and psychological effort."[43] When this is taken into consideration, the highly uncertain benefits that might come out of the effort to share one's value knowledge with an entrepreneur (or other producer), weighed against the much more certain and visible costs in the effort to do so, should probably leave us wondering why anyone provides feedback at all! So let's try to unravel the psychology of consumers to understand what might be driving them to share (or not) their value knowledge.

The most commonly observed motivator of consumer sharing in marketing research is their self-interest – to get for themselves a better product. In part, this is why dissatisfied customers are more predisposed to share their negative feedback – they want a better product (or, at least, to be recompensed). Such self-interest inspires more and better information sharing when a consumer believes the information sharing would be sufficiently likely to elicit a beneficial response from the producer.

---

42 Zaki, J., Bolger, N., & Ochsner, K. 2008. It takes two: The interpersonal nature of empathic accuracy. *Psychological Science*, 19(4): 399–404.
43 Hoyer, W. D., Chandy, R., Dorotic, M., Krafft, M., & Singh, S. S. 2010. Consumer cocreation in new product development. *Journal of Service Research*, 13(3): 283–296, p. 288.

But some consumers are pro-socially motivated, such as by a desire to help other consumers (e.g., social contribution or altruism) or to help a producer that they identify with. Sharing their knowledge may also produce financial, social, technical, and even psychological benefits.

These potential benefits are counterbalanced by the costs of providing the feedback. Generally, the costs of information sharing are inversely related to the complexity of the information. Some value knowledge, such as their specific and explicit demand, is comparatively simple and easy to convey, entailing a specific willingness to pay for a specific product at a specific price. Such information is relatively easy and costless to communicate. In contrast, value knowledge concerning more general or abstract wants (e.g., "I want something to cheer me up") or, even, needs can be difficult and, thus, costly to put into words in a way that communicates what, specifically, is wanted or needed. Sufficient motivation to surmount these costs is less likely, especially when the expected benefits are uncertain.

Even when consumers are motivated to share their value knowledge, some trigger may be necessary to instigate the sharing, especially when the potential for self-benefit is limited. The most common trigger is solicitation, which can trigger reciprocity motives that impel a response. As Satish Nambisan writes, "customers rarely offer new product ideas without being prompted."[44]

However, solicitation may *reduce* instead of enhance information-sharing efforts as it can replace or inhibit intrinsic or pro-social motivations might have already held. Perhaps more importantly, solicited questions can constrain the information communicated because it constrains what is perceived as relevant to the questions asked, as I'll explain in a bit. Also, solicitation tends to be temporally removed from the experience in question, which means that it relies on experiential memory from a while back, and may suffer from recall error.

In short, communication costs (including time and effort) mean that consumers will always convey at most only a portion of the value knowledge they actually hold with respect to any value experience. They're simply not going to sit there for hours telling you every little detail of their value experience unless you make it worth their while.

This implies a few practical things that you might do to improve your customer feedback – and the greater the motivation to share more and detailed value knowledge, the greater the resultant empathic accuracy. One thing to do right off the bat is *avoid* solicitation as your primary go-to method of collecting feedback. It's problematic for a few reasons. For example, unless you're being very careful and selective, you may be soliciting value knowledge from customers that do not have very much, and what they have may be incorrect or misleading. Remember that may be

---

44 Nambisan, S. (2002). Designing virtual customer environments for new product development: Toward a theory. *Academy of Management Review, 27*(3), 392–413, p. 394.

at a much lower level on the value learning cycle than even you are regarding this particular need. A random sampling of consumers is liable to get feedback from low-knowledge consumers just as much as high-knowledge consumers, and it's often not obvious which one is which. Instead, seek out and solicit help from specifically high value knowledge consumers – again, those lead users. Don't listen to customers that don't know what they're talking about. They're almost certainly going to lead you astray.

Another thing to consider is that your customers' time and effort are valuable to them. If you want real and deep help – which you should – you need to keep their motives in mind. Many of these consumers, the lead users in particular, *want* to help you because if you succeed, they will be better off in addressing a need that they really care about. But make sure that you and they are on the same page on this. Make sure they know and understand that they are helping themselves by engaging in the process. You might offer them free or severely discounted access to the prototype and/or the first production run. If they can clearly imagine how their help in your efforts will lead to a much better solution for themselves, they will be highly motivated to communicate effectively.

Entrepreneur's Intention to Acquire Knowledge

On the flip side of consumer's intent to share is your own motivation to learn from them. Some of this may seem obvious, but let's dig into the entrepreneur's motives to learn also because this is actually where a lot of mistakes happen. Learning from feedback also involves costs and tradeoffs, including your own time, effort, and research costs that, again, generally increase with the complexity and tacitness of the value knowledge sought. So there are strategic tradeoffs to pursuing different types of value knowledge. What type of value knowledge should you be seeking and what are the costs involved? Let's discuss.

Perception is consciously focused – we tend to perceive only that to which our attention is aimed. This was illustrated with Simons and Chabris's famous experiment,[45] where observers watched a scene of people passing a basketball around. Observers were asked to count the number of passes in the scene. Most were able to count the number of passes correctly, but almost none of them noticed that someone dressed up like a gorilla had wandered right into the middle of the activity! When your attention is directed toward a specific goal, your mind conserves its efforts and does not attend to the minutiae surrounding you. But, interestingly, even

---

45 Simons, D. J., & Chabris, C. F. 1999. Gorillas in our midst: Sustained inattentional blindness for dynamic events. *Perception*, 28(9): 1059–1074. For the video, see https://www.youtube.com/watch?v=vJG698U2Mvo.

when you're focused, your mind appears to have an emergency system that will warn you of real dangers and arrest your attention to those dangers, like if you see something about to hit you out of the corner of your eye.

The point of this is that what you hear and learn from communications is very dependent on what you *want* to hear and learn. Your intentions direct with whom you will communicate, the nature and form of communications pursued, the questions asked, and what information is heard or dismissed – all of which impact what is heard and learned.

Empathic accuracy can, in this way, be limited or undermined by an entrepreneur's overly narrow learning intent. For example, an entrepreneur, (over)confident in her/his recognition of a real and valuable opportunity, may be unmotivated to expend time, effort, and other costs in pursuit of further opportunity refinement via new value learning, supposing his or her empathy to already be accurate.

But even if and when the entrepreneur desires to learn, overly narrowly learning intent can constrain learning about other needs and preferences that might affect wants and demand. In other words, your market research is severely biased toward your priors, toward your own understanding of what your product does (or should do). Kimberly Clark's misreading of the toilet paper market (from Chapter 8) is a good example of this.

As another example, consider what happened when Coca-Cola's executives learned of taste tests suggesting that most consumers preferred the taste of Pepsi in the early 1980s. They set out to identify a new flavor that blind taste-testers would prefer, and, in 1985, altered their recipe. But there was a massive consumer backlash to the change, and Coca-Cola was forced to bring back the classic recipe, rebranding the new recipe 'New Coke' to contrast it from the traditional 'Coca-Cola Classic' recipe. The execs were, perhaps understandably, so focused on understanding taste preferences that their research overlooked all other factors that might have led their customers to prefer Coke to Pepsi. When the recipe was changed, some customers reported feeling as if they had lost a family member.[46]

Entrepreneurs are generally inclined to prioritize more easily accessible value knowledge, which can constrain what is learned, for several reasons. Perhaps foremost are the costs of learning sufficiently rich value knowledge to engage in successful empathic imagination, and the energy required to do so. Where new empathic understanding is perceived to be less important – e.g., in stable industries where demand is well-established – the costs of nuanced value knowledge learning may not be warranted. Also, because demand produces sales, knowing current demand – an explicit form of value knowledge – is the most certain and immediate route to profitability and, so, it has a strong draw. Resource-constrained entrepreneurs may be inclined to pursue the cheaper route of seeking simple and explicit demand value

---

46 Oliver, T. 1986. *The Real Coke, the Real Story*. New York: Random House.

knowledge rather than more nuanced and complex value knowledge about needs experiences needed for empathic imagination. In other words, why not just have customers tell you what they'll buy instead of having to guess with some roundabout empathy process? This is how most entrepreneurs tend to think.

But it's mistaken thinking for reasons that I've already explained – that customers typically *don't* know what they really want. Their preferences are fickle because they themselves are trying to figure out what to want and are learning as they go. They can at best tell you what they want *at that moment*. If you're in a position to give it to them at that very moment, then great. But don't count on them always putting their money where their mouth is.

In short, what entrepreneurs want to learn directs and constrains what is asked, perceived, and learned. Getting good, trustworthy factual value knowledge needed for empathic accuracy requires an intention toward truly understanding the consumer, rather than, for example, toward confirming your own beliefs. It demands open-mindedness. To the extent that entrepreneurs hold strong priors about what they believe consumers want, they will tend to find only confirmations from others, and empathic accuracy (and new opportunity recognition) is prone to be limited.

This is an ever-present challenge for entrepreneurs, who must balance a conviction that they have really good idea (which conviction is needed to initiate and sustain the long and difficult path to commercialization) with an openness to new learning, to being wrong. This balance underpins issues of over- and underconfidence that are often associated with entrepreneurship (overconfidence more so than underconfidence, but they both can happen).

To overcome these potential issues, you may benefit from practicing techniques for gaining self-awareness of your own intentions. Learn to question the premises underlying those intentions. Ideally, you would approach consumers with minimal preconceptions of what you expect to find. You might even try going into conversations with customers expecting to be surprised, to be wrong. Press consumers to go beyond just the obvious and primary reasons for their preferences. Try to learn about secondary and tertiary reasons. Make sure to watch the basketball passes, but keep an eye out for those gorillas too!

Communication

Let's now turn to the crux of the communication process, the information-sharing interaction that we call *communication*. Your ability to communicate will be significantly augmented by simply knowing how communication really works so you can avoid the errors that are so prevalent in social discourse.

Remember that only the explicit aspects of knowledge can be readily transferred in communications. So, in order to communicate any knowledge (such as value knowledge), that knowledge must first be stripped of its tacit elements, such as subjective experience and personal meaning, leaving only the expressible information. This explicit information is then translated from whatever state in which it resides in one's brain into expressible language. Primarily, this translation entails finding the right words to convey the intended meaning. But the meaning of words can be augmented with, e.g., tone and body language.

Of course, finding the 'right' words is often a severe challenge, especially when describing complex and nuanced knowledge, such as value knowledge. Even if a 'perfect' word can be found, the meaning of that word must be shared by the receiver for it to convey the right meaning. Thus, language barriers tend to arise when communicating complex phenomena – even when it's a shared primary language!

Once the value knowledge is stripped of the tacit elements and translated into an expressible message (which generally happens as you go), the message is then transmitted via some communication medium. That medium might be text, it might be audio, it might be some other form.

Whatever the medium or channel of communication, there is a high chance of *noise* of some sort. Noise refers to a distortion of a communication. Obviously, noise typically refers to audio distortions that come in the form of other sounds from various sources surrounding the audio message that can make hearing the message difficult. To hear it, the mind must filter out the other sounds to focus only on that single sound wave. But when noise is loud, the mind cannot filter it all out. But this same noise phenomenon occurs for other forms of communication also, albeit in different manifestations. There can be, for example, visual noise that can draw an observer's attention away from the focus of the visual message. This is why strictly visual commercials (e.g., for television) will often clean out all the visual noise and create an essentially blank background so that consumers will focus their attention on the featured product.

Textual messages generally have a different problem – a lack of visual or audio 'tone' to complement the message. We use tone to convey a deeper meaning in a message, such as sarcasm. Much of one's emotions are 'worn on their sleeves,' which convey a deeper meaning to messages they convey. "I just love getting up at 6 a.m. every morning" has a very different meaning depending on the tone, i.e., if expressed excitedly versus sarcastically. Text, of course, cannot easily depict such tonality. Many an email or text message has been misconstrued because the receiver mistook the tone of the message. The introduction of emojis has done wonders to begin to clear these confusions up, but it is still a highly fallible process.

At the other end, the receiver must be able to receive the message without loss, understand the symbology (e.g., words) used, and reconstruct the meaning of the message from what was heard. Recall that this message has already been stripped into a mere skeleton of explicit information, and then translated from that into the communicator's choices of meaningful symbols. The receiver now has to reconstruct what they believe the communicator intended by filling in the missing gaps of the expressed message. We do this intuitively, filling in the gaps of interpretation to produce a more complete and meaningful message. But from what? Like empathy, we fill most of these gaps with our knowledge of the other person where we can, and with our own experiential knowledge where we can't.

If I don't recognize a person's sense of sarcasm, I might construe their statement that they love getting up at 6 a.m. every morning as indicating that they're a morning person, that they're a go-getter, and early riser, a workaholic, or some other interpretation. But if I know them, their sense of sarcasm, and their propensity to stay up late most nights, I can derive from the statement the more accurate meaning of it – that the truth is the *opposite*.

So much of communication is, again, knowledge-based. This includes language and base knowledge to know the meaning of words. But it also entails contextual knowledge of culture and person. As Liyanage and colleagues note, "if you do not understand the context you will always misinterpret the embedded situation to a greater or lesser extent."[47]

Recognizing these challenges will enable you to avoid some of the more common pitfalls. What we call 'jumping to conclusions' is perhaps the most common, where the meaning of an expressed message is presumed when the message was in fact ambiguous, and the intended meaning was different than was received. Clarifying questions are vital, especially where communicators are of different backgrounds.

To this latter point, communication is greatly facilitated by sharing a common culture and background. Each culture and subculture has its own symbology and iconography. Words and symbols mean different things and convey different messages. When communicating across cultures, misunderstandings are bound to happen. To avoid such misunderstandings, you might first embed yourself within their culture and learn it to enable communication. Or, perhaps, you might employ a market researcher with the appropriate background knowledge to enable such communications and avoid misunderstandings.

Finally, take the messaging channel into consideration. Text, such as an online survey, can reach a broader audience, but it is no substitute for a face-to-face discussion. Also, survey scales can give you large quantities of aggregate data, but they only answer the questions you have provided and are, thus, confirmatory. You can't learn much that's new from a survey.

There are other pitfalls and ways around them that I might bring up, but this is not a book about better communication. Just remember how difficult it is to communicate perfectly with people you know very well, such as a spouse or a sibling. Do you really think you know exactly what some stranger from a different background really thinks and means? Be careful.

---

47 Liyanage, C., Elhag, T., Ballal, T., & Li, Q. 2009. Knowledge communication and translation–a knowledge transfer model. *Journal of Knowledge Management*, 13(3): 118–131, p. 129.

Entrepreneurial Learning

The last stage is the learning stage, where the receiver of the communication takes the interpreted message and electively generates from the message new knowledge. Knowledge is really one's mental model of causal reality. In this case, we're talking about value knowledge, and the value knowledge about the *consumer* specifically. We're not trying to solve our own needs and wants directly here, we need to solve the consumer's needs and wants if we're going to have a viable venture.

The main point in this stage of the communication process is that learning is *elective*. You decide what you will learn from the information that was communicated to you.

In much the same type of learning cycle as discussed in Section 2, one's learning from communications is, essentially, a hypothesis-testing process – the new information confirms or rejects their expectations (according to their current mental model). This means that new information can result in three possible learning outcomes.

First, you may interpret new information, as you understand it, to be consistent with your already held value knowledge, confirming and strengthening it. In a sense, this is learning, but without actually changing the mental model. Instead, it solidifies the current structure of it, adding credence to the current causal interpretation. Contradictory evidence in the future, then, would have a harder time displacing the current causal interpretation because of the evidence collected in support of it.

Second, if the information cannot (or will not) be interpreted to conform to or confirm you present mental model (i.e., it is disconfirmatory), you may discount the information as inaccurate or anomalous and ignore it. This is akin to removing outliers from a dataset, which is common (but questionable) practice in statistical science. Such dismissal of the information results in no new knowledge. You may scoff at this possibility, but I guarantee that you do it all the time. We get new information all the time from all kinds of sources. Often that information contradicts our worldview, and we dismiss it due to an unreliable source, because it's a one-off exception to the rule, etc. We preserve our worldview by rejecting challenges to it.

Third and finally, you may find the information new, meaningful, and important, and elect to modify your mental model accordingly, producing new value knowledge. This knowledge can span a spectrum of magnitudes, from minor and inconsequential additions to major overhaulings of fundamental beliefs, depending on the assumptions being challenged and the extent to which the current mental model depends on them. Once interpreted information is accepted and integrated as new knowledge, it becomes the new hypothesis against which new feedback and information are judged.

It is perhaps worth elaborating that making severe changes to fundamental beliefs is excessively difficult – it is what is often referred to as a 'mental crisis' or 'having your world turned upside down' – and it can take a long time. Basically, when you finally decide that a fundamental assumption is flawed and needs to be replaced, all of the causal knowledge that you had built atop that assumption also comes crashing down and needs to be rebuilt. You don't understand the world anymore. Things stop making sense to you until you can reconstruct a new causal knowledge structure with the revisions that you had to make. This is why the second learning outcome is actually so common.

Over time, your customer value knowledge – your value knowledge of what other customers value – evolves with repeated and aggregated collections of feedback from various sources. This learning process can occur serially – considering, interpreting, and integrating shared feedback individually – or in parallel, through the quantitative assessment of 'bulk' feedback. With more data comes, presumably, more inferential accuracy, although this is not necessarily the case. At any one time, a producer has a 'present state' of an ever-evolving customer value knowledge based on their consideration, interpretation, and integration (or not) of all information so far obtained from consumers, in aggregate. This knowledge may be parsed individually, with the entrepreneur's interpretation of consumers' needs, wants, and demands being ascribed to customers individually so as to tailor solutions accordingly; or it may be abstracted and generalized, the producer taking stock of the 'average' or 'typical' customer so as to evaluate standardized solutions to customer segments.

There are a few pitfalls that you can certainly fall into here. For one, be careful what information you dismiss. Those 'outliers' are often your most important source of knowledge. Bill Gates wrote, "Unhappy customers are . . . your greatest opportunity. Listening and learning rather than being defensive can make customer complaints your best source of significant quality improvements."[48] Don't dismiss outliers just because they don't conform to your priors.

With that said, don't overhaul your value knowledge on the challenge of a single outlier either. First, not everyone has the same needs, values, or expectations, so you can't please everyone. And second, some people are just ornery. Their opinions probably *should* be dismissed.

Perhaps the best advice is, before dismissing a datapoint, it's probably wise to dig deeper into *why* it's different. If it is different for legitimate reasons, that is something to learn from.

A second and related implication is that inferring from incomplete information is always dangerous. Be wary of jumping to conclusions. Make sure you understand *their* reasons and reasoning. You don't have to agree, but don't just presume to know what they think or why.

Finally, learning from single data-points can mislead if it is not trustworthy or if it is not representative. Depth of communication is extremely valuable, but don't completely discount the value of multiple datapoints. Scholars have espoused

---

48 Gates, B. 2001. *Business @ the Speed of Thought*. Essex: Pearson, p. 60.

triangulation as a powerful method for grounding your learning. Get different per-spectives from people of different backgrounds and beliefs. Although 'the truth is somewhere in the middle' is usually a pretty good rule of thumb, finding a 'middle-ground' conclusion is not always the best option – sometimes a middle option doesn't appeal to anyone. But it is important to get value knowledge from different perspectives so that you can more deeply understand what the underlying needs are and why.

Summing Up

Communication is not really as easy as we social beings make it look. We do it all the time and so we're pretty good at it. But all of us are, or ought to be, all too famil-iar with the propensities to misunderstand or misconstrue. Communication is a complex interpretive process.

Perfect communication is, in fact, impossible – and even if it were possible, we could never know if or when it happened.

So be careful how much stock you put into communications. It is all too com-mon for companies to collect mounds of datapoints from surveys and customer focus groups and derive inferences from them. But such 'learning' is superficial. Those firms tend to really learn only if their customers claim to be satisfied or not – a conclusion they probably could have reached just by looking at their performance metrics. Good communication can get you much more, provided you are careful not to stumble into communication's many pitfalls.

Learning as much as you can about customers is vital for accurate empathy – if you're going to truly understand your customer. So talk to them. A survey just won't cut it.

Chapter 10
Learning from Observation

If consumers don't know or understand what they want or, at least, what they *should* want, how can we figure that out? In other words, given the limitations of communication just explained in the previous chapter, how else can you learn about and from your customers? One of the more common and increasingly important sources of information is customer *observation*. That is, scholars and marketing gurus have started to recognize the benefits of observation as a supplement to fallacious market surveys and customer interviews. Various techniques and methods, like journey mapping for discovering consumer needs, have emerged to advocate ethnographic observation as a core mechanism for learning what customers experience and need that they themselves might remain unaware of.

In this chapter let's explore what can be learned from observation, and how you can make your observations more empathic and, thus, more accurate and helpful.

What You Can (and Can't) Observe

In the previous chapter, we discussed how better communication can get us as far as accurately learning what consumers *think* they want and even how and what to read between the lines. But really you can't use communication to effectively learn what consumers *should* and *will* want when the time and opportunity comes, which is why so many products still struggle and fail despite extensive market research (like the moist toilet paper roll).

There are several important problems, as we learned in the previous chapter. The first is that what is at the heart of the matter is needs and value experiences, which are *tacit* knowledge. The second is that consumers don't know themselves as well as, sometimes, we (or they) think they do. They are merely at a particular stage in the value learning journey discussed in Section 2. They are themselves looking for that next better thing. Unless one of them has had some radical and brilliant insight, they're as much in the dark as anyone else.

So communication only gets us factual knowledge that we can then use in empathic imagination. But even then, it's rare to have such communication prowess to purvey such nuance and details as is desirable for profound empathy. There is just so much that gets 'lost in translation,' no matter how good at communication you and your customer might be.

The social sciences face a similar dilemma. A significant amount of the data that scientists collect are self-report data – communications from those they study, of one form or another. Most of these data are surveys, which of course convey extremely basic and limited information. Social scientists have been struggling with

https://doi.org/10.1515/9783110750805-010

this problem for decades. Most scholars have resigned themselves to the simplicity of the data we collect. The nuance, they argue, is captured in the variance of the survey responses. So scientists ask very simple questions to get at basic phenomena to answer straightforward hypotheses.

This is, perhaps, fine for scientists, whose job is to add incrementally to scientific knowledge. But there are, of course, huge drawbacks and limitations. Perhaps most importantly, you can't see below the surface.

If you approached your customers like a social scientist, you would come to them with a hypothesis – maybe about their dissatisfaction with a current product or perhaps about some new idea that you have – and would hand them a survey of statements where you would rate 1–5 how much you agree with each one. By the end of the process, you would be able to run some statistical regressions to determine, at least statistically, whether your hypothesis is supported by the data or not. But what have you really learned about your customers?

Some social scientists have recognized these shortcomings and have worked on trying to find better ways to get deeper into how people think and act. Fortunately, some have come up with some pretty interesting and useful insights. In social science, like in entrepreneurship, we're trying to figure out how and why people behave as they do. But those we study often don't know or can't articulate exactly what or why they're doing it. After all, if they already clearly knew and understood the reasons, they wouldn't require much study.

One insight that has come out of this dilemma is that there are things that can be *observed* beyond what is communicated. These things include mannerisms and behaviors that subjects don't even realize they're doing. A lot of things we do subconsciously or habitually. Other things we can observe are things they do differently than other people. We often don't know we do things differently, either because we've never seen other people do it or because we haven't noticed the differences. So observation can entail a rich set of factual knowledge beyond what actors are conscious and aware of.

We do a lot of things out of rote habit or by instinct. For other things we do, we know why we do them in some abstract sense, but we can't really put those reasons into words. Observation allows us to glean at least some of these insights, insights that very likely others have missed in their market research.

So why don't consumers recognize the problems that you might be able to spot? Well, the main reason is that they're just used to doing it the old, inefficient way. It works for them well enough that they don't even begin to wonder if there's a better way. Think about all the things you do throughout the day by rote. How much time do you spend thinking about those activities? You have other things to wonder and worry about than whether you might be able to clean your teeth more efficiently and effectively than brushing them with toothpaste. Because you're accustomed to doing it one way, you don't begin think of trying to find a better way.

And even if you did, your mind is so entrenched in how it's always been done that it is difficult to see any other way of doing it.

A couple of decades ago, Thomas Ward did a study where they asked participants to draw an alien life form.[49] Almost all of them drew aliens that had two eyes, arms, legs, etc. They were humanlike, or at least resembled earthly creatures. Why? When we are so accustomed to something being a certain way, even given the chance to change it we still think in the terms of the old way.

Observation can help you see things that others don't, or to make sense of something through a different lens. Like the gorilla in the study, most of us are simply missing the forest for the trees when we do things the same old way.

Let me give you an example. Rob Campbell was a software engineer who developed the software that became PowerPoint. But how did he come up with the idea? As he tells the story, he was on a flight and, as he sat in his seat, he noticed people taking out transparency slides for overhead projectors. Clearly, these were business people heading to some meetings. They were thumbing through the slides and working on them, marking them up, making notes and changes, all by hand – and on a bumpy flight no less.

He realized that the ability to visually present ideas was a core aspect of effective meetings and teaching. But the current method of using printed transparencies really didn't allow for professional last-minute adjustments. Of course, with a background in software, he had some idea of how to design a better solution. The technology for PowerPoint had existed for years, but the connection was never made until some outsider, Campbell, observed people working inefficiently.

Now think for a second what he might have learned by merely asking those people what they wanted. Most of them would probably have said this method was fine, that they didn't mind doing it this way. But if pressed, some might have come up with an idea or two, something to the effect of a portable transparency printer – doing it the same way, but on the go. The apocryphal account of Henry Ford's statement – "if I had asked my customers what they wanted, they'd have said faster horses" – rings true. Can you simply ask your customers? You can, but they might not be able to come up with a good idea of what they *should* want. They often will not have a sufficient technical background to know what is possible or what would work. They are, as we saw in Section 2, themselves learning what to want.

But you don't really want or need to know what they *want*. You need to know what underlies their want – what do they actually *need*? What is the real job that they're trying to do, and why? Once you grasp the fundamental problem, you can apply your own technological expertise to it. You'll be able to see and think past 'how it's always been done' and begin to see new ways of doing it that may be better.

---

49 Ward, T. B. 1994. Structured imagination: The role of category structure in exemplar generation. *Cognitive Psychology*, 27(1): 1–40.

Observation can get you to see needs at a deeper level than your customers now understand. But it's not easy. Typically, we see what they see. To see past what they see, we have to be in a different frame of mind. And of course you can't 'see' needs at all – all you can see are behavioral indicators of possible needs. Observation is itself an interpretive process. So let's get into how you can do this well.

Ethnography

One of the most important developments in social science that scholars have come up with in response to this problem is a technique called *ethnography*. Ethnography is a methodology for studying human actors by embedding yourself in their life and simply observing it. There are, of course, variations of this technique and disagreements among scholars about which approaches are best. But the basic premise is that we can better discover the purpose and nature of behaviors through careful, in-depth and embedded observation techniques. I won't give you a formal introduction to ethnographic methodology here. I will just provide a brief introduction and overview of the general premise. You are certainly welcome and encouraged to dig deeper into these techniques.

The basic idea of an ethnographic study is to embed yourself in the situation you're studying and to closely and carefully follow what that person does for a fairly long period of time. Most ethnographic methods espouse prompts by the ethnographer to ask the person being studied *why* they're doing things. Some have instead advocated 'think-aloud' protocols, where the person studied is constantly speaking their thoughts aloud as they go, explaining everything they do. The researcher keeps a journal-like record that is as detailed and precise as possible. They might also or instead record the subject with audio and/or visual recording technology. If an audio recording is taken, the words the subject speaks are fully transcribed for content analysis.

These types of studies can last a long time sometimes. It has to at least last as long as it takes for the activity or experience that you're interested in to occur, hopefully many times. Some researchers spend months or even years doing such a study. This is one of the reasons why these qualitative studies are rare in the social science journals – very few are willing to spend the time to do them. Collecting a survey is much easier.

So how and why can ethnography be useful to you? If you're having a hard time understanding what your customer really needs, or if you're not sure your customer really understands what he or she really needs, you can glean some really useful insights into those needs through careful observation.

One of the fundamental tenets of many ethnographers is that the method is inductive – that the observations tell the story. But this is nonsense. The principle behind this notion is a good one – we should avoid letting our biased priors influence how we interpret what we see others do. To the extent that they can tell us why, we should probably believe them. But observations don't interpret themselves. You have to do some interpreting – even of the reasons they give you.

Furthermore, ethnographers are not blank canvases, they are *looking* for something. Maybe it's not something specific, and certainly the idea is to have an open mind. But they are looking for breakthrough insights.

Similarly, you can ethnographically study consumers to learn breakthrough insights about them and what they need. The idea is to keep your own interpretive lens free from the biases of the consumers themselves that are accustomed to how it's always been done. If you're *looking* for needs to solve, if your attention is pointed toward those routine efforts and looking for different ways those jobs might be done, then you may be able to see things they haven't.

Examples

Let me offer you a couple of examples of how observational ethnography can help you see things that will improve your empathy and better understand your customers.

One example comes from Continuum, a design firm that was hired by Proctor & Gamble (P&G) to help come up with some new products for floor cleaning. P&G had been working on this problem for a while but was having a hard time coming up with a chemical solution that cleaned floors better, but didn't also damage the floor. While P&G engineers plugged along trying to find a better chemical solvent for mopping, Continuum suggested they try ethnography.

Continuum researchers went into people's homes and watched them clean their floors. They took detailed notes and even videotaped their customers mopping. Maybe not the most exciting movie to watch. One woman they observed would clean her mop in a bathtub. This process was clearly difficult for her for a few observable reasons. The mop and long pole were difficult to maneuver in the narrow bathroom, for example. Also, the mop itself was designed to trap dirt, not let it go. So rinsing the mop clean took extensive effort. And kneeling over the bathtub scrubbing the mob just didn't seem like an efficient method or use of time. In fact, based on their observations they found that many consumers were spending more time cleaning the mop than using it!

This observation led to a breakthrough for the research team. Yes, a better cleaning solvent might be useful. But the real problems of floor cleaning weren't going to be solved with a new mop solvent. They needed an entirely new solution altogether – a new way to mop. But coming up with a solution proved difficult for the team – as I've explained, it's hard to come up with revolutionary ideas, especially when thinking is bounded by traditional solutions. So they went back to their observations. But this time, their mindset had changed. They were now looking for a mop alternative. With this mindset, they saw something new in the observations.

One particular woman had spilled coffee grounds on the floor. After sweeping them up, she wet a paper towel and wiped the linoleum to pick up the dusty remains. With the mindset right, this provided that needed spark of insight and the Swiffer was born.

Let me give you one more example. Toothbrush manufacturer Oral-B was the first modern toothbrush manufacturer, with Dr. Robert Huston patenting the familiar toothbrush design in 1950 with the name Oral-B 60 for the oral brush with 60 nylon tufts.

Since that time, however, there was little innovation to the standard design other than the electric toothbrush, which had limited popularity. By the mid-1990s, however, one key issue had emerged in the customer feedback they received as one of the most common and frustrating – kids. Parents were frustrated with their kids refusing to brush their own teeth. Oral-B saw dominating the kids' tooth-brushing market as an opportunity to grow their market share. So they enlisted the design consulting firm IDEO for some help.

IDEO consultants jumped immediately into ethnographic research, a core component of the 'design thinking' method they espouse. They went into the homes of families to observe kids as they brushed their teeth. The hope was to catch some difference in the way kids would brush their teeth that made it a challenge. Brushing teeth would always be a chore, one kids would prefer to skip if they could. But if Oral-B could make the chore easier, they could improve kids' oral health and potentially lighten the burden on parents.

What they saw was immediately apparent. Kids didn't hold their toothbrushes like adults do. They *couldn't*. They didn't have the finger strength or dexterity. Instead, most of them held the brush in a closed fist, which greatly limited how and where they could brush. It's tough to get the back of the teeth with a fist around the brush.

Having observed a key problem, they went about working on a solution. Clearly, the problem was not a lack of training children to hold a toothbrush properly. It was a problem of capability. They needed a toothbrush that kids could handle better. Their solution was the *squish gripper* handle, which was a fatter, softer, and textured handle that kids could much more easily maneuver than the hard, skinny grips of adult brushes. With some market testing, the new design proved far more effective for kids. So it was that Oral-B changed the way kids brush their teeth.

Summing Up

Observation is a key tool in your toolkit of value learning. We learn from observation frequently in our daily lives. For example, we watch what others consume and evaluate their satisfaction with those things so that we can determine if we might benefit from consuming those things too. Most of the products we have purchased we learned about from seeing others consume them.

To reiterate, observation is not a silver bullet. You can't observe *why* people do what they do. You might be able to get at why from asking. But they don't always know or understand why. And when they don't, they can't tell you much. In fact, they probably don't even realize what they're doing.

Ethnographic observation is useful for seeing things consumers don't see (and, so, can't share). You have to have the right mindset to be able to see anything. But observation can lead to breakthrough insights that communications generally cannot.

If you're having a hard time figuring out how to better serve your customers, go observe them. Look for pain points. Look for inefficiencies in how they do things. Look for frustrations or difficulties. Almost everyone has some. And once you see them, you then have an opportunity to facilitate new value for those customers.

Chapter 11
Learning from Yourself

In this final chapter of Section 3, let's turn to one of the most important customers to learn from – yourself. Generally, research has found that user entrepreneurship and innovation tend to be far more successful on average than innovating for others. Perhaps by now it is somewhat intuitive why that may be, but let's dig into it to make it clear and obvious why this is. By doing so, we'll uncover some less-obvious implications for how to do it well.

The Consumer Sovereignty Principle

To begin to understand the benefits of user innovation approaches, let me introduce you to the concept of *consumer sovereignty*. Now consumer sovereignty, if you're familiar with Austrian economics, is generally understood to mean that consumers are the directors of an economy, that it's consumers, and not producers, who determine who succeeds or fails by their choices in what to buy and from whom. This is, of course, a key conclusion of the principle, but the principle of consumer sovereignty is actually a lot deeper than this.

The notion of the sovereignty of the consumer dates, at least, to Adam Smith, and is recognizable in popular slogans such as "the customer is always right." It was formalized by economist William H. Hutt,[50] who suggested that it is through consumer demands (or refraining from demanding) that production is directed.

Hutt perceived that economic actors have a twofold relationship to society: (1) as a consumer and (2) as a producer. As producers, we are servants to the community of consumers, utilizing our resources, skills, and knowledge to produce consumable outputs for consumers. As consumers, we command other producers, demanding from them products and services to satisfy our needs. We each perform the role of producer so that, ultimately, we can consume, creating (or contributing to the creation of) consumable goods for ourselves or else for others in exchange for money that can then buy consumables. It is the consumer's job to determine *what* to consume – whether products, services, or enjoyable activities – in order to maximize well-being. In other words, it is the role of the consumer to discover their needs and the best solutions to them. The role of the producer is, then, to enable the consumer role through production activities to create those things demanded by your consumer self, typically through market exchange.

50 Hutt, W. H. 1936. *Economists and the Public: A study of competition and opinion.* New Brunswick, NJ: Transaction Publishers.

https://doi.org/10.1515/9783110750805-011

We operate *both* of these roles actively throughout the day. We consume constantly. Not just the products we actively consume, but all the things we passively consume also – the air we breathe, the food we've already eaten, the clothes we're wearing, the furniture we're occupying, and so forth. Similarly, we actively and passively produce throughout the day. In fact, we're very often producers for our own selves. It's your consumer self that tells your producer self what to produce when you're hungry – what kind of lunch to make, for example. Once your consumer role has decided what he or she wants, your producer role takes over to make it happen.

Let's follow Hutt's framework and specifically define the role of the consumer as the seeking out and consuming of solutions to their various perceived needs for the general improvement of their well-being. At all times where a person is performing this role, he or she is acting as a consumer. We can define the role of producers, then, as the acting toward the production of consumable outputs. The individual is a producer, then, only when he or she produces (or attempts to produce). While these roles are distinct and are generally performed separately, they are interrelated and inform one another.

Because it's the consumer role that is tasked with maintaining the individual's well-being, it is the consumer who dictates valuations and who experiences the value, as I argued in Chapter 3. It is also the consumer's job to tell producers what to make for them. This is the essence of the consumer sovereignty principle.

In a free market, producers do not have power to dictate to consumers what they must buy. Consumers instead have ultimate power over producers in their choices to buy or withhold their money from those producers – we vote with our wallet who will succeed and who must fail. Ludwig von Mises, in his important treatise, *Human Action*, explains:

> In the political democracy only the votes cast for the majority candidate or the majority plan are effective in shaping the course of affairs. The votes polled by the minority do not directly influence policies. But on the market no vote is cast in vain. Every penny spent has the power to work upon the production processes. The publishers cater not only to the majority by publishing detective stories, but also to the minority reading lyrical poetry and philosophical tracts. The bakeries bake bread not only for healthy people, but also for the sick on special diets. The decision of a consumer is carried into effect with the full momentum he gives it through his readiness to spend a definite amount of money.[51]

Even concerns about monopoly power are overblown. Monopolists must keep their customers placated or else there is an opportunity for competitors to arise. Economist Joseph Schumpeter[52] explained that the mere threat of competitive entry

---

51 Mises, L. v. 1949. *Human Action: A treatise on economics*. New Haven, CT: Yale University Press, pp. 271–272.
52 Schumpeter, J. A. 1942. *Capitalism, Socialism, and Democracy*. New York: Harper (see Chapter VIII in particular).

disciplines monopolists from the exploitative pricing that some economists have always feared. History bears this out. The only companies that were close enough to a
true monopoly in a market economy (e.g., Standard Oil, Carnegie Steel) never raised
their prices – in fact they historically fell the entire time period of their so-called
monopoly position. The only monopolists to have sufficient power over consumers
to enable the exploitation that economists fear have been state or state-backed monopolies, with the backing of the state's policing power. The power of the consumer, in all other cases, is ultimate.

The Advantages of User Innovation

It follows from Hutt's consumer sovereignty framework that the most important
consumer for you to know and understand is yourself. This also follows, of course,
from PVT as explained in Section 2. Your goal in life is to maximize *your own* well-
being.[53] To make any progress in this ultimate goal is to discover yourself as a consumer, as per the value learning cycle.

Here understanding the PVT value learning cycle pays some really big divi-
dends. Because in this process we also find the origination of entrepreneurship.

Here's a big claim that might seem dubious at first – entrepreneurship originates as a *consumer* process. Let me back that claim up. Remember how I've defined the consumer function and distinguished it from the producer function.
Producers are mere servants to consumers, who make the decisions. Entrepreneurship is one of those consumer decisions – a decision to put productive resources to
some *new* and *uncertain* use. So entrepreneurial judgment, I propose, is actually a
consumer judgment, and the entrepreneur-consumer then instructs the entrepre-
neur-producer role to carry it out.

This is somewhat of a tangential point, but it highlights something that I think is
important. Your capacity to see what are often called 'entrepreneurial opportunities'
is through the lens of your consumer role! Your understanding of unmet consumer
needs is phenomenal knowledge that you have only as a consumer – firsthand or
empathically.

If you don't have an idea for a new product or service, if you don't see any unmet
needs in your life, it may be because you're too placid a consumer. While that's probably a good mindset for life in general, as an entrepreneur you need to be constructively
dissatisfied with the status quo. You need to be perpetually dissatisfied with the value

---

53 Some, like parents, might object that they desire the well-being of others more than their own.
Within our subjectivist framework, you desire others' well-being because it makes you feel happy.
This isn't an attempt to cast your selflessness as selfishness. It's just a better theoretical framework
to understand why you act as you do.

that you and your customers attain from current solutions. Placidity breeds complacency, which breeds entrepreneurial failure.

I don't mean this to say that you should turn into a whiny jerk, always complaining about everything. But constructive dissatisfaction breeds entrepreneurial insight – necessity is the mother of invention. By becoming more introspective, you can perhaps discover new areas for improvement in your life.

One of the more common origination approaches to entrepreneurship is what is often called user entrepreneurship. That is, you start your entrepreneurial journey by solving your own needs and problems in a way that is much better for you personally, and then further develop and take that solution, designed originally for yourself, to a broader market.

There are a lot of good examples of this approach. Travis Kalanick and Garrett Camp came up with the idea for UberCab, later to become Uber, when they were stuck in the rain at a conference in Paris, trying to hail a cab. They couldn't find one. Interestingly, the reason they were there was to attend a tech conference. So the timing was just right for them to put their heads together to create a ride-hailing app. Their idea would undergo a few more evolutions before it would become the Uber app that we now all know, but the origination of Uber is a user entrepreneurship story.

There are plenty of other such stories. Drew Houston kept forgetting to bring his flash drive during his college days at MIT and so he created Dropbox. Kevin Plank hated the feel of his sweaty cotton t-shirt after football practice and developed the Under Armour athletic clothing line. Nick Woodman wanted to get some action shots of himself surfing, and developed the GoPro. And on and on. I love hearing entrepreneurs' origination stories. Not all are user entrepreneurship stories, but a great many are – a problem that they had and couldn't find a good solution for on the market, so they decided to create one.

Research on user entrepreneurship has been around for a few decades now, led perhaps foremost by Eric von Hippel. The bulk of this research finds, generally, that user entrepreneurship tends to have a higher rate of success. But why?

Our value-as-a-process theory from Section 2 offers a few reasons. Perhaps most importantly, users of a product understand the needs that the product is meant to satisfy better than non-users. Their own experiential value learning cycle is very likely to lead to deeper and better value knowledge than could be achieved by empathy alone. The subjective experience of the need and its satisfaction are gained firsthand – no empathy needed. Your empathic accuracy is 100%.

The effect of this is that you can produce great products that satisfy real needs, and as a result, others are likely to want them. In a 1985 interview, a young Steve Jobs explained how the Macintosh was designed:

> We think the Mac will sell zillions, but we didn't build Mac for anybody else. We built it for ourselves. We were the group of people who were going to judge whether it was great or not.

> We weren't going to go out and do market research. We just wanted to build the best thing we could build.[54]

In other words, Jobs' and Wozniak's early success with home computers wasn't because they were some incredible visionaries, or because they had some superior understanding of the market. They succeeded because they designed their computers *for themselves*. Did you know how Jobs met Woz? They were both members of the Homebrew Computer Club – they were huge computer nerds that geeked out to this stuff. So it is no surprise that their designs *for themselves* proved superior to others' designs. *They* were the lead users.

But let's be clear that being a user entrepreneur doesn't mean your value knowledge is perfect – as Section 2 hopefully makes clear, it's always and necessarily imperfect – nor does it mean that you don't still need empathy and empathic accuracy. You still have to empathize if you're going to take the product to market to sell to others. Do they all have the exact same experience that you do? I'll come back to that in a moment.

But the point is that you don't have to empathically imagine the experience to understand it. You are the consumer you're trying to understand. Again, that doesn't mean that you understand your need perfectly or even well. But you do know what the experience is like.

Another plausible reason that user entrepreneurs tend to do better is that they tend to be more passionate about their product. Because it solves a real problem for themselves, they see, understand, and believe in its value. That recognition of value inspires a passion that can often be sensed by others, including investors and other consumers. That passion may inspire greater effort and perseverance throughout the entrepreneurial journey that is often needed during the initial stages of high uncertainty and arduous and sluggish growth.

But von Hippel and colleagues point out that it is not just users who are most successful, but *lead users*, which I introduced in Chapter 9. To remind you, lead users are those consumers that are at the cutting edge of a market, grabbing up every incremental improvement to the market's leading products. In other words, it's the users of a product that are at the forefront of its consumption, those who need it the most, who love and enjoy it the most, who are best at devising new and better solutions to consumer needs. For example, researchers found that avid and competitive mountain bikers have most often been the designers of the best and most successful mountain biking advancements.[55]

---

54 https://allaboutstevejobs.com/verbatim/interviews/playboy_1985.
55 Lüthje, C., Herstatt, C., & von Hippel, E. 2005. User-innovators and "local" information: The case of mountain biking. *Research Policy*, 34(6): 951–965.

Learning from Your Consumer Self

There are two important implications of our value-as-a-process learning cycle that was developed in Section 2 that are helpful in understanding how to become a better user innovator. The first is that it gives us the fastest way to the value knowledge you need for entrepreneurship. And the second is that it points us in the right direct of *where to look*, specifically, for ideas. Let's discuss these further.

First, the firsthand value learning cycle is the fastest way to learning and understanding specific needs. Others' value knowledge is very difficult to access and acquire, as I've explained in the last two chapters. It is difficult to know which consumers have that value knowledge that makes them worth talking to. It is a profound challenge to learn what they know, since the most important aspects of that value knowledge are tacit. Observations can sometimes provide some deeper insights, but only if you infer correctly what those observations mean – and that's only if you manage to see something interesting and important. In short, third-person value learning is extremely difficult and problematic, and there's always a good chance – even if you avoid all the pitfalls, that what you learn will be wrong or, at least, incomplete.

But you have *your own* value learning cycle that you can leverage. If you want to better understand a particular need or value experience, how well do you understand *your own* experiences regarding that need and its satisfaction?

Once you realize this, one very promising way to advance your value knowledge is to immerse yourself in the consumption activity. Try different solutions. Compare the cutting-edge technology to the traditional solutions. What really works? What doesn't? Why? Depending on the market, this can get a little expensive, but most ventures require up-front costs in developing an idea.

Because you are a consumer, you can leverage your own consumer experiences to ascertain key insights into how and how well current solutions work. Of course, the magnitude of the experiences you will have as a consumer will depend on your own needs, so some needs and value experiences will be easier to learn from than others.

This leads me to the second key point – that the value learning cycle points us to what markets we should be considering first and foremost in our search for an entrepreneurial idea. Your value knowledge is going to be the most advanced – the deepest and most accurate – in markets that you have the strongest needs and interests in, where *you* are a lead user or, if you are not already a lead user, where you could and would like to become one.

Finding Ideas in Your Own Experiences

If you don't already have a great idea, or if you're still willing to consider other options, your own consumer experiences are a great place to look. This is how I suggest you start. Ask yourself, what needs am I most passionate about? What products am I most excited to buy? Examine yourself as a consumer before you start going to other consumers for information.

Starting with the consumer segments that you are most interested in has several advantages. First, it ensures that you end up in a market that you're passionate about. You don't dread waking up and going to work in the morning when you love your work. This passion will help you to dig deep and find ways to persevere and succeed.

Secondly, you're already ahead of the game here in terms of value learning. These consumer spaces are the ones you know most about. You follow the trends in the market. You're on the lookout for the latest and greatest. You have opinions on which products and features are better and why. This value knowledge will be an important asset as you try to create something even better.

And third, you're much more likely to understand other consumers in this space, having some shared experiential background. You understand the industry jargon and can better communicate with those consumers. You interact with them enough and have similar enough needs that you can much more easily empathize with them. You already know your customers, and can get to know them better than anyone.

So let me quickly walk you through what this process of finding an idea looks like. To start, list your most important needs for your own well-being, as you understand them. What are your favorite products and services? Why are they important to you? In essence, you're trying to introspectively determine where your greatest value knowledge already is and why.

A quick word of caution when you do this: don't pigeonhole yourself into only art and entertainment solutions, which are typically more exciting and have high staying power in memory. The arts and entertainment are great and fun, and you'll be tempted to put those as your greatest passions. Don't discount these as possibilities, but be aware that the stimulation that these provide are merely aesthetic and hedonic pleasures. This is not to say that they aren't real or valuable. So this is a potential space to work in. But it's a difficult and saturated one.

You're likely to do better by being broad in your consideration of your various needs. Consider various types of needs that you have. In Chapter 4 I introduced three basic need types: physiological, psychological, and spiritual. These subsume all kinds of other, more specific needs. But let's walk through a few specific need types to jog your mind.

Do you have any particular physical needs that you've worked hard on, such as specific food and dietary needs, medical problems, physical discomforts, and so forth? Perhaps you have a hard time falling asleep at night, or have trouble attaining or maintaining the body weight you want. Maybe you have some kind of medical condition that prevents you from enjoying certain things in life. These are things that matter to you and that you likely know more than the average person about. How many others are suffering from similar physical challenges?

Next, turn to your intellectual needs. Do you have easy access to all the knowledge and information you need for your various endeavors? If not, what don't you know? Why don't you know it? Why is it so hard to find or to learn? What sort of knowledge would be valuable to you if you could more easily know it? It's often not easy to pinpoint what you don't know, but you can often think of at least a few things right off the bat. And if you choose to go down the path of satisfying intellectual needs, your journey will take you into a world of intellectual discovery that you had no idea existed. There is so much to know in too short a lifespan. Going down this path will lead you to what you'd wished you could have known sooner, which you can then make a business of helping others to know.

What about your psychological and social needs? Here's where you might consider entertainment and other hedonic ideas. But this category is much vaster. So introspectively dig into what brings joy and happiness into your life. What do you love doing? Why do you love it? Who do you love spending time with, and why? What's missing in your social life? Are you sometimes depressed or otherwise psychologically unsatisfied? Can you pinpoint where and why? You don't have to be a psychologist to be able to see when and where you are struggling mentally or socially. If finding better mental health is something you are passionate about, this may be a promising path for you. A deep dive into how to find better mental health for yourself may reveal solutions that could help many others.

Finally, what about your spiritual needs, your search for purpose, meaning, and hope in your life? What gives you purpose and meaning? Why? Are you making a difference? How could you do more? Can you help others find purpose and meaning in their lives?

Once you've generated a list of various needs, which ones are you most interested and passionate about? Which ones do you know the most about? Narrow your list down to, say, two or three. For these 'finalists', introspect about why they matter to you. How do current solutions work for you? Why do you like them? What could they do better? Or could there be a very different solution altogether that satisfies the same needs better all around? Which of these needs do you, or could you, have the technical know-how to better address?

After this process, you should have a pretty good idea of what market space you may want to be in and what direction you might go with it.

You're of course far from ready to go just yet. Now it's time to dig deep into the market and learn all there is to know. You might have an idea already for a new product, but don't hold fast to that idea. Just keep it to the side for now and learn more about others in this segment, how and what they think and why. You may very well find that the initial idea you had is not as good an idea as you first thought.

Here are some questions to ponder as you work through this process. Do other consumers experience this need the same way that I do? What differences can I pinpoint in our experiences? Do I really understand this need correctly? How would my own experience be improved? How can others' experiences be improved? Are they the same improvements, or different?

Here the insights from the chapters in this section will be very important to keep in mind. This is where those other tools we've already discussed need to come into play. But you're already off to a great start in an area that you're passionate about and where you already have strong initial value knowledge.

Entrepreneurial Empathy: Consumer to Consumer

You may have noticed that this process drifted from innovating for yourself to innovating for others. Although it is often the case, it is not wise to simply presume that others have the exact same needs and problems you do. There is simply no getting around the fact that entrepreneurship entails predicting what others will want.

To this point, I want to add one more insight that I think will be useful to you in your search for an idea, which pertains to the distinction between producers and consumers explained earlier in this chapter. Entrepreneurial empathy is *consumer to consumer*. That is, you empathize with other consumers in your role as consumer. Philosophically and pragmatically, this makes sense – you can only empathize with others through the same mindset as them.

But this insight has some interesting implications. One, which I've already mentioned, is that you are better able to empathize with other consumers like yourself. This is intuitively obvious, but somehow many entrepreneurs and managers have gotten into their heads that they don't have to have any commonalities with their customers – they can understand their customers with just a little market research! Sorry, it's not so simple.

Throughout your entrepreneurial journey, you will need to put yourself into consumer mode quite often. This is how you understand the market. If you want to succeed, embrace your consumer role. Become the most knowledgeable consumer you can be. Don't just let others do the consumer tasks for you. Learning value knowledge from other consumers is just too hard and problematic to rely wholly on. If you become your own lead user, you will not only learn from your own experience, but it will enable you to vastly improve your empathic learning from other consumers. You will get them. And that will lead you to much more clearly figuring out what they really want and, more importantly, what they actually need.

Section 4: **Facilitating Real Value**

Chapter 12
Innovating a Value Proposition

In Section 2 I walked you through what value is and how consumers learn what to value, and in Section 3 I discussed how to use this understanding of value toward achieving more and better value knowledge about what people really want and need. Here, in Section 4, let's move on to the next stages of the entrepreneurial journey, the innovation and entrepreneurial judgment processes. First, in this chapter, let's talk about how innovation works and why the better value knowledge you can now obtain will equip you for better ideas.

Innovation as Imaginative Problem Solving

Before we get into the specifics of how entrepreneurial innovation or 'ideation' (idea generation) works, let's first lay down some groundwork. First, what is innovation? Innovation is a specific type of creative imagination, which is a specific type of imagination. Let's unpack this a bit more.

Imagination underpins a bunch of different cognitive processes. Recalling our representationalist foundations, we can define imagination as a mental representation of something not real. This distinguishes it from *sensory* representation – the mental representations that our brains create from our sense stimuli. Sensory representations are *intended* to be real, to reflect reality as it is.[56] Imagination, in contrast, is a mental representation from *non-sensory* inputs – representations of things other than our immediate perception of reality.

Understanding imagination this way, we imagine all sorts of things. Memories are imaginations that mentally play out past experiences. Expectations are imaginations, playing out causality from present conditions to future outcomes. Counterfactuals, such as dreams and empathy, are imaginations, simulating some sort of alternative reality. And problem solving is imagination, the creative application of logic and knowledge to generate a not-already-existing solution to a known problem.

Innovation is, specifically, a *creative* imagination in that it generates something essentially novel and inserts it into the world. Whereas counterfactual imagination creates an alternative reality that you can manipulate or assess, creative imagination entails devising some presently non-existing entity – an imaginary construct – and inserting it into your mental model of reality. In a sense, then, creative imagination is

---

56 Cognitive scientist Donald Hoffman has argued that, in fact, our sensory representations are optimized for survival and not for realism, purposively skewing our perception of reality to ensure more likely survival.

https://doi.org/10.1515/9783110750805-012

actually a counterfactual – an artificial reality.[57] But this is a special type of counter-factual, one that is reality as it would be with the existence of this new creation.

The primary component that makes a creative imagination an *innovation* is that it is purposive, the creation of a *new solution* to a particular problem.

The Cognition of Innovation

Cognitive scientists have been deeply fascinated by creativity and innovation for several decades. There are mountains of research on these topics, which I will mostly avoid. But I have a good reason to do so – it is not especially helpful. The vast majority of this research concerns, for example, what parts of the brain light up when doing creative tasks, or what types of personalities are more predisposed to more creative ideas, for example. The underlying hope of these large streams of research has been that we might accelerate innovativeness by, for example, better identifying those who are more creative or by better facilitating the cognitive conditions necessary for such creativity. But if these hopes are valid at all, they are still a very long way from realization.

But there's enough there that's useful that I should at least briefly review it. And, rather than reinvent the wheel, I'm not going to take the time to do my own extensive review of the literature. Keith Sawyer put together a pretty good summary of this literature in his book *Explaining Creativity*.[58] In it, he unpacks the innovation process into eight steps:
1. Find and formulate the problem.
2. Acquire knowledge relevant to the problem.
3. Gather other related information.
4. Incubate.
5. Brainstorm ideas.
6. Combine ideas.
7. Select the best idea.
8. Externalize the idea.

Some of these steps may seem obvious. Others might be less so. I don't want to spend time on each one of these. Broadly, I think this summary is both an accurate reflection of the current state of research *and* probably very close to correct in depicting the innovative process. However, not all innovative insights come in this

---

57 In a similar sense, an expectation is a counterfactual – a reality that will be.
58 Sawyer, R. K. 2012. *Explaining Creativity: The science of human innovation*. New York: Oxford University Press.

way, and so I think it is not perfectly representative. Instead, I think a simpler framework is probably more correct.

Innovation as Knowledge Combining

A lot of scholars have argued that innovation is merely combining existing knowledge in new ways. Some go so far as to argue that there is no *ex nihilo* knowledge creation, that all new ideas are combinations of old ones. I think that's nonsense, but there is something to the idea that new ideas are combinations of knowledge.

So far, however, creativity scholars have simply argued that novelty comes from combining and repurposing seemingly unrelated concepts. Sawyer gives the example of "PANCAKE BOAT." Clearly the concepts of pancake and boat are, in general discourse, completely unrelated. But it is easy enough to cognitively connect them in a new way. Sawyer writes:

> Maybe a pancake boat is a very flat boat, with a low profile that allows it to go under low-lying bridges. Or, it could be a new kind of restaurant that serves breakfast while touring the harbor.[59]

In this way, scholars have argued that all innovations are new combinations of existing concepts that spark new ways of thinking about things. Specifically, these combinations generate 'emergent attributes' that would or might be true of the new combination that are not true of either concept individually. Thus, new combinations generate new knowledge and implications.

The problem with this notion of innovation as concept merging is that the *innovation* does not happen until the new, merged concept is given a *purpose*. A 'dirt fork' is a combination of two concepts, but unless I find a meaning and purpose for the combination, it is just gibberish. Keith Sawyer's pancake boat example illustrates this well. The key insight to both of those possible concept combinations is in their *solving a problem* – the flat boat in skirting low bridges and the breakfast on the lake idea as a fine tourist option.

This was one of the key insights I made in my dissertation[60] – the *type* of knowledge that is combined matters. Specifically, I identified two key types of knowledge that are combined in every innovation process: problem (or needs) knowledge and technical knowledge. *Problem knowledge* specifies the problem to solve. Without a problem, there is no innovation, as innovation is always a solution to a problem. *Technical knowledge* references one's knowledge of resources and their affordances.

---

59 *ibid*, p. 116.
60 Packard, M. D. 2016. *Consumer Sovereignty and Entrepreneurship*. University of Missouri, Columbia, MO.

'Affordance' means what something can do. A spoon *affords* scooping and holding a small amount of liquid.

Innovation, then, is the combination of knowledge about a problem to solve and knowledge about resources that have properties that can solve the problem.

This solution is, I think, intuitive and even obvious, but it has so far evaded scientific perception. And it is not such a wonder, I suppose. Many innovative solutions to problems *are* novel combinations of other resources. But some innovations are novel applications of existing technologies to new problems, no combination needed – that is, other than the problem and technical knowledge. Other innovations, similarly, are novel applications of new technologies to existing problems.

But innovation occurs at the intersection of problem knowledge (knowledge of a problem) and technical knowledge (knowledge of resources that can be organized to solve the problem). The more of both of these types of knowledge, the more likely you are to 'see' an innovation and the more innovative your solution is likely to be.

Cognitive Schemas

Let's go deeper into this process so you can really see what's going on. Our brains are perceptually limited. Remember the gorilla study I discussed in Chapter 9? The reason participants could not see the obvious gorilla walking through the basketball passes is because our minds are capable of only a limited amount of information processing. When that cognitive capacity was set to the task of counting passes, other observable phenomena were filtered out so that the mind could focus on the task assigned. Participants in the study probably also weren't listening to chit chat going on in the room or smelling the lunch that someone in the next row had brought, or whatever other ambient sensory stimuli surrounded them. Because our mental capacities, as extremely powerful and remarkable as they are, are limited, we cannot focus on all things at once and must pick and choose what to focus on and think about at a given time.

Our knowledge and memory have a similar mechanism. To preserve mental acuity, our minds classify knowledge into categories or domains of related and associated information, termed cognitive *schemas* (or schemata). A schema is a group of various concepts that are causally connected within our mental models. When we access a concept in a schema, we typically bring with that concept the entire schema to our 'active memory,' which lets us quickly access those things which we have classified as similar or related. There are neural ties between these parts of memory which activate as the memory is accessed. For example, my schema 'car' includes what I know about cars – its attributes (4 wheels, seats, steering wheel, engine, etc.), how it operates, different car types (sedan, minivan, SUV, etc.) and brands, etc. I 'know' these things about cars, but I don't have them in my active thought *unless and until I'm thinking about cars*. But when I am thinking about cars, I can easily think about those related concepts.

Computers work in a similar way. Hard disk drives (HDDs) are extremely slow in computer terms, but they can hold and semi-permanently store immense amounts of data. In contrast, random access memory (RAM) is extremely fast, but cannot hold a whole lot of information in its limited space. So the way computers optimize their performance speed is by storing all program data on the HDD, but downloading the data that it needs for the programs that it is actively running into RAM. So the programs you're actively using are running from the fast RAM memory, and the computer only goes back to the HDD when it needs to get more data from it. This is why your computer runs slowly when you don't have enough RAM, or if you are running too many programs at the same time. Once its RAM is full, the computer needs to go back to the HDD more frequently for the information it needs, which slows everything down.

In much the same way, our minds 'download' schemas to active memory when we're thinking about those schemas and related topics. This lets us have fast memory access to all the knowledge we need to know relating to that topic. When I'm driving, for example, my driving schema includes *how* to drive and all the rules of the road. I don't have to sit and think about what a particular sign means – I won't often find those driving concepts at the metaphorical tip of my tongue when I'm driving – my active memory has that information already at the ready.

But when thinking about different knowledge schemas, the causal connections between them, if there are any, tend to be weak. Again, this lets the mind bring a more limited subset of knowledge to active memory. This preserves cognitive activity to focus only on that information which is considered relevant.

But such mental efficiency generally precludes the innovative connection of typically unrelated knowledge sources. Consider, for example, these three words: *nurse*, *lemon*, and *bull*. What is their connection? At first or even second glance, they appear unrelated. But they do have something in common. Only when the mind possesses the knowledge necessary to make the connection, and only when it is pushed to consider connections outside the realm of immediate intuition, can the connection be made. These are all species of sharks.

Many of you probably did not know all three types of shark and, so, were unable to make the connection. I suspect several of you knew of one or maybe two of the shark types, but because you were not familiar with all three, you were not, and could not be, able to connect them. But even if you have heard of all three shark types, the connection is not obvious and the mind has to break free from considering the words strictly within the cognitive schemas in which they typically reside (i.e., a medical worker, a sour fruit, and male cattle). If your mind evoked those schemas and tried to find a connection between them, you were probably out of luck or, if you came up with one, it was probably tenuous. You would have to instead search your memory for other schemas that have those terms in them. And if you were lucky, you might have found the *shark* schema.

Activating Problem and Technical Knowledge Schemas

The point I'm getting at is that, in order for you to see a connection between a particular consumer problem – your problem knowledge, which is in this case really your *value knowledge* – and some technology(ies) that can address that problem, you have to be able to make new connections that, so far, have remained unseen. You have to make connections between schemas that are so far, in your mental model, not causally connected.

In other words, your brain will *not* bring to mind these other schemas when a problem schema is brought to active memory. Again, you will have to practice abstract thought in searching for different, seemingly unrelated schemas that you can connect. When disparate schemas are connected in a new way to create and provide a sought-after solution to a problem, the formation of that neural connection is accompanied by that exciting 'aha!' insight experience.

The trick, then, is to figure out how to bring to active mind these seemingly unconnected schemas such that a connection can be forged. It's not practical in most cases for someone to spend the time trying to search their entire memory for a strange causal connection – it would take days or longer! Typically, our mental searches for possible connections is ordered. We look at other related schemas first, since those would seem to have the highest likelihood of providing some insight. This makes some sense, but often there are only incremental solutions in such proximal schemas.

Researchers have found a few things that may increase the likelihood of bringing different and more 'outside-the-box' resources to mind when problem solving.

Recency

The first is called *recency*. We tend to search recently-used schemas before delving into our memory archives for solutions. So it's easier to bring a particular schema back to active memory if we were thinking about fairly recently.

To illustrate this phenomenon, researchers[61] gave participants a difficult puzzle to solve, but few of them were able to solve it. For example, here's one such problem as conveyed by Gick and Holyoak in a 1983 article in *Cognitive Psychology*:

---

[61] Here are three research articles that show this effect:

Gick, M. L., & Holyoak, K. J. 1983. Schema induction and analogical transfer. *Cognitive Psychology*, 15(1): 1–38.

Lung, C.-T., & Dominowski, R. L. 1985. Effects of strategy instructions and practice on nine-dot problem solving. *Journal of Experimental Psychology: Learning, Memory, and Cognition*, 11(4): 804.

Weisberg, R. W., & Alba, J. W. 1981. An examination of the alleged role of "fixation" in the solution of several "insight" problems. *Journal of Experimental Psychology: General*, 110(2): 169–192.

Suppose you are a doctor faced with a patient who has a malignant tumor in his stomach. It is impossible to operate on the patient, but unless the tumor is destroyed the patient will die. There is a kind of ray that can be used to destroy the tumor. If the rays reach the tumor all at once at a sufficiently high intensity, the tumor will be destroyed. Unfortunately, at this intensity the healthy tissue that the rays pass through on the way to the tumor will also be destroyed. At lower intensities the rays are harmless to healthy tissue, but they will not affect the tumor either. What type of procedure might be used to destroy the tumor with the rays, and at the same time avoid destroying the healthy tissue?[62]

Without any help, few participants were able to solve this puzzle. But, prior to attempting this puzzle, some participants were told this story (*The General*):

A small country was ruled from a strong fortress by a dictator. The fortress was situated in the middle of the country, surrounded by farms and villages. Many roads led to the fortress through the countryside. A rebel general vowed to capture the fortress. The general knew that an attack by his entire army would capture the fortress. He gathered his army at the head of one of the roads, ready to launch a full-scale direct attack. However, the general then learned that the dictator had planted mines on each of the roads. The mines were set so that small bodies of men could pass over them safely, since the dictator needed to move his troops and workers to and from the fortress. However, any large force would detonate the mines. Not only would this blow up the road, but it would also destroy many neighboring villages. It therefore seemed impossible to capture the fortress.

However, the general devised a simple plan. He divided his army into small groups and dispatched each group to the head of a different road. When all was ready he gave the signal and each group marched down a different road. Each group continued down its road to the fortress so that the entire army arrived together at the fortress at the same time. In this way, the general captured the fortress and overthrew the dictator.

Whereas the solution to the tumor problem was very difficult for most, it came much more quickly and easily to mind for many who had read *The General*. If you didn't get the tumor puzzle the first time, go back now and see if you can solve it.

Arguably, the reason the solution came to mind was that the solution, the way to think about the problem, was still fresh in memory in the story they had just read. Had those participants read *The General* years ago, it is unlikely they would have performed any better than the other participants that had never read it.

The implications of this are that you will be able to make connections with more disparate cognitive schema *if you've been using them more recently*. If I was learning about ketosis and the ketogenic diet one morning, and in the evening my wife coincidentally suggested we both go on a diet together, it would be very easy and likely to recall what I'd just recently learned as a solution to her suggestion (and, if you're wondering, *yes*, this really did happen).

---

62 Gick & Holyoak (1983, p. 3). This puzzle was first proposed by Karl Duncker in 1926.

Schema Size

Another factor that plays into how easy it is to bring a schema to mind is the *size* of the schema – how much you know about a particular subject – and its prominence in your normal thought. The more expert you are in a subject – the more connections you can make to it. And, related to recency, if it is a subject that you think about often, its schema will tend to be your go-to for first looking for answers. In other words, you're most likely to search for solutions to these problems in the areas you're expert in first.

But there is a big drawback to expertise also in that it can lead to what's called *cognitive entrenchment* or *Einstellung effects*. In 1968, Edward de Bono described Einstellung thus: "too much experience within a field may restrict creativity because you know so well how things *should be done* that you might be unable to escape to come up with new ideas."[63]

This interesting effect was, as far as I know, first discovered by Abraham Luchins in 1942.[64] He presented participants with a series of water jar problems where the goal is to achieve some given volume of water using only the jars available. Consider the jars (in quarts) in Fig. 12.1:

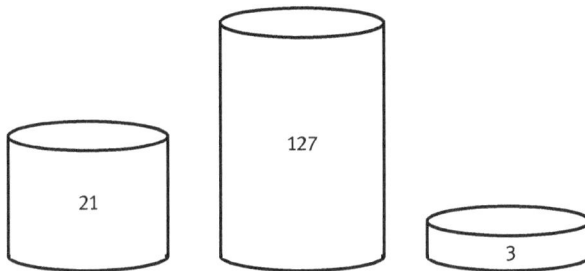

Fig. 12.1: Water Jar Problem 1.

Participants were asked to find a solution using only these three jar sizes to obtain exactly 100 quarts. The solution is given in Fig. 12.2:

---

63 De Bono, E. 1968. *New think: The use of lateral thinking in the generation of new ideas.* New York: Harper Collins.

64 Luchins, A. S. 1942. Mechanization in problem solving: The effect of Einstellung. *Psychological Monographs*, 54(6): i–95.

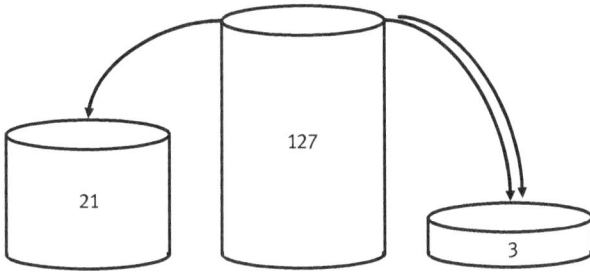

Fig. 12.2: Solution to Water Jar Problem 1.

That is, the 127-quart jar is first filled, then emptied once into the 21-quart jar until filled, and then the 3-quart jar is filled twice from that jar also, leaving exactly 100 quarts in the large jar.

Other problems were then presented with similar solutions. For example, obtain exactly 20 quarts from the jars in Fig. 12.3:

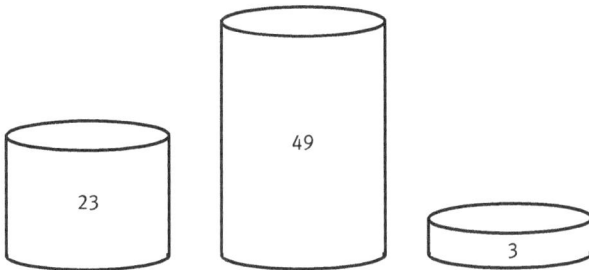

Fig. 12.3: Water Jar Problem 2.

More than 80 percent of participants solved this problem in the same way: fill the middle jar, then empty once in the left jar and twice in the right. That certainly works, but this problem could also be solved with a much more efficient solution: fill the left jar and then fill right one from it. It's obvious once I point it out, but did you see it? Knowledge can lead to what we call 'cognitive entrenchment.' Once we know something, it is often hard to see other ways of looking at it.

More recently, scholars have replicated this effect in studies of the game of chess.[65,66] Experienced chess players tend to fall into cognitive routines of how

---

65 Bilalić, M., McLeod, P., & Gobet, F. 2008. Inflexibility of experts – Reality or myth? Quantifying the Einstellung effect in chess masters. *Cognitive Psychology*, 56(2): 73–102.

66 Saariluoma, P. 1990. Apperception and restructuring in chess players' problem solving. In K. J. Gilhooly, M. T. Keane, R. H. Logie, & G. Erdos (Eds.), *Lines of Thinking: Reflections of the psychology of thought*, Vol. 2: 41–57. Oxford: Wiley.

they play the game. In the experiment, skilled and less skilled players were shown different situations and asked to make their next move. The more experienced and expert players, of course, did well, but like the jar experiment, many of them failed to see the even better move, which many of the less experienced players found.

Expertise is important and helpful to seeing ways to use your expertise in novel ways. But sometimes, because that's your expertise, that's all you can see. As the saying goes, when all you have is a hammer, everything looks like a nail.

Strategies for Out-of-the-Box Thinking

Given what we know about creative thinking toward generating novel combinations of needs knowledge with useful technical knowledge, how can we improve how we go about trying to problem solve? Assuming that, after getting through the previous chapters, you've been able to learn at least one unmet consumer need, can we use what we've learned in this chapter strategically to generate better and more novel ideas?

I want to give you two important implications. The first is a simple and straightforward one: get interested in technologies. I mean 'technologies' very broadly to refer to the science of what things can do. If you're having a hard time innovating a new solution, it is either because you don't know a problem to solve or you don't know enough to solve a problem.

The brightest and more successful innovators are highly savvy in the technology world. They can see not only some groundbreaking solution, but also have the wherewithal to assess its technical and economic viability.

So stop sitting there, waiting for ideas to just come to you. They probably won't unless and until you have enough technical knowledge to start actually solving problems when they come to you. Even if you do have some clever idea, without enough technical knowledge this could be just a wild goose chase over some solution that just isn't feasible.

Find tech websites that can keep you up to date on the latest-and-greatest new discoveries. Subscribe to tech periodicals if that's your jam. You might 'specialize' in certain technological areas – chemistry, mechanical physics, electronics, etc. Breadth of knowledge is very helpful, but you need to get deep enough into some technology (ies) that you know and understand what can and can't be done. The more you understand about the properties of resources and technologies, the better you can leverage those properties and what they do to your advantage.

The second implication is a specific method I've devised to help you combine your existing knowledge more broadly and effectively.

Knowledge-combining Method

The first step of this method is to list as many different resources, technologies, and skills you know about. This'll be a long and arduous process for some of you, since I expect you'll know a lot of things. But list as many as you can think of: software skills, hardware skills, people skills, technologies you've worked on or with, processes that you've used, various resources that you've used and are familiar with, etc. Chisholm uses the helpful acronym STARS: skills, technologies, assets and accomplishments, relationships and reputation, and (inner) strengths.[67]

If you find this strategy helpful, it may be worthwhile to keep and update this list over time with all the new things you learn about, so you can come back to it and reuse it again and again.

Once you have a pretty complete list, turn your focus onto the problem, the customer need that you're looking to solve. Think deeply about it. Try to remember all the details and nuances of what that need experience is like for your customer(s). If it's your own problem, find a time to put yourself into that situation such that you can actively experience it. This gets your value knowledge about that need fully activated in your mind.

At this point, you'll then mentally step through your list of resources and bring each of them to active memory. Try to think of a possible solution to the consumer need using each one. In many cases it might seem impossible. Try anyway. The solution you devise might be crazy, but that's okay. Write it down, no matter how wild. If a solution came fairly easily to your mind, try to think of another way to use that resource or skill to solve the problem, maybe even a few. Do this for your whole list of knowledge areas. Don't just stop at one that seems promising. Keep going and get through the whole list. The point of this is that you are bringing to mind your various technical knowledge schemas while holding your problem knowledge in active memory. This will give you the opportunity to have 'aha!' insight moments by making new connections to different resources and technologies.

Once you've been through the whole list, look at all of your solutions. Go back through them. Do some of them stand out to you? Do they have certain advantages over others? If so, can those advantages be combined somehow? Some of the best ideas are combinations of multiple technologies that are designed in effective ways. Write down as many combination solutions as come to mind.

---

67 Although I devised this method on my own from my dissertation work, I was very surprised and happy to find a very similar method developed independently by John Chisholm in his book *Unleash Your Inner Company*. His method is better and more fully developed than my own here (although I bring additional insights here that should be considered), so I highly recommend the book to readers.

Chisholm, J. 2015. *Unleash Your Inner Company* . Austin, TX: Greenleaf Book Group.

Hopefully by now you'll have a pretty good list of solutions, ranging from the wild and crazy to the practical and boring. Which ones seem most promising? Don't just consider the most obvious. Choose at least one or two that are outside-of-the-box ideas. If a solution doesn't seem possible right now, is it really *impossible* or just limited by current technology? If it is the latter, don't discount it! Not only is technology marching forward a breakneck pace, but you might be the one to move it even further.

With a short list of your most promising ideas, it's time to do some more research. What advancements have been made in how the resources, technologies, or skills in your solution can be used? Learn as much as you can about that technology. What new insights does that new knowledge give you for your idea? If you're going to succeed, you need to become an expert in your solution. This may require some significant effort on your part if you're not already an expert in the field. But it's easier than ever to learn about all kinds of technologies.

Once you're pretty well versed in the technology, it's time to put it into action and develop a prototype. Prototype development is a critical learning process where you really get to dig into the technology and see how it works and what doesn't work. At this stage, you're just trying to get proof of concept. Skimp on the features. Start with a bare bones model. If it works, you can use it to get help (investment money, team members, etc.) in moving to the next, more advanced stage of prototyping.

Eventually, you should have a working prototype that's ready to market test. This should no longer be the bare-bones model, but should be a (close to) market viable solution that offers a significant advancement over current solutions. Take it to your lead users and see what they think. Does it solve their need any better than existing solutions? If so, you're on your way! If not, what's are the limitations and drawbacks? Can they be fixed? You're learning more and more about your customers' needs here, so don't just keep going with your initial design. Go back to the drawing board with your new understanding, over and over again if necessary. Don't accept the first okay design that seems to work either. Build the best solution to your best understanding of those needs. 'Okay' will not sell.

It'll take time, commitment, and resources. I hope you're passionate about it. But all that extra time and effort will pay off big time if and when your solution succeeds.

Wrapping Up

Creativity and innovation are hard to teach. It's just too spontaneous. But once you get the basics of how innovative insight works, you can use that basic understanding to your advantage. I can't promise that this chapter is going to make you a brilliant innovator. It's up to you to have the right knowledge and break out of your 'cognitive entrenchment' of thinking of things in the same way they've always been understood. Novelty is often weird to think about. Don't be afraid to think a little weird.

Chapter 13
Managing Value Uncertainty

By now the hope is that you have an idea that is both highly promising and interesting to you. But you still have a decision to make – *are you going to go for it?* We call this the 'plunge decision' (i.e., are you going to 'take the plunge'?).

At this point, you don't have to be *right* about your value knowledge and expectations. It's not too late to learn and change what you know about and will offer to customers. But you have to commit to the process here – commit your time and at least some of your resources to it.

Recall from Section 2 that consumers learn about their needs over time through a cyclical experiential process, and that entrepreneurs learn what needs to solve from those consumers. One of the key take-aways from our value-as-a-process theory is that value is uncertain, both for the entrepreneur and for the consumer. I'll discuss consumers' uncertainty more in the next chapter, but in this chapter I want to focus on *your* uncertainty.

First of all, what do we mean by uncertainty? What is uncertain? As we learn more about the world, things begin to be more and more predictable. We know, for example, exactly when the next lunar eclipse will occur. We know what will happen when you add baking soda to vinegar. We probably even know the air-speed velocity of an unladen swallow. But entrepreneurs don't deal much in this world of scientific predictability. That's because entrepreneurs' judgment depends on *people*.

Let's elaborate on these points.

What *is* Uncertainty?

Uncertainty is a term that has been widely bandied about. It has various meanings in common parlance, and perhaps even more in academic work. It has been notoriously difficult to study and understand, and I've heard some conclude that maybe we *can't* really study it because uncertainty is unknowable by nature. That conclusion was an interesting one to me. But it stems from a confusion of language more than anything. It's true that the *content* of uncertainty (what one is uncertain *about*) is unknowable *a priori*, but the *concept* of uncertainty is within comprehensibility. But this concept of uncertainty has proved really hard to pin down, which has made it essentially impossible to parse the confusion to develop a comprehensive and comprehensible theory of entrepreneurial uncertainty.

But some clearer thinking within the framework of our Austrian subjectivism and representationalism can, I think, really help us clear this confusion up. Together with some of my friends and colleagues, I've been working on trying to get

https://doi.org/10.1515/9783110750805-013

at the true essence of uncertainty, and I think we've made some groundbreaking progress.

The first point of confusion is that the term 'uncertainty' is commonly used to describe *different* things. If I say, "There's uncertainty in the electronics market," I'm saying something different than saying, "I have some uncertainty about the electronics market." I probably *mean* the same thing, but those statements are different. This is where the confusion stems from.

Uncertainty is a phenomenon of the mind. The electronics market, or the ocean, or the weather *can't* be uncertain – these things don't think. The weather, can be *unpredictable* – it can be complex and volatile in such a way that some thinking actor can see it and be unable to be certain about it. This is what the phrase "the weather is uncertain" actually means.

But it doesn't matter how complex or dynamic or otherwise unpredictable the weather is *if there is no one to be uncertain about it.* If we removed all thinking beings from the earth, would there still be uncertainty? No, of course not, because uncertainty is a phenomenon of the mind.

Using the term 'uncertainty' to describe unpredictable phenomena is the linguistic confusion I was talking about. This isn't uncertainty, it is *unpredictability* or, more correctly, *unknowability*. The term unpredictability can be used insofar as the thing we want to know, but can't, is a *future outcome*. But we don't have to be uncertain only about future states. I can also be uncertain about who really shot JFK or what really caused the extinction of the dinosaurs. These are not *unpredictable*, but they are *unknowable*. We simply cannot go back in time to observe these historical events as they really played out. Similarly, what is happening right now in the kitchen of some home in rural India is unknowable to me. I have no way to see or otherwise observe it, so I cannot know.

The key point here is that I am uncertain about these things *because* they are unknowable. Unknowability is a *cause* of uncertainty, but it is not the uncertainty itself. In fact, if we're being especially careful and precise, the causal relationship between unknowability and uncertainty is indirect, mediated by *ignorance*. Unknowability causes ignorance, which causes uncertainty.

This matters because these causal relationships are *contingent*. Not all ignorance causes uncertainty. It is possible for you to be uncertain despite having sufficient knowledge to be certain. Or, more commonly, it is very possible for you to be *certain* despite in fact having large gaps in your knowledge that should preclude you from such confidence.

Entrepreneurs are notorious for their overconfidence. Now, if we're being fair to those entrepreneurs, research on overconfidence is problematic. Studying overconfidence *as if* we were these strictly 'rational,' computational beings isn't fair. Our brains are extremely powerful in dealing with the complexities and ambiguities of real life. If we feel as if we have more control over outcomes than we really do in some artificial situation, if we have greater hopes than are warranted in some experiment that doesn't really matter to us, it's a little unfair to dismiss our complex brains as inefficient. We just don't think that way. And we shouldn't.

Cognitive scientist Beau Lotto argues in his book *Deviate*[68] that our brains evolved to see the world optimistically. If we were too rationally afraid to explore what's on the other side of the mountain, we would never discover anything. Taking risks is *better* for us and for humankind. As I'll explain in Chapter 15, risk-taking entrepreneurs are what drive economic growth. We are *meant* to take risks. So, perhaps the overconfidence research is a bit too overly dismissive of the *advantages* of overconfidence. It's okay to be confident in yourself and your chances. Yes, the rate of new venture failure is pretty high, but it's not as high as some will tell you. It depends on how you define 'failure,' of course. But very few entrepreneurs regret it. And that tells you something.

But let's get back to what *uncertainty* is. If it's not what we're now calling *unknowability*, what is it?

To explain uncertainty, let's recall the philosophy of representationalism. Our conscious minds perceive nothing but representations. Even our immediate, sensory experience is actually a representation that our minds create for us from sense stimuli. But we don't have to represent only reality. We can also represent counterfactuals and imaginary worlds. And sometimes it's tough to tell the difference.

But not only do we consciously experience representations, but as we do so we *assess* them. As I explained in Section 2 (particularly Chapter 7), we assess them for their desirability and for their usefulness. We assess them for their interestingness and relevance for our interests. But perhaps most fundamental and important of all, we assess them for their *veracity* – if it's *true*, if it represents reality accurately, or not.

Veracity assessments are made, specifically, for what philosophers call *knowledge claims*. A knowledge claim is, essentially, a representation that is intended to be true, to represent reality as it really is. But really, it's a claim *about* the representation rather than the representation itself: "that is a tree" rather than the mental picture of a tree *per se*. It is a belief or claim that a representation is true.

The *result* of a veracity assessment can be one of three outcomes: that the knowledge claim is *true*, *false*, or *uncertain*. If a claim is assessed as either true or false, those claims are *certain*. If and to the extent that there is any room for doubt about the truth or falsity of the claim, there is uncertainty. Uncertainty is greatest at the midpoint between certain truth and certain falsity.

This may seem somewhat of a tangential point, but misunderstanding uncertainty has been the source of endless confusion and debate among scholars. More importantly, it has led entrepreneurship scholars to mistake how uncertainty affects the entrepreneurial process and what can (and can't) be done about it. There isn't

---

68 Lotto, B. 2017. *Deviate: The science of seeing differently*. New York, NY: Hachette Books.

some uncertainty 'out there' impinging on your capabilities as an entrepreneur. Your uncertainty is your own.

My goal for you in this chapter is to help you *match* your uncertainty to the unknowability conditions of the venture so that you're not making 'unreasonable' judgments that could cost you. I put 'unreasonable' in quotes there because 'reasonable' is of course subjective. There's no objective 'right' or 'wrong' answer when there's unknowability at issue, as is particularly true for entrepreneurship. But if you can properly assess unknowabilities, you can set your expectations well and prepare properly for the unpredictable – not overly uncertain, but not overly confident either.

Entrepreneurial Uncertainty

So now that we know what uncertainty *is*, let's discuss why it's understood to be so central and necessary to entrepreneurship. The plunge decision is made over an *entrepreneurial value claim*. The entrepreneurial value claim is a particular and specific knowledge claim with a *future empathic contingent*.

Let's break that down further. There are *two* contingents in an entrepreneurial value claim – a future contingent and an empathic contingent. Either one renders the entrepreneurial value claim unknowable. Together, the two contingents make the entrepreneurial value claim *highly* unknowable – one of the most unknowable activities we can do. That's not to say it can't be estimated or predicted – you can and should, of course, form expectations. But you cannot *know* for certain if it will be valuable or not to others. It requires, in the end, some leap of faith to some extent. Thus, your expectations should be tempered to the level appropriate of a particular degree of unknowingness.

Predictive Uncertainty

The first contingent is a *future contingent* – the decision to buy and consume is a future one – and may result in what we might call *predictive uncertainty*. A future contingent within a knowledge claim, as you might guess, is a contingent whose resolution occurs at some future date. Aristotle famously depicted such future contingents with the statement "there will be a sea battle tomorrow." Such a knowledge claim is *intended* to reflect reality as it will be, but its veracity – even if it can be observed and known – cannot be observed and known *yet*. The contingent 'tomorrow' precludes a veracity assessment from concluding certainly true or false, except by overexuberant expectation, until 'tomorrow' comes and the contingent is resolved.

The future is unknowable. We all know this. The further into the future we look, the more unpredictable it appears to us. We have to act *now*, in the present, while the relevant consequences of our actions and inactions (those things we elected not to do) will only play out down the road.

The reason the future is unknowable to us is that, even if we could know precisely what our actions would do, there are all kinds of things that could happen between now and then that might affect the outcome. This is, of course, why more future outcomes are harder to predict than nearer ones – outcomes further out into the future have many more opportunities for something to unexpectedly turn the course of events astray.

Causality is one of the most important things we learn over the course of life – we need to know how the world works so that we can make it work better for us (see Section 2). But no matter how much we know and understand what leads to what, that causal knowledge can only lead to perfect knowability in a *closed system* – an environment that is perfectly shielded from any outside influence – and where nothing within the system can be characterized as indeterminate. In other words, perfect knowability requires that we know all actions and interactions of all potentially relevant things. Otherwise, factors outside of our knowledge could interfere in ways that we do not expect.

Closed systems are important for engineering, where it is important that outside factors don't interfere with the designed processes. But not only is such a closed system virtually never actually the case in human life, entrepreneurship is essentially the *opposite* of a closed system. Entrepreneurship is the injection of novelty and unpredictability into the economic system. The entrepreneur's future is always highly contingent on factors far beyond the entrepreneur's control or knowability, including and especially other people's choices.

Empathic Uncertainty

The second of the entrepreneurial contingents is an *empathic contingent*. Because an entrepreneurial value claim is ultimately about *another's* value experience, knowability hinges on our ability to know and predict other people. But people are inherently unknowable, even in the present. Their decisions are their own to make, and they don't always make the decisions we think they will or should make. No matter how much we *think* we know what someone else is thinking or feeling or will do, it's always possible – and in fact common – that they surprise us. Parents, for example, can certainly attest to the fact that, despite knowing their own children just about as well as possible, those children never cease to surprise them.

Many scientists believe that people are essentially biological machines, reacting instinctively to the various stimuli that they perceive. The goal of the human sciences, then, is to unravel the mysteries of human physiology and psychology in such a way that we can understand and predict human behavior. But in fact, the debate over free will has been highly inconclusive. Whatever evidence scholars have found to support this determinist position – that free will is only an illusion, and that human behavior is predetermined by social and physiological processes – has been countered by careful arguments that the evidence is either tenuous or faulty or that the inference to the determinist position is not as compelling as first thought.

Over 70 years ago, Ludwig von Mises concluded that, given this inconclusive state of science on the free will question, the only justifiable position for social science is to assume that free will exists. I concur for at least two reasons. First, we clearly can't fully predict people if we can't even tell for sure if they have free will or not. We are much further from actually being able to scientifically predict people than most people – scientists especially – tend to think.

The positivist paradigm that I critiqued in the first chapter has given us a wealth of scientific knowledge of human behavior that is either useless or just wrong. The 'Reproducibility Project'[69] concluded that most of our psychology and behavioral research doesn't replicate – most of what we thought we knew was just false positives. I can only laugh to myself when some exuberant behavioral scientist gets excited about how predictable people seem to be. But what they're actually talking about are extremely small *statistical* effects contrived from highly artificial experiments that have little semblance to the reality we actually encounter. What's more, people in fact behave very differently (heterogeneously) even in those experiments. But if the scientist can extract a slightly upward-sloped trend in the mass of messy data, he or she will typically conclude that there is an effect, and infer from it that virtually all people react in a similar way (even though their own data dispel such a conclusion). In other words, the 'predictability' of people in the behavioral sciences is an aggregate compendium of a great many non-universal behavioral quirks that scholars have found in unrealistic experimental situations.

Second and perhaps more importantly, there are some pretty important ethical implications in one's belief or not in free will. Perhaps not surprisingly, scholars have found that people will behave much more unethically when they disbelieve in free will.[70,71,72] The classic excuse 'the devil made me do it' has been replaced with

---

69 Open Science Collaboration. 2015. Estimating the reproducibility of psychological science. *Science*, 349(6251): aac4716.

70 Baumeister, R. F., Masicampo, E., & DeWall, C. N. 2009. Prosocial benefits of feeling free: Disbelief in free will increases aggression and reduces helpfulness. *Personality and Social Psychology Bulletin*, 35(2): 260–268.

Monroe, A. E., Dillon, K. D., & Malle, B. F. 2014. Bringing free will down to Earth: People's psychological concept of free will and its role in moral judgment. *Consciousness and Cognition*, 27: 100–108.

71 Vohs, K. D., & Schooler, J. W. 2008. The value of believing in free will: Encouraging a belief in determinism increases cheating. *Psychological Science*, 19(1): 49–54.

72 Krueger, F., Hoffman, M., Walter, H., & Grafman, J. 2013. An fMRI investigation of the effects of belief in free will on third-party punishment. *Social Cognitive and Affective Neuroscience*, 9(8): 1143–1149.

'circumstance made me do it' – if people can justify shirking responsibility for their misdeeds, they will. Mises's conclusion stands – if we do not have full and incontrovertible evidence against the free will hypothesis, which we don't, then the theoretical and ethical obligation is to accept it.

If we accept this conclusion and accept the free will hypothesis, what does this mean for entrepreneurship? It leaves the entrepreneur in something of a predicament. Because the outcomes that we're interested in, value preferences and experiences, are the consumers', consumers' free will matters. Entrepreneurs *do not* control their own destiny – they are at the whims of consumers' choices. Entrepreneurs typically have to make their own judgments and commit resources to productive activities before the consumer has to decide whether to buy it or not. No matter how much marketing and advertising the entrepreneur can muster, the choice remains the consumers' only.

The consumer, again, is also uncertain about the expected value that your solution will provide, and they'll have to somehow mitigate or bear that uncertainty if they're going to buy it. I'll talk more about this in the next chapter.

But the point of this is that you cannot know what others will do. Your predictions are based on an empathic contingent – what those others, your customers, want is outside of your purview and is not within your control. Again, the goal of this chapter is to help you better recognize what you do and can know, and what you cannot. Most entrepreneurial failures are a result of entrepreneurs presuming to know more than they really do and failing to temper expectations to what they really do not and cannot know.

The Many Uncertainties of Entrepreneurship

Entrepreneurial judgment is, specifically, over an entrepreneurial value claim, which is innately unknowable. But of course the value of your idea is hardly the only uncertainty that you will experience. In fact, you will need to deal with many different uncertainties throughout your entrepreneurial journey. Let's look at some of them.

Value uncertainty corresponds also with *demand* uncertainty, which is the uncertainty you have about how many others will value and want your solution. *Technical* uncertainty concerns whether the imagined solution is technologically feasible. *Economic* uncertainty questions whether it can be produced economically (i.e., at a lower cost than the price it can command). *Resource* uncertainty entails uncertainty about whether you have or can acquire the necessary resources to bring your idea to fruition, which of course include the financial resources you will need. *Capability* uncertainty wonders whether you and your team have, or can get, the combined skills needed to achieve a successful launch. And *competitive* uncertainty concerns what competitive response you might get from other market actors.

Each of these uncertainties reflects some lack of knowledge that you will need to somehow manage if you are to be successful.

Better Uncertainty Management

Ultimately, you, the entrepreneur will have to manage the uncertainties that you will face, culminating in the uncertainty that the consumer may or may not buy your solution when all is said and done. There is no getting around it. These things are simply unknowable at the time of your entrepreneurial judgment. Managing this uncertainty is one of the primary economic functions of the entrepreneur.

But you can bear the uncertainty in different ways, and how you bear it over time should really depend on what type of uncertainty you're facing. I've already explained why the free will hypothesis should be accepted – even if we *think* it's just an illusion. If it's an illusion, we're still so far from being able to account for all the variables at play that it is no different, theoretically, than if we had just accepted the free will hypothesis.

Accepting the free will hypothesis implies two different types of uncertainty – those that are *ignorance*-based and those that are *indeterminacy*-based. Ignorance-based uncertainties arise simply because we don't know enough (knowable) information to determine the outcome with certainty. Certainty increases with more and better information. Indeterminacy-based uncertainties are those with unresolved contingents, which means that the information you need to be certain is not just unknown but *unknowable*.

Mitigating Ignorance-Based Uncertainty

Some of the uncertainties you will experience are ignorance-based – technical, resource, capability, and economic uncertainties for example. These are uncertainties that are *not* due to unknowabilities, but only due to a present lack of knowledge. These are uncertainties that you will want to deal with by *mitigating* them. That is, you will need to work to figure these out. Collect the information you need in order to know what works and can be done in order to make a decision.

Technical uncertainty, for example, you would not want to leave unmitigated. You need to *know* if your solution can and will work before investing significant financial resources toward its development and production. Theranos is an example of insufficient technical uncertainty mitigation prior to entrepreneurial judgment. Elizabeth Holmes's idea – kiosk blood testing – was, of course, a very good one. It would have saved consumers significant time and money. But while she was very successful at wooing investors, her team simply could not get the technology to work. She had jumped the gun, bearing the technical uncertainty rather than miti-gating it, and it landed her in a heap of trouble.

Capability and resource uncertainties are similarly ignorance-based and mitiga-ble, and *should* be mitigated. You may not be able to mitigate them completely be-fore entrepreneurial judgment must be made – at least some resource commitments must be made up front just to even mitigate these uncertainties. But such uncer-tainty mitigation ought to be the goal of early investments.

Resource uncertainty is an interesting one because it may only be *partially* miti-gable. Do you have or can you get the resources you need to bring the idea to fru-ition? Part of this resource uncertainty is ignorance-based – you need to know what those resource costs will be, which you can mitigate with research. But if you don't have those resources at hand already and will need to procure them from others, then it becomes an indeterminacy-based uncertainty, where you can only *hope* others will be willing to financially support your venture.

As a final note here, some ignorance-based uncertainties are costly to mitigate. You may not have the resources to fully eliminate them. These you might have to *manage* rather than mitigate using the tools I'll discuss next.

Managing Indeterminacy-Based Uncertainty

Some of the uncertainties you will experience will be based in indeterminacies – primarily other people's choices. These include value and demand uncertainties, as well as, e.g., competitive uncertainty. Because those whom you are uncertain about have not yet made their choice, you cannot yet know what their choice will be. Again, that's not to say that you can't have expectations about those choices – we often predict what other people will do, even though we can't know for certain. But not knowing for certain is a difficult position to be in when dealing with huge com-mitments and investments.

These types of unknowability can only be *managed* – you cannot eliminate them. Managing uncertainty entails planning for and putting yourself in a ready po-sition for if and when your predictions are wrong. And they *will* be wrong, at least to some extent. So it is wise and important to have a management approach in place for when things do not go quite as expected. I'll walk you quickly through some of the approaches advanced in entrepreneurship scholarship.

One approach is called a real options approach. Essentially, the idea here is to not commit too much to any single idea or plan, and to develop contingency plans ("real options") for if and when things don't play out as expected. This allows you to cut smaller losses and to pivot more quickly when you find that you've made a wrong prediction. In fact, one of the possible reasons entrepreneurs don't pivot when they should is the *sunk cost fallacy*. This fallacy has been widely studied in financial investment markets, where investors hold on too long to an investment because they don't want to fold when the chips are down, holding out a hope and expectation that the investment will go back up. Entrepreneurs do this too – they become unwilling to simply abandon their idea and their venture because they've already invested so much time and money into them.

A real options strategy lowers the sunk cost, making it easier to abandon a losing idea and to pivot quickly. It tries to help you stay above water long enough to figure out what's the right track and get on before the resources run out. Of course, you only can have a few real options, each of which is a prediction with some resource commitments tied to it. So you can't be wrong too many times or you'll run out of resources.

Another approach is called effectuation theory, where the idea is to commit to the venture only up to the resources you're willing and able to lose – your *affordable loss*. Never commit more than you're really able to lose. Don't put yourself and your family into dire straights if things go poorly. I think this is sound advice for any approach to entrepreneurship. There are others with money to invest that will be willing to invest in you if you have a compelling idea and message. If you can't find others to invest in your project, it may be because you, your idea, or your message are wanting. If investors can't see the value in your idea, will consumers?

With those limited resources you are willing and able to commit, you would then innovate whatever market solutions you can come up with. With some ideas in hand, you'd then go out and get feedback from others and recruit new stakeholders, pitching your ideas and trying to get others to commit additional resources. You don't want to be too committed to your idea here because, again, it might not be all that great – especially given the limited resources you started with. You just have to have something that's *promising*, and to be compelling enough as a personality that others can see you as a capable leader and entrepreneur. The others you speak to and recruit will then contribute additional resources, and help you discover new and potentially better ideas for that now larger pool of available resources.

This effectuation process is an iterative cycle where you keep redefining your value proposition, enrolling new stakeholders, collecting new resources, and then redefining the value proposition again and again until you have a really strong value proposition *and* the resources to make it happen. This method is great because it limits your potential loss to only those resources that you committed at the very beginning, your affordable loss. But it is time consuming, and having a large pool of stakeholders can make decision-making a challenge.

There are also other approaches to uncertainty management (such as the lean method and design thinking), but the basic intuition is generally the same: relatively low up-front resource commitments and high adaptiveness to new information. These approaches acknowledge your uncertainties and account for them in different ways to mitigate losses where expectations fail, as they very likely will at times.

Choosing between Approaches

In the more traditional entrepreneurial approach, you start with a problem to solve, design some solution, and then procure the resources that you would need to bring that solution to market. This traditional approach is highly predictive and doesn't have the evaluative feedback processes that an uncertainty mitigation approach – such as effectuation, with its cyclical redefining processes – would entail. So this approach is riskier, but it's also generally faster and more efficient, avoiding the often arduous processes of finding more and more stakeholders and responding repeatedly to feedback.

The point here is that you don't want to waste time and resources on less-efficient uncertainty management approaches if you can perhaps avoid it. Recent research suggests that, often, the optimal approach to entrepreneurship is not exclusively one or the other decision approach, but a combination of both. After all, entrepreneurship isn't just a single judgment but a series of many decisions and judgments over time over different uncertain circumstances and possibilities, and few decisions are irreversible.

But it's not always clear what decision strategy is ideal for which situation. Many entrepreneurs just make their decisions and move on. Some would even argue that decisiveness is a critical attribute of good entrepreneurs. But quick decisions can be extremely costly if they're wrong, and decisiveness can put your venture at too much risk.

A quick and general rule of thumb is this: ignorance-based uncertainties should be mitigated with cost-effective information gathering, while indeterminism-based uncertainties should use uncertainty management techniques.

But costs and risks also come into play. If information gathering is overly costly to effectively mitigate the ignorance-based uncertainty, then a management approach is apropos. On the other hand, if an indeterminism-based uncertainty is very low-risk – if the consequences of being 'wrong' are low – then spending time and resources on contingencies or adaptive processes may not be worth it. So take the costs and risks into consideration when choosing how to deal with the uncertainties that you face.

Dealing with Uncertainties Sequentially

As a quick and final note, there appears to be a common pattern to how successful entrepreneurs deal with uncertainty. In some collaborative research with colleagues, we've found that many successful entrepreneurs deal with those many different uncertainties in a common or typical pattern (see Fig. 13.1).

First, they work on the value uncertainty first, attempting to gather impressions and information about others' thoughts and feelings about the idea. Next, they take

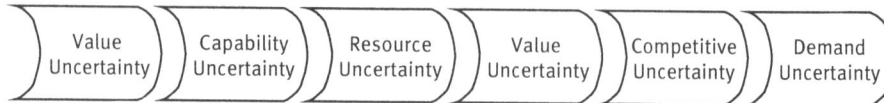

Fig. 13.1: The Typical Uncertainty Management Process.

on capability uncertainty, trying to find the right team to develop the idea and bring it to fruition. Third is their resource uncertainties, working to get enough financial backing and support from investors to get the idea to market.

Fourth is a deeper dive into value uncertainty, working on taking the idea from concept to a real, deliverable value proposition for consumers. Do we really have consumers' actual needs figured out? Do we really have the best and most effective solution to a particular need? Are there adjustments that we can make to improve the value proposition?

Fifth and sixth are competitive uncertainty and demand uncertainty. Are others looking to enter this same space? Or, if others are already there, how are they going to respond to my entry? Will they imitate? How can I guard against this? And will people really prefer my product to others at the price I'm asking? How many?

This is, I think, a useful roadmap of the uncertainties you will need to deal with in your journey. You don't have to deal with them in this order, of course, but it is a sensible sequencing, where you start with determining whether the ignorance-based uncertainties are worth pursuing and then go to work on pursuing each of them to ensure that you will be able to create and deliver the value proposition envisioned in an economic manner. Finally, work to manage those remaining uncertainties that you can't mitigate. This sequential approach minimizes your losses in failure, while maximizing your potential to succeed.

In short, pay attention to the type of uncertainties that they are and deal with them accordingly. Don't let yourself get overconfident. But don't let yourself get paralyzed with fear either. These uncertainties are significant roadblocks, but you *can* work through them. Just be sure that you understand them when taking them on, or you can get tripped up.

Chapter 14
Customer Uncertainty and Value Diffusion

Although my primary intention in this book is to help and guide you toward achieving a solution that will prove truly valuable to consumers – that better addresses a real need that others have – as we near the end of this book, let me offer a few more words of strategy for the later stages of your venture emergence process. Even if you have succeeded in creating something that would be highly valuable to consumers, your success is hardly foregone. This is because it's not only you who suffers from unknowability and, thus, uncertainty – *customers* have their own uncertainties.

In this chapter I'll discuss some new insights on innovation diffusion processes from our Austrian subjectivist perspective. 'Diffusion' refers to the process of a new product's dissemination across a market population. A new innovation 'diffuses' from its origination out to the local market, and then to a broader national market, and then on to a global market. Research on diffusion has studied what are the differences between who buys early and who buys late and why.

Classical diffusion research suggests various simple mechanisms such as marketing and word of mouth processes. But it's missing the underpinning mechanisms of *why* and *how*, which has led to misguided conclusions and implications for entrepreneurs. In other words, the classical theoretical approaches to diffusion are likely to lead you astray, to direct your efforts toward marketing activities that are not as effective as you need them to be. A better understanding of these processes from our subjectivist foundations offers more compelling advice.

The Limitations of Diffusion Theory

Given the arguments I've made about the missteps of economics, it shouldn't be surprising, perhaps, that I would find much about prevailing diffusion theory also wanting. The definitive work on this question has traditionally been Everett Rogers's book, *Diffusion of Innovations*, published first in 1962 and then again as a new edition every decade thereafter. The fifth and final edition,[73] published in 2003, is still widely read by scholars and business owners around the globe. But that work is riddled with assumptions and conclusions inconsistent with the Austrian school of economics, and which I find to be highly problematic.

Rogers, and the research behind his book, explores who are the earlier versus the later buyers or 'adopters' of new innovations and why see (Fig. 14.1). The first adopters of a new innovation are called 'tech enthusiasts' and are, Rogers argues,

---

73 Rogers, E. 2003. *Diffusion of Innovations* (5 ed.). New York: Free Press.

https://doi.org/10.1515/9783110750805-014

motivated by having the latest and greatest technologies. These are the ones who line up at the Apple Store the night before a new release of the iPhone so they can be the first to have it. These singular people pay close attention to the news of the tech world to stay at the cutting edge of consumer technology.

Just after those tech enthusiasts are the early adopters, who are highly motivated and willing to buy the new product, after learning of it from marketing and information diffusion processes. After this early phase, word starts to spread more quickly, and a larger number of people start adopting the new product – the early majority. At this point, competitors have entered and more and more people have heard about the new product. The late majority comes next, these consumers being in the further outreaches of society and, thus, slower to learn of and adopt the new innovation. Finally, you have the laggards, who are resistant to new technologies generally, or are simply far removed from society such that they learn of and want new products much later than others.

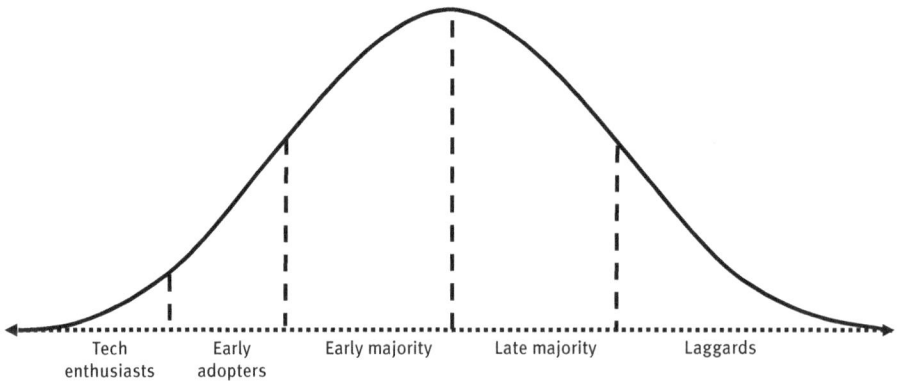

| Tech enthusiasts | Early adopters | Early majority | Late majority | Laggards |

Fig. 14.1: The Standard Diffusion Distribution.

Returning to the challenges to classical economics that I made in the first chapter, this traditional diffusion model is a positivist approach called a 'contagion' model – a new innovation spreads through the market via communication like a virus. Based in the traditional and erroneous value-as-utility concept, Frank Bass[74] and others devised a model of diffusion that assumed real and objective value to diffuse contingently based on the extent to which consumers have access to information about that value. In other words, what keeps a valuable product from diffusing is just that consumers don't know about it. Value diffuses with and as a result of the diffusion

---

74 Bass, F. M. 1969. A new product growth model for consumer durables. *Management Science*, 15(5): 215–227.

of information about it. The temporal process of information diffusion, and its sup-posed direct effects on value diffusion, produce the famous S-curve model.

But this process doesn't play out as expected for a lot of new products, which fall into what Geoff Moore has called a "chasm"[75] between the early adopters and early majority and fail. But because they have relied upon the current contagion model, Moore and scholars have supposed that, to cross this chasm, the entrepre-neur should pursue relentless marketing and advertising to spread the word far and wide. That is, new products fail because they don't get the contagion process going soon, fast, or hard enough, and the spreading of information peters out. There is a vicious cycle where lack of marketing leads to insufficient sales, which further starves marketing efforts. To overcome this defeating cycle, you need to get the word out hard and fast through guerilla marketing techniques.

Now, although there is certainly something intuitive to this theory, looking through the lens of subjectivism allows us to intuitively grasp some of its prob-lems. Of course, the primary issue underlying this contagion model is that value is actually *subjective*, and not objective. But what does this mean for diffusion theory?

Our value-as-a-process theory, and the Austrian understanding of subjective value, implies that value is actually uncertain, not just to the entrepreneur but also to the *consumer*. As explained in Section 2, the consumer is learning what to want, and every action and purchase is a prediction of future consumption value. Con-sumers can predict the value of some existing products pretty well, since they have consumed them maybe many times before. If we can reasonably expect the product, and the experience it produces, to be consistent with previous experiences, we can predict its value fairly accurately. But *new* value, such as that which you, the entre-preneur, might offer, is typically very difficult for consumers to predict. It's a lot safer for your prospective customers to just return to familiar value in order to sat-isfy their needs. For you to succeed, then, you need consumers to see the value that you offer in such a light that they see it as worth the risk that it might not really sat-isfy. In other words, it's not an information chasm as typically understood, it's an *uncertainty* chasm (see Fig. 14.2)!

The Uncertainty Chasm

The value of a new innovation is inhibited by value uncertainty. Certain value is more valuable than uncertain value, all else equal. And the greater the uncertainty, the more wary and less willing the consumer is to purchase the innovation. See, the

---

75 Moore, G. A. 1991. *Crossing the Chasm*. New York: HarperCollins.

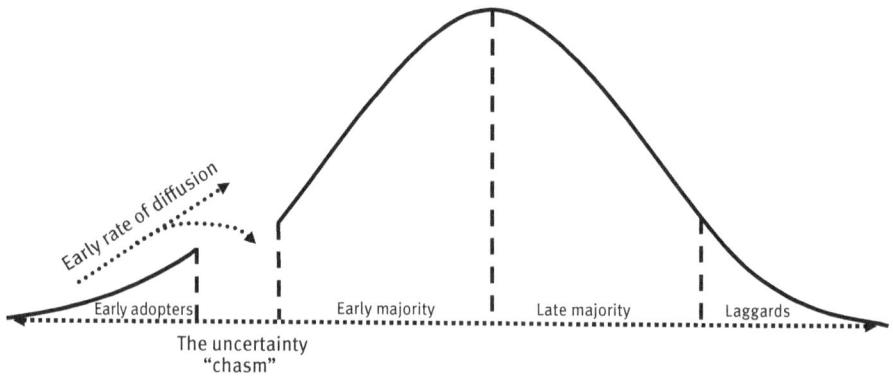

Fig. 14.2: The Uncertainty Chasm.

problem is, if you'll recall, that there's an opportunity cost to trying a new product. If it doesn't work as hoped, the consumer is out the price paid, which precludes other satisfactions that they would have enjoyed. This might even mean forgoing the satisfaction that they would have gotten with the safer option.

Most ideas are 'incremental' innovations – they find a minor, but valuable way to augment existing solutions. Such ideas are usually easy to grasp, so it is not difficult to explain how and why the product is better. But incremental ideas are easy to imitate, and new entrepreneurs are unlikely to displace the incumbents, who can rely on their brand familiarity to give them enough time to develop the change. If your idea is too similar to existing products, you'll have a hard time getting enough traction fast enough to really compete with the established products.

But if your product is too novel and uncertain, not even the early adopters will be willing to forego their opportunity cost unless they can get some help. These are the so-called *radical* innovations that are often difficult for consumers to understand.

The Uncertainty of Edison's Light Bulb

In a 2001 article, Hargadon and Douglas detail the history of Edison's efforts to overturn a strong and entrenched institutional gas light industry. It is a fascinating case example of how Edison intentionally designed his product in a way that was *less* effective, but which made the value potential of the innovation easier to grasp and accept. They note:

> While Edison's notebooks reveal that he envisioned an entire constellation of electric gadgets that would one day be powered by his burgeoning electrical system, he deliberately designed

his electric lighting to be all but indistinguishable from the existing system, lessening rather than emphasizing the gaps between the old institutions and his new innovation.[76]

For example, early prototype light bulbs were able to generate a fairly bright light, but the product that Edison landed on was designed to be a mere 13-watt bulbs, a single watt brighter than the gas lights of the day. He insisted on metering the consumer's usage of electricity, just like the gas industry, even though he didn't have any idea how to do so at the time (which meant that the earliest customers got several months of electricity for free until he could figure it out!). He even designed his electric lamps to *look* like gas lamps.

When you have something radically new, you may need to make it *feel* familiar – otherwise, if the value is too unfamiliar, consumers will resist it in favor of the more familiar. Generating such familiarity may mean temporarily sacrificing some functional utility. But you can reintroduce these once consumers grasp the value potential of the new solution. But the general mindset – the consensus value knowledge – has to shift first. And that can be quite the challenge.

Crossing the Uncertainty Chasm

So let's get into how to help consumers rethink their value knowledge and become more amenable to a new solution. Getting across this uncertainty chasm is not just a matter of guerilla marketing. Remember, it's about uncertainty, not just information. Learning about the product doesn't mean that consumers are going to buy it. They'll still have important uncertainty about its value, as we learned in Chapter 4. They can know all about a new product, but not be sure about whether it's worth the price. In fact, a lot of us do this all the time – we think we might want a new product, but we'll wait until others try it first. I'll come back to this point in a bit.

So there's more than just spreading the word far and wide that you'll need to do. Consumers need to ameliorate their value uncertainty, and you need to help them get there. In fact, getting that first customer is one of the most challenging and important aspects of the entrepreneurial process that you'll have to do. But how can you help them reduce their uncertainty about products they've never tried?

The key is precisely those first customers. *Your first customers are the primary linchpin to crossing the uncertainty chasm.* It is their experiences and reviews that others are waiting on. Others may have thoughts and opinions on the potential value of a new product, but they are unwilling to risk the cost of the new product given the remaining uncertainty of it. They are waiting for the value uncertainty to be resolved sufficiently before they'll feel confident and comfortable with some new

---

76 Hargadon, A. B., & Douglas, Y. 2001. When innovations meet institutions: Edison and the design of the electric light. *Administrative Science Quarterly*, 46(3): 476–501, p. 489.

value proposition. You need your first customers to love your product enough to highly rate it and tell others about it.

Your own efforts to mitigate uncertainty are simply not enough, and can never be. That's because they don't trust you. You're a biased source of value knowledge. You have an underlying motive – your motives are to sell them a product, not to maximize their well-being. They may listen to your marketing and advertising pitches, but they will not trust them, at least not fully. That final step in reducing their uncertainty are the testimonials of others they trust. Celebrity endorsements are sometimes helpful, but everyone knows that these are paid endorsements – they're bribes and seen as such. Testimonials on the website are helpful but known to be highly selective and deceitful. Most people just will not fully trust anything that you might do to convince them.

This means that, ultimately, your crossing that chasm of early failure, and igniting the diffusion of your product into the larger market, hinges on the experiences and testimonials of others that you have no control over. It's difficult to leave your fate in others' hands in this way. But it is inevitable. Per the consumer sovereignty principle that we discussed in Chapter 11, consumers ultimately decide the market's winners and losers in a free and open economy.

But understanding this, there are some things you can do to give yourself the best chance at success. Let's get into these.

Pick your First Customers Well

The first principle I want to convey is that it matters who your first customers are. Again, most scholars follow Rogers in segmenting the market into five groups. Let's focus on the early adopters first, because as I've just explained, they're the key to success. Here I'm lumping the tech enthusiasts in with the early adopters. There are, of course, some who are 'techies' that get some value just from being the first to have a new tech gadget. But this is only true of certain industries, and even they are typically motivated foremost by some underlying need that the product solves. In most industries, the first adopters are the *lead users* that we've talked about, those who have the strongest needs for a solution, and so they're most willing to bear the value uncertainty of a new product. In other words, it's worth the risk to them that the product might not actually improve their situation if it shows even a little promise that it *might*.

Let me elaborate briefly on these types of people. They're at the cutting edge of their fields. Often they make their incomes from being and staying at that leading edge. They are the Olympic athletes, the world-renowned artists and designers, the competitive racers, and so forth. For them, having the absolute best matters, even if seemingly small and costly differences. For example, professional tennis players are very selective about the type of strings they use on their racquet. Different strings offer different ball spin, power, and feel that the average tennis player will not notice. But it matters to the competitive player – they notice the difference.

The point, then, is that, if your product is really better than what's already out there, you want lead users to be your first users. If it's not better, then it better be cheaper, and you *don't* want lead users to use it at all – you want to target the early–late majority and laggards. But let's assume that you've created a better product, one that solves consumers' needs better than what's out there. Lead users are going to be the most interested in, sensitive to, and benefited by the advantages your product offers over existing solutions. That is, lead users will experience the greatest value from your product.

So how can you entice these lead users to give your solution a shot and become early adopters? The first step is, of course, *finding* them. You don't want to sell your first products to 'average' consumers who won't appreciate as much the value that you've developed so carefully. You want to sell it to lead users, those who need it the most and who will be highly sensitive to the advantages that your solution facilitates.

Finding such lead users is easier than ever in today's hyper-connected world. There are online communities for just about any consumer market. The lead users will be the experts and the influencers in their niche segments. Finding them shouldn't be hard – you just need to know where to look. It's getting their attention and making a connection that is going to be the trick.

Once you've found them, it shouldn't take too much convincing to get them to try it. Remember that they really *want* any improvement you can proffer, so they will tend to be very open to trying new options. I don't recommend approaching these as a paid sponsor – an endorsement that is paid for just isn't as compelling. But a paid endorsement, if genuine, is certainly much better than nothing.

Relieving your Customers' Uncertainty

If lead users are still hesitant, you may need to do a little more to help them get past the uncertainties they have about your product. Let me go over a few things you can do. But be very careful with these tactics – you do not want to come across as cheap or gimmicky. Your product is worth the price because it satisfies a real need better than other products. If it doesn't sell itself, it at least shouldn't require gimmicky sales tactics. These tactics are meant to get the ball rolling only. They are not a winning long-term strategy. If your first customers don't get the ball rolling, you probably don't have a good enough product.

The first tactic you might consider is careful and strategic pricing. Remember that subjective value is assessed with respect to its opportunity cost. That is to say, the consumer has to give something up in order to purchase your product. The higher the price you ask, the bigger that opportunity cost that they have to give up, and so the greater the risk to themselves. If your value is both uncertain and costly, it's going to be a really tough sell. So be careful how you price your product. If you set the price too high and the product doesn't deliver on the promise of value, then you've set yourself up to fail.

Strategic pricing is underdeveloped as an area of research, and it can be tough to know where to set your initial price. I've discussed pricing and how to 'relativize' value in Chapter 5. As a quick summary, if you're not sure where to set your price, one good way to do it, aligned with our value-as-a-process theory, is to set the price based on the existing market solutions that consumers now use to satisfy the need(s) that you're addressing. Unless your solution addresses the same need(s) so much better than existing solutions that it's obvious that the products aren't comparable, you'll probably need to price your product in the same ballpark. For your very first customers, you may have to give a few free or discounted products in order to get the ball rolling.

A second way to reduce lead users' uncertainty is to show them that you get them. Part of this is providing them with the information they want – even details that they probably don't really need to know. This is important to effective marketing. Building a brand is important, but you have to establish legitimate market value first before you can effectively build a brand. So at this stage of your entrepreneurial journey, your marketing needs to be all about information – what is it about your product that's better than what's already out there? How does it work? Why does it work? These are the questions your prospective customers are asking themselves. Make it easy on them, and give them the answers right up front, and they'll be more likely to give it a try. "Just try it" isn't an effective slogan – *why* should they try it? Because you should have such a profound understanding of their needs at this stage, it will be much easier to formulate a marketing message that will connect with consumers – they will believe and trust you if you can show them you understand their needs. So communicate this to them – show them that you really get it.

The third and, perhaps, most effective way to reduce lead users' uncertainty is through firsthand experience. Can they demo the product? Can they have a free trial? If you can, you need to make sure that this experience is done in as perfect of conditions as possible. This is a big mistake that a lot of entrepreneurs make. If your customer won't be trying your product in optimal or, at least, very good consumption conditions, then their demoing the product is not going to deliver the value experience that you will need in order to get them excited and actively talking about the product.

For example, food companies offering free samples is great, but pushing samples onto people who aren't hungry is going to result in them not enjoying the experience as much as they would if they were hungry. The saying that 'hunger is the best of seasonings' is derived from the fact that things really do taste better – the eating experience is significantly more valuable – when you're really hungry. So try your best to deliver your sample or your demo to consumers at *peak need* – when the uneasiness of the needs experience is at its maximum.

It's particularly useful to demo the product in the *context* of their own need. For example, if you have a new solution for a business, bring the demo to their site and let them try it there and see it in the context of their own work. Let them see clearly how it improves the way *they* do things.

Diffusion as Uncertainty Mitigation

Once lead users have given your product a try, other consumers now have a fourth source of uncertainty reduction, and the most important to the success of your business: observation and word of mouth. Consumers observe others using the product, they read reviews, they see the brand loyalty of others. In other words, the early majority – who need it less than the early adopters – are waiting for those early adopters to let them know whether it's really worth it. And the late majority – who need the solution less than the early majority – wait for word from that early majority about its value. The laggards basically would rather just keep things as is, and are only eventually forced kicking and screaming into the new technology by the rest of the world moving to it. But generally, people trust their own eyes, and they will tend to trust what apparently unbiased consumers are saying about it.

Because each preceding segment needs it less, their value experiences are less potent. So to get the product to fully diffuse, it needs to be that much more valuable than prior solutions – it can't be just a little better, or it will only diffuse to the lead users. Said differently, the extent of the market to which your product will diffuse depends on *how much better* it is than prior solutions. It will only *fully* diffuse if it is proves to be clearly and unambiguously better. And even then there will be a populace that will resist it – the old dogs that don't want to learn new tricks.

So this is the most important key to your success: *you have to get those who need it the most to love it enough to tell others how great it is*. The reviews of the first customers are a vital signal to the rest of the market, who need the solution less, of the value of the product. In other words, the number one reason new products fall into the chasm and fail is that they just weren't better enough than what's out there to warrant the switch for most consumers. The value uncertainty was greater than the predicted value, and was not mitigated sufficiently in most consumers' minds to warrant risking the opportunity cost for the new solution.

What often happens with a lot of new products is that they will get the attention of the lead users, the value that the lead users gain is just not enough for most others to warrant the change. So the lead users will enjoy the product, that that small market segment is not enough to fund the further development of the product. The money dries up, and the entrepreneur is forced to abandon the project. The lead users will often keep using the product if they don't need to be on the market standard, but will remain (as ever) on the lookout for something better. In other words, most innovations are a better solution, but just not better enough for most consumers. If you want to cross the chasm, you will need to be better enough.

This mechanism is the main reason I'm not a proponent of the Lean Startup method. There's a lot to like about the Lean method. For example, it is great at getting entrepreneurs to be fast learners and adaptive, which I think is critical given how much entrepreneurs don't really know at the onset. But Lean tends to push entrepreneurs to market too soon. It advocates that you go to market with a 'minimum viable product' or MVP – a bare-bones prototype that addresses the core of the perceived need – and then develop and add revisions from the market feedback you would get from the early adopters. This *can* work, as long as the core of your solution, which the MVP encapsulates, is already significantly better than current market solutions. And it does start cash flow early, which allows you to reinvest and further develop the product. But because you need your early adopters to love the product, not just like it, selling a bare-bones product can be very risky, especially if it's a large price tag. If your MVP is only marginally better than existing solutions, you can't use your first users to reduce others' uncertainty. This leaves an often insurmountable mountain for the entrepreneur, who has to use marketing efforts to overcome the still-remaining uncertainty barriers.

If and when the early adopters love your product, you're ready to build your brand on top of that core customer segment. If the early adopters' value is high enough, you may not even need to spend money on marketing at all. For example, Tesla Motors, Ben & Jerry's ice cream and Krispy Kreme doughnuts each blew up without spending a dime on advertising. Word of mouth was extensive and they built their brands organically with very little effort of their own, but simply because their products were better.

But this organic diffusion, while most effective, is also slower. You can accelerate it with brand-building efforts. But be careful with such efforts. Some entrepreneurs will grow too quickly, and overextend themselves before they're ready and able to meet the growing market demand. They find themselves creating frustrations for consumers who get delayed or shoddy products, or don't get the customer service they might need to learn how to use the product most effectively, which ends up killing their growth momentum. And be careful with the expectations you make for yourself. If you build a brand that you can't live up to, that is a recipe for disaster.

Summing Up

One of the primary reasons so many new ventures fail is that their new product or service is comparatively uncertain to consumers. Because of this, their product just doesn't appear as valuable to consumers as the market solutions that they are already familiar and happy with.

You will have to overcome this inevitable uncertainty that consumers will have about your product. Perhaps the most important thing will be to ensure that your product is much better than those existing solutions. If it isn't, then the best you can do is a short-lived spurt of sales due to hard and clever marketing efforts. But your product is destined for the chasm.

But even if it is much better, you still have some work to do – you will need to help your customers mitigate their uncertainty about the product's value. It is rare for such value to be so obvious and apparent that others readily see and understand it. Your efforts to reduce their uncertainty will inevitably be weak because you have an underlying motive that consumers will naturally distrust. So how can you help them reduce their uncertainty without pushy marketing? This is a key challenge that you will have to take on.

Section 5: **Understanding Entrepreneurial Economics**

Chapter 15
The Market Process

In this final section, let's discuss the economics of entrepreneurship. This will be important to you because you will be affected by socioeconomic forces outside of your control. The more and better you understand these changing forces, the more able you will be to navigate and manage them.

As you might guess based on the discussion in Chapter 1, I'm going to give you a heterodox take on the economic process. But again, the orthodoxy of economics is to assume entrepreneurship away! So that's not especially helpful for us. Modern entrepreneurship theory is derived from the Austrian school, which has a rather different take on the market process.

General Equilibrium Theory is Unhelpful

One of the most central arguments of the Austrian school is its explicit rejection of general equilibrium theory in favor of a market process theory. General equilibrium theory is the idea that the market is, at all times, in a state of 'general equilibrium,' where all supply and demand have, at that moment, been reconciled as well as can be. This theory is used to explain the tendencies of markets, generally, and market phenomena specifically. For example, it tries to explain prices – if there is a supply shortage, supply and demand intersect at a higher price level. The value of general equilibrium theory is in its simplicity and usefulness in economic modelling, which allows economists to take historical data and formulate general predictive models of what can or will happen under, say, present economic conditions.

The problem with it, though, is that it's *overly* simplistic and doesn't reflect reality well at all. As a result, economists' predictions have an extremely poor track record – you'd do just as well flipping a coin. For example, none of the major schools of economics understood or predicted the dot-com or housing bubbles. In fact, general equilibrium theory doesn't make sense of bubbles at all because a bubble is essentially an economy in persistent and growing *disequilibrium*, which general equilibrium theory of course denies.

But the Austrian school doesn't assume the economy is in some artificial equilibrium state. In fact, it explicitly rejects such a notion as conscribing some of the most important economic processes: learning, innovation, entrepreneurship, failure, and so forth. Bubbles, to the Austrian school, are the consequence of artificial manipulation of markets, primarily by government intervention – particularly by the Federal Reserve's manipulation of interest rates. For example, the government's response to the dot-com bubble crash was to stimulate new growth by lowering housing interest rates

https://doi.org/10.1515/9783110750805-015

and accelerating lending to prospective homeowners. Paul Krugman famously argued in 2002, "To fight this recession the Fed needs . . . soaring household spending to off-set moribund business investment. Alan Greenspan needs to create a housing bubble to replace the Nasdaq bubble."[77] He got his wish.

Proponents of the Austrian school very quickly recognized the house of cards the Fed was building. In 2003, Congressman Ron Paul argued in front of Congress (at a Financial Services Committee hearing) that the housing bubble that the Fed was creating was going to crash and that it was going to hurt. Introducing his Free Housing Market Enhancement Act, which would have removed government subsidies for home loans, he concluded:

> I hope today's hearing sheds light on how special privileges granted to GSEs distort the housing market and endanger American taxpayers. Congress should act to remove taxpayer support from the housing GSEs before the bubble bursts and taxpayers are once again forced to bail out investors who were misled by foolish government interference in the market.[78]

That bill never made it to the floor.

The point is that prevailing economic theory is highly artificial and unrealistic. As a result, it is generally unhelpful as a predictive map of economic conditions and outcomes. My belief is that you will be vastly more benefited from a foundational understanding of Austrian economics.

The Market as a Process

The central tenet of Austrian economics is that the market is not in some stable, stagnant equilibrium, but is instead constantly in motion. It is a *process*. This conclusion, of course, also follows from our value-as-a-process framework.

Ludwig von Mises offered the most comprehensive exposition of Austrian market process theory in his seminal tome *Human Action*, first published in English in 1949 (published originally in German in 1940). Although it is very much worth reading, it is a difficult read, heavy in philosophy, history, and economic theory. A more accessible presentation of the same arguments is made in Robert P. Murphy's *Choice*, which I will highly recommend.

Here I'll offer a very brief overview and introduction to the basic insights. Let's start with Mises's own explanation of the market in *Human Action*:

> The market is not a place, a thing, or a collective entity. The market is a process, actuated by the interplay of the actions of the various individuals cooperating under the division of labor. The forces determining the – continually changing – state of the market are the value judgments of these individuals and their actions as directed by these value judgments. The state of

---

77 https://www.nytimes.com/2002/08/02/opinion/dubya-s-double-dip.html.
78 https://www.minnpost.com/politics-policy/2008/09/ron-paul-saw-financial-mess-coming/.

the market at any instant is the price structure, i.e., the totality of the exchange ratios as established by the interaction of those eager to buy and those eager to sell. There is nothing inhuman or mystical with regard to the market. The market process is entirely a resultant of human actions. Every market phenomenon can be traced back to definite choices of the members of the market society.

The market process is the adjustment of the individual actions of the various members of the market society to the requirements of mutual cooperation. The market prices tell the producers what to produce, how to produce, and in what quantity. The market is the focal point to which the activities of the individuals converge. It is the center from which the activities of the individuals radiate.[79]

Mises's analysis is clever and brilliant in that he starts with an artificial foil that he calls the 'evenly rotating economy.' In this economy, we introduce the basic players of a simple economic system: owners (of land and capital), producers, and consumers. But for this analysis he ignores time and change – supply and demand are constant. There are no exogenous shocks and no entrepreneurship. Even in this artificial system the economy is not in constant equilibrium, but cyclically reaches what can be called an 'equilibrium' (Mises calls it a 'plain state of rest') over and over again. It's still a process, but it's a recurring process.

Now let's add time and change back into the equation. The dynamism of the market system becomes even more apparent and important. Bob Murphy gives an apt example in his book *Choice*:

Suppose we are in an initial equilibrium situation where oil is $100 per barrel. Suddenly, an energy company discovers vast new crude deposits off the coast of South America, which eventually will allow for a large increase in global annual oil output. After the news of the discovery spreads across financial markets, the spot price of oil falls to $80. Once everyone has adjusted to the news, the oil market will again be in a plain state of rest. The new price of $80 per barrel fully takes into account the oil discovery.

However, the situation doesn't stop there. For example, deep-sea platforms may not be profitable when oil is less than $90 per barrel. The platforms continue with their previous operations because they had already scheduled the personnel months in advance, but given the new reality in the oil market, the owners of the platforms are gradually rotating the personnel out and slowing down extraction, waiting for oil prices to rise. In a longer term adaptation to the oil discovery, the sharp fall in crude prices may lower the retail price of gasoline at the pump. Motorists in the market for a new vehicle end up buying more gas-guzzling SUVs and fewer fuel-efficient hybrids and compact cars than they would have if crude had remained at $100 per barrel. Consequently the demand for gasoline grows more quickly than it otherwise would have done. Changes such as these put upward pressure on the world price of crude oil, so that eventually – years after the new oil discovery – it would settle into the final price of $88 per barrel, if no other outside disturbances affected the oil market in the meantime.[80]

79 Mises, L. v. 1949. *Human Action: A treatise on economics*. New Haven, CT: Yale University Press, pp. 258–259.
80 Murphy, R. P. 2015. *Choice: Cooperation, enterprise and human action*. Oakland: Independent Institute, pp. 119–120.

We see in this example the temporal processes by which the actors that comprise markets continuously reconcile changing conditions in order to more efficiently and effectively facilitate value for their customers and, thereby, earn a profit for their efforts. As a result, the disparate knowledge and information that people have are more effectively used in servicing consumers.

The Role of the Entrepreneur

Now that we have introduced changes into the market process and can see how markets adjust to change in time, let us finally introduce entrepreneurship into the market process. In Chapter 11 I argued that entrepreneurship is first and foremost a *consumer* function, that it is consumers who are tasked with discovering what to want, which is the origination of the entrepreneurial process. This value learning process is, of course, the focus of Section 2.

But the important implication of Section 2 is that demand is constantly changing – not only because prices are going up and down, but also and more importantly because we are constructively dissatisfied with the status quo. We want better things, and we keep looking for them. And if we don't find them in the market, we set out to create them.

The primary reason why we invest in and do research is to discover new ways to better satisfy our needs. Modern science today has, to some small extent, become seeking knowledge for knowledge's sake. But even those that advocate this acknowledge and argue that ultimately the goal is its application, to generate knowledge that will make the world a better place – their argument is essentially that we can't always predict *ex ante* what will and won't prove valuable, which is fair enough. But the point of scientific advancement is the improvement of life, the advancement of well-being. For example, about 56% of all research funding is spent on medical issues such as cancer. Other spending goes to discovering and developing new technologies. Other research funding is about understanding the social and physical world that we live in so that we can live better in it.

In other words, we actively pursue new and better things, and create them, as part of the market process. I wrote in a 2019 article:

> Knowledge discovery – of resources and their technological affordances, or of personal needs and their satisfaction – does not occur by chance (except, perhaps, in rare circumstances). It is *sought*. Scientific knowledge and resource discovery are economically intentional because such knowledge can facilitate a higher state of well-being. Similarly, consumers intentionally seek to learn their innate needs in an effort to know what to want in order to better satisfy those needs.[81]

---

81 Packard, M. D. 2019. Entrepreneurship and the Nirvana state of rest. *Mises: Interdisciplinary Journal of Philosophy, Law and Economics*, 7(3): 523–543, p. 531.

This is, of course, referring to the PVT process as well as the scientific process. But the *application* of whatever new knowledge is learned – its innovation and presentation as a market solution to real problems – is done by entrepreneurs.

The role of the entrepreneur in the market process is the pursuit of betterment, of new economic value. It is to try new things and see how we can move from the present state of welfare to a higher one. In other words, entrepreneurs are the engine of economic growth.

Entrepreneurship and Economic Growth

Economists, within the framework of general equilibrium theory, have struggled to explain economic growth. In remaining true to the framework of general equilibrium, they have had no entrepreneur to explain such growth. The best they've devised is an *evolutionary* model, where growth comes in Darwinian fashion from natural variations in economic activities and, as a consequence, variance in their outcomes. In other words, because people are naturally different, companies will do the same things differently, which will lead to somewhat different outcomes. In the Darwinian process of survival-of-the-fittest, those companies that do well will outlast those that do not, and the processes that led to those superior outcomes survive and are propagated.

Of course, the problem with this explanation is that it is excessively slow. Yet, history shows that economic growth occurs at a rate that does not seem to be explained by such simple variance.

Take a look at this chart (Fig. 15.1) from Our World in Data (ourworldindata.org), from data provided by the Maddison Project. It shows the estimated GDP per capita over the last millennium or so. It is one of the most important charts I've ever seen.

Human history has been, for almost all of recorded history, an endless fight for mere survival. Most people lived hand-to-mouth through their entire lives. Life for all but a very few was what we would today call extreme poverty.

It is only in the last ~200 years that the situation of humankind has changed dramatically. Not even the poorest in so-called first-world countries are really scraping by for survival. We have such abundance that the poor today live lives of extreme luxury compared to those of only a couple hundred years ago.

Today, people complain about having to work a whole 40 hours a week, or that they don't have as nice and new a car as that other guy over there. Our biggest health challenges are the opposite of malnutrition, i.e., obesity. We have so much time on our hands and information at our disposal that everyone seems to be an expert in everything – at least they know enough to believe they are.

Economist Per Bylund put it this way: "What causes poverty? Nothing. It's the original state, the default and starting point. The real question is, what causes

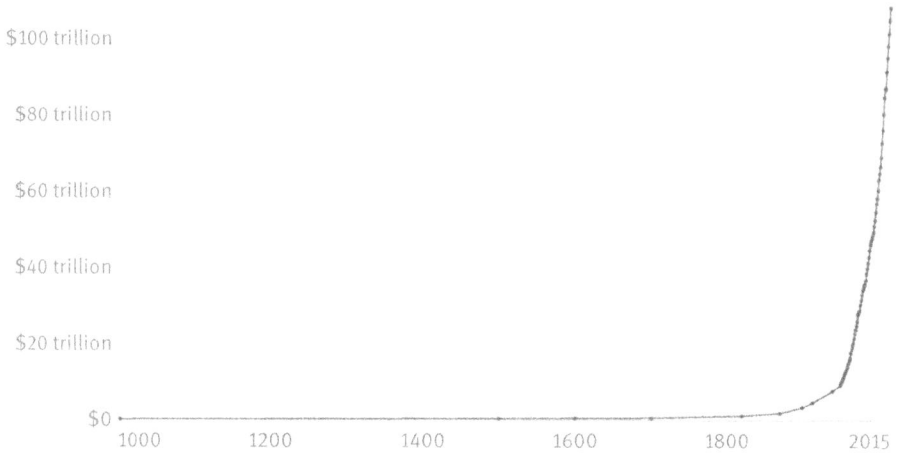

Fig. 15.1: World GDP Per Capita Since 1000 A.D.
Source: World GDP – Our World in Data based on World Bank & Maddison (2017).

prosperity?"[82] This is the right question: what causes prosperity? What has allowed so many to escape the impoverishment of human history and live a life of comparatively extreme comfort?

The answer, as I will put forward in the remainder of this chapter, is *entrepreneurship*. I have so far built my argument on rational, theoretical grounds. I have explained how and why entrepreneurship is the engine of growth, that entrepreneurs are those who pursue and apply new knowledge more effectively to solve humankind's various needs and problems. I hope and expect that you are already persuaded by these arguments. But, if you are not, let me now turn to the historical data – let me show you that entrepreneurship is the driver of economic growth.

France

Let me start with the history of France (see Fig. 15.2), which was for much of the medieval period the wealthiest nation in the world. Note the flatness of the line from the beginning of the chart to the French Revolution (which began in 1789, where the data are missing). This medieval time period was marked by the traditional feudal system, where a monarch essentially owned everything, but delegated control of lands to 'lords,' who managed productive activities on those lands. Serfs were a lord's subjects, who performed the economic activities delegated to them.

This system of economic management worked insofar as it goes. In many ways it is reflective of the modern corporation. But it stifled innovation and entrepreneurship.

---

82 https://twitter.com/PerBylund/status/665900726388785153.

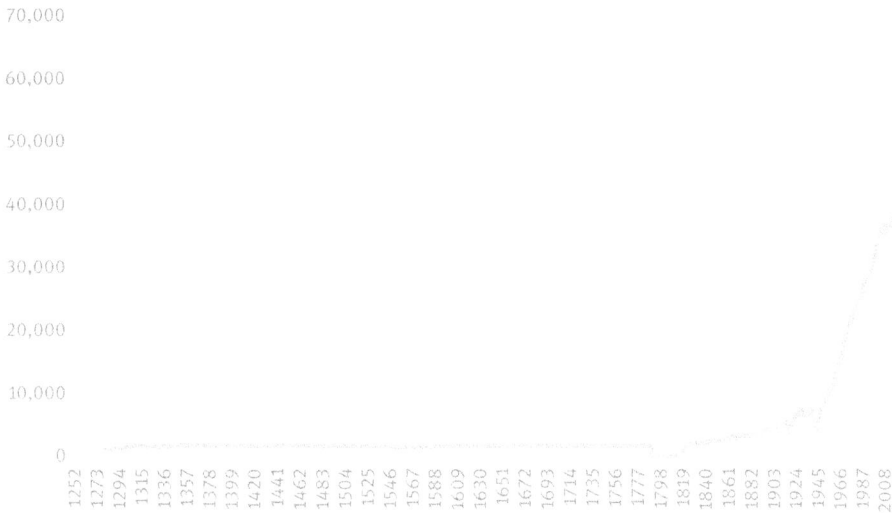

Fig. 15.2: France GDP Per Capita (in 2011 U.S. dollars).

Serfs had no leeway to innovate, and were disincentivized to do so as they could not own the land or the products of their labor.

The trade guilds in France, the *corps de métiers*, were the 'middle class' of the era. They were comprised of the skilled artisans and merchants – the metal workers, the armorers, the shoemakers, the glaziers, the masons, and so forth. By the 14th century there were some 350 guilds in Paris, each of which operated as essentially a modern union. They each bargained with the monarchy to gain monopolistic control of the market and strictly controlled the markets in their jurisdiction.

Again, innovation in these sectors was disincentivized. The guilds held such control that they would not tolerate deviations from standard practices. Entrepreneurship was disallowed by the political charters granted the guilds, which gave only guild members legal rights to operate. Becoming a member of a guild operated through apprenticeship, which also served to ensure that standard practices were followed.

Like other industrialized nations, France's growth trajectory begins essentially after the French Revolution with the Enlightenment age. But France's growth trajectory did not keep pace with the U.K. or U.S. in this same time period. But this is interesting, because France in the 18th and early 19th century boasted the best and brightest minds of science at the time. For example, in Paris, the École Polytechnique employed some of the most important academic figures of the natural sciences, such as Lagrange, Laplace, Poisson, Fourier, and Ampere.

But entrepreneurship was still stifled. Napoleon financed some innovation, but virtually all of it was on military armaments, and Napoleon's massive war debts led to high taxes on the private sector. Moreover, the French aristocracy disdained and antagonized entrepreneurs because entrepreneurs threatened their positions of power and authority.

It was only after World War II, after France's economic structure was severely disrupted and destroyed, that economic reform (the Marshall Plan) opened up the gates for entrepreneurs. Charles De Gaulle and his 'dirigiste' would of course claim credit for the 'Trente Glourieuses' – the 30-year period of rapid economic growth. But it was, in fact, the entrepreneurs, who were finally left free to pursue innovations, that were truly responsible for the growth.

United States of America

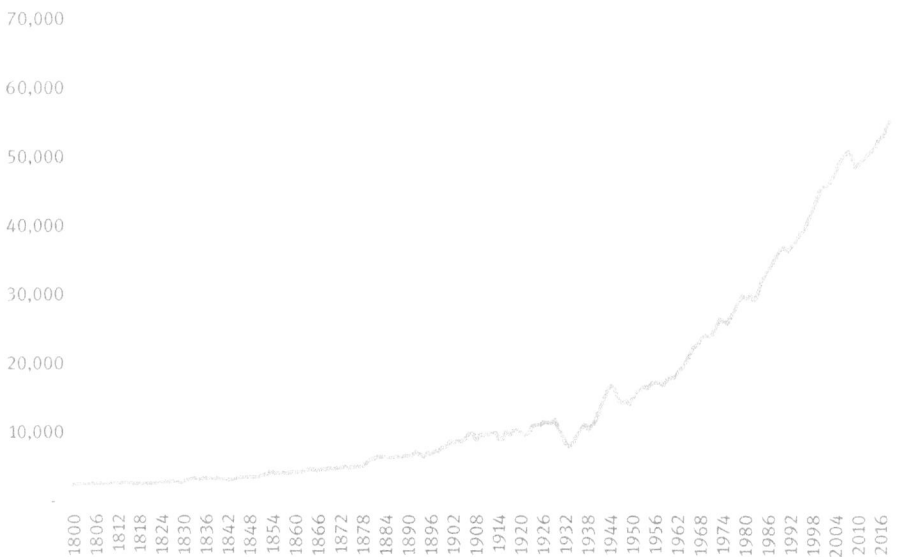

Fig. 15.3: U.S. GDP Per Capita (in 2011 U.S. dollars).

The U.S. (see Fig. 15.3), of course, gets its start right in the middle of the Enlightenment and industrial revolution. In fact, its founding principles were based in Enlightenment philosophers. The Declaration of Independence is straight out of Locke, as is the 3-branch system of government that its Constitution established.

The culture within the early U.S. had already grown to be highly entrepreneurial. There was already a culture of reverence and romanticism for entrepreneurship that had emerged, with many of its most revered founding members being successful entrepreneurs and inventors. American children are taught about American inventors and entrepreneurs that had a significant impact on the quality of life of Americans – Benjamin Franklin's various inventions and discovery of electricity,

Eli Whitney's cotton gin, Alexander Graham Bell's telephone, Andrew Carnegie's steel, Thomas Edison's gramophone and incandescent light bulb, Henry Ford's automotive assembly line, the Wright brothers' airplane, and on and on. As a result, exponential economic growth began immediately and quickly vaulted the U.S. into top billing as the richest country in the world and a politico-economic superpower.

This growth trend was disrupted, of course, by the Great Depression, when FDR's New Deal took over the entrepreneurial function from private investors and entrepreneurs, who were taxed at massive rates and, thus, prevented from investing in their own ideas and solutions. Government, of course, does not perform the entrepreneurial function very well. Resources were mostly reallocated to failing sectors of the economy, and not to innovations of new solutions to consumers' needs.

The U.S. is still very entrepreneurial. But its government has learned the wrong lessons from history, and has become the largest government in human history. Recently, the entrepreneurial sector has begun to be crowded out by public spending, and the economic growth rate in the U.S. has tapered.

Singapore

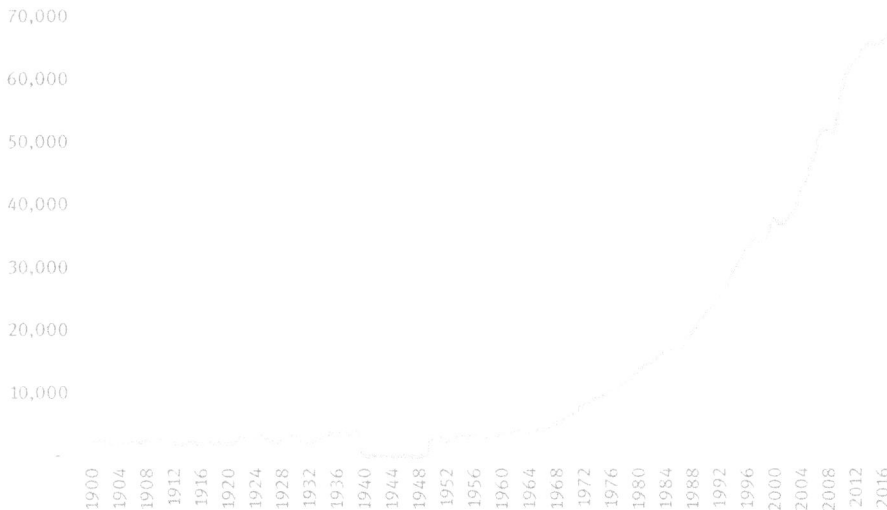

Fig. 15.4: Singapore GDP Per Capita (in 2011 U.S. dollars).

Singapore is a fascinating example because it jumped from one of the poorest in the world to one of the richest in record time (see Fig. 15.4). It has a land area of a mere 580 square miles and lacks the natural resources that other nations boast – including water! Yet, today Singapore is one of the wealthiest nations in the world, its estimated GPD around $100K per capita, compared to the U.S.'s ~$65K per capita.

Singapore was a British colony up until 1959 (the data from 1940–1949 are missing, not zero), when it declared independence and formed the Federation of Malaysia in 1963 with other nearby Pacific islands. But this political union proved problematic, and Singapore was expelled from the federation two years later in 1965. At this time, Singapore's major industry was opium, and so the island was dominated by the opium gangs. There was high unemployment and widespread poverty. Trade was difficult due to its contentious relations with the other islands. GDP per capita was only about $500.

In the new and independent Singapore, the new leadership, led by Prime Minister Lee Kwan Yew, turned its focus and attention to economic reform. The focus of this reform was explicitly to encourage and facilitate entrepreneurship. The government lowered taxes and made starting a new business comparatively painless. Economic regulations were abandoned and trade and investment relations with, e.g., Europe were encouraged and facilitated. Fiscal and monetary policy has been highly stable.

As a result, industrialization and economic development took off, the economy growing by ~10% year after year. In a few short decades, it had caught up to the rest of the first world and, soon, would surpass it. It has only had a single recession in its short history, in 1985. It was brief and constrained to the domestic economy, but led to reforms that only promoted more entrepreneurship and further accelerated growth. For example, service sectors such as finance, telecommunications, and utilities were deregulated.

Entrepôt trade and shipping have emerged as the dominant industry for Singapore, followed by tourism, banking, biotech, and other manufacturing. Due to its deregulated economy, its tourist attractions include casino resorts and medical tourism. People from around the world visit Singapore to have surgeries that are overly expensive or delayed in home nations. Its financial sector, deregulated in the late 1990s and early 2000s, has made Singapore banks an attractive alternative to Swiss banks, which have instead been faced with growing regulations.

Entrepreneurship continues to be one of Singapore's driving values, and its economic growth has continued unabated by changes and disruptions, such as global crises.

China

In stark contrast to Singapore's economic history, China's economic history is rather dark. Historically, China was a world leader in innovation and ingenuity, boasting one of the highest GDPs per capita throughout the Middle Ages. But its progress was hampered by frequent changes in leadership and polity such that economic welfare remained stagnant for centuries.

In the modern era, China's economic history (see Fig. 15.5) begins in 1949 with the communist revolution and the rise of Mao Zedong. Mao and the communists promised vast economic advancement under communist economic principles. The

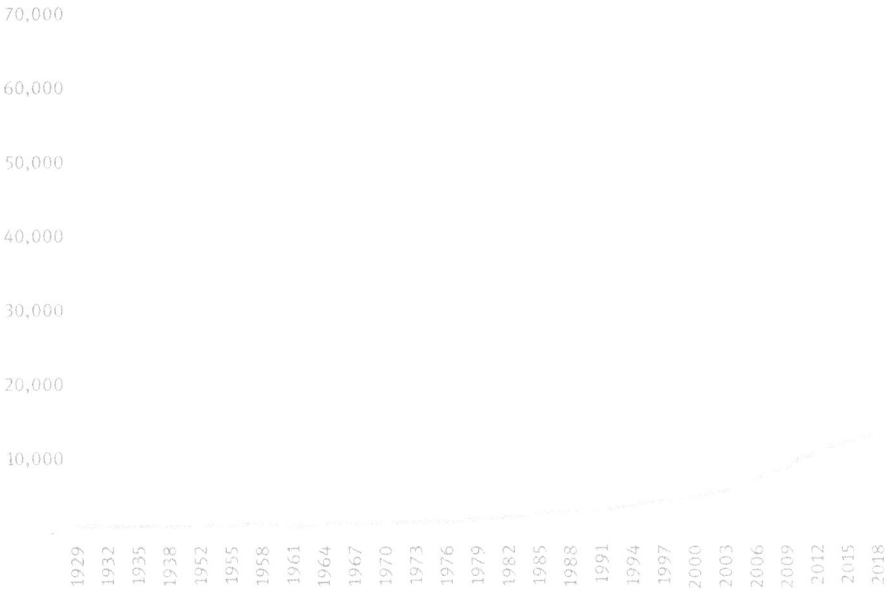

Fig. 15.5: China GDP Per Capita (in 2011 U.S. dollars).

Communist Party actively rooted out the 'capitalist' business owners, landlords, and other wealthy entrepreneurs and confiscated their possessions. Entrepreneurship was not just frowned upon as contrary to egalitarian ideals, but was also actively eliminated by political coercion and violence.

In 1958 Mao launched his Great Leap Forward to complete China's transition into a fully and uniquely Chinese communist state, which Mao believed would finally stimulate economic growth to match that of other industrial nations. All private properties were coopted and reorganized as people's communes, which collected and redistributed all agricultural produce. Simultaneously, Mao hoped to launch China's own industrial revolution by making use of China's cheap labor supply to avoid having to import costly machinery.

The plan was a disaster. Despite favorable weather and good crops, agricultural production plummeted as farm labor had been diverted to manufacturing projects. Moreover, the Four Pests Campaign – which worked to eliminate the overabundance of rats, flies, mosquitoes, and sparrows – chased out many of the local sparrows who were the natural predators of locusts. A nasty locust swarm in 1958 devastated the still unharvested crops. Even then the Chinese had managed to harvest a decent amount of food. But under communist rule local officials were under extreme pressure to report record output, and so exaggerated their harvests. These exaggerated reports were then used for food redistribution by the central planners, who prioritized the cities and party officials. The peasant class was left with nothing, and starvation ensued. Estimates range from 15 to 55 million people that starved in this 'famine.'

After Mao's death in 1976, Deng Xiaoping began to introduce various market reforms that moved China toward a market economy. Ownership was again permitted, and entrepreneurs were allowed to pursue opportunities. Reforms began with "Special Economic Zones" (SEZs) of free trade along the southeastern coastline. By 1981, over 70% of rural farms had been returned to private owners, and 80% of state-owned enterprises were allowed to retain and reinvest their profits. But these opportunities were still constrained and limited by the still-communist regime.

But the successes of such policies bred growing dissent. Growing trade with foreign nations invited increased foreign interaction and involvement, including foreign investment and foreign products. The ideologies of Western market economies incrementally crept in largely unchecked by the communist government. Ultimately this led to disenfranchisement, unrest, and demonstrations, including the infamous student march on Tiananmen Square in 1989.

Partly as a result of these protests and growing acknowledgement of markets and entrepreneurship as the engine of economic growth, Chinese leadership turned to the Singapore model – which decentralized economic activities, but maintained tight socio-political control with strict social regulations. The Chinese communist leadership recognized that they desperately needed to allow economic growth, but feared losing power and control of the nation. They sent some of their leaders to Singapore to learn of its methods, and have attempted to closely emulate Singapore's model.

A refocusing on entrepreneurship was the result. Deng proclaimed, "It is honorable to become wealthy" (致富光荣). The social stigma toward entrepreneurship that Mao had carefully nurtured was abandoned, and pent-up entrepreneurial energy was unleashed into the market. But the party still keeps careful control of its political economy and is wary of leaving entrepreneurs completely alone to their own devices. It reins in economic freedom when ambitions seem to get too unwieldy, and many of the leaders of the business world (such as Jack Ma and Ma Huateng) remain advocates of communist ideology. Communism is still the aim, and capitalism is seen by Chinese leadership, as it was by Marx, as a mere stepping stone to those ends. Thus, while the growth of China has been noteworthy, it cannot match the meteoric rise of its neighbors, Singapore, Japan, and Hong Kong.

Hong Kong

Finally, it's useful and interesting to contrast China's economic development process to Hong Kong's, given their shared culture and heritage.

Hong Kong gained its independence from China as a British colony after the First Opium War in 1841 as a surrendered land. In 1940, many of the British colonists were evacuated in the lead-up to WWII. It was attacked by the Japanese the

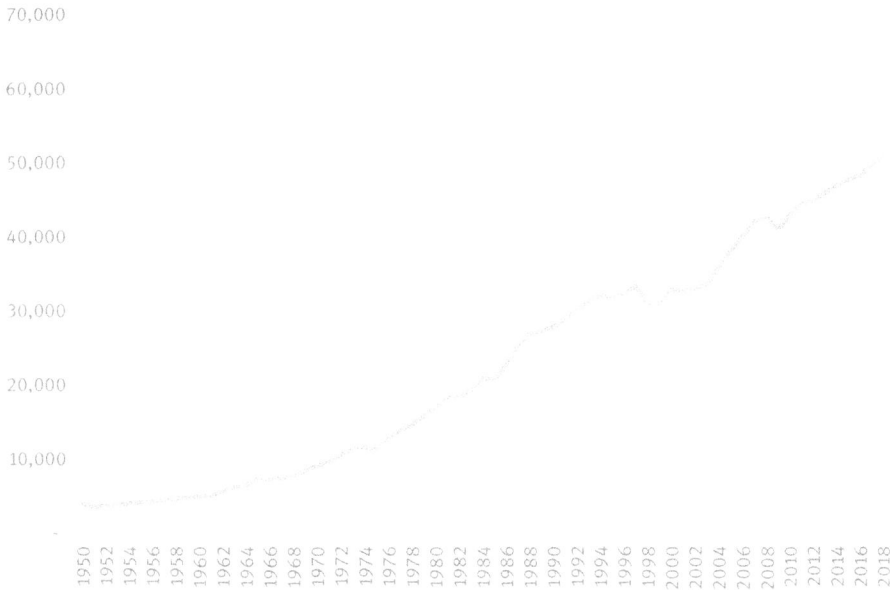

Fig. 15.6: Hong Kong GDP Per Capita (in 2011 U.S. dollars).

next year who occupied it until 1945, when Britain regained control. Eventually, in 1984, diplomatic negotiations with China resulted in the Sino-British Joint Declaration, in which Britain agreed to transfer control of the colony to China in 1997 with the promise that China would guarantee Hong Kong's economic and political independence for 50 years thereafter. Although the transition was somewhat messy, Hong Kong has so far maintained most of its independence from China, albeit with various disputes from time to time.

Its modern economic history (see Fig. 15.6) really begins with China's Communist Revolution in 1949, when Hong Kong received an influx of Chinese immigrants fleeing the new communist regime. This influx was welcome, as Hong Kong was still suffering from the exodus during WWII. While the colonial government was preoccupied with managing the immigration, the economy was virtually left alone – taxes and regulations were very low. Although economic integration of such a large population influx was difficult, the immigrants brought with them (perhaps out of necessity) an entrepreneurial spirit and energy that would serve the 426-square-mile island well. Most immigrants didn't find jobs, they made them. Industrialization was thus spawned primarily by small and medium enterprises (SMEs) rather than large, consolidated corporations.

The economic growth that ensued prompted political leaders to maintain the regulatory structure that facilitated it. They have kept their tax rates low and have resisted economic regulations. Hong Kong has ranked at the top of economic freedom indices for several decades. This economic freedom has unleashed the entrepreneurial potential of its small population, which has grown Hong Kong's economy into one of the largest in the world.

But the transition to Chinese rule seems to have stymied the exponential growth trajectory that Hong Kong enjoyed from 1950–1990. For example, over a half a million fled the country in the lead-up to Chinese control in 1997, which dampened its economic growth. That growth flatlined in the transitional period until a new political stability was reached. Growth has again ensued, but it does not appear to be reaching the same exponential trajectory that it once enjoyed.

Summing Up

Entrepreneurship is the engine of economic growth. The tendency of markets is toward growth – we as consumers are constructively dissatisfied with our state in life, and we keep looking for new and better ways to solve our needs. To the extent that we are left free to pursue such solutions as we can find, and are unburdened by barriers to new venturing, we increase economic productivity – we facilitate a higher state of well-being among consumers – through such entrepreneurial efforts.

Understanding value-as-a-process highlights the centrality of entrepreneurship within the market process in a way that subjective utility- and equilibrium-based economic theories do not. Entrepreneurship, as described by economist Joseph Schumpeter, comprises the innovation – the introduction of 'New Combinations' – of resources, of means, in value experiments. This implies an *accelerating value learning cycle* – more entrepreneurship implies faster value learning, and vice versa.

On the other hand, entrepreneurship, as expounded by economist Israel Kirzner, is also the process by which new value learning is more broadly diffused across the market. Thus, new value knowledge facilitates economic growth – a higher state of general well-being among a society's members – through entrepreneurship's generation and diffusion of new value knowledge and, correspondingly, more effective economic solutions. In other words, entrepreneurship, as understood by Austrian economists, is both a primary source of new value knowledge and its purveyor across and throughout an economy, thereby facilitating a new and higher economic state.

Countries thus grow wealthiest that unleash their entrepreneurs on the economy. I have selectively reviewed the economic history of several countries. But this same pattern can be found in every country – as many countries as I've reviewed have told the exact same story, that their growth periods are periods of higher entrepreneurial activity, and that declines or stagnation are periods of inhibited entrepreneurship. An economic decline or recession isn't always or necessarily due to a lack of entrepreneurship, but its delayed correction and recovery is.

Economic growth can't be manufactured. I hear politicians discuss their plans to achieve economic growth all the time. They try to sell a narrative that they're to credit for such growth. It's nonsense. In fact, the numbers show that the more politicians do, the less entrepreneurs can do and, as a result, the slower the economic growth. The best thing politicians can do for economic growth is to get out of entrepreneurs' way. I'll discuss the problems of regulation more in the next chapter.

Chapter 16
Regulation, Markets, and Entrepreneurship

There is, of course, much more to learn about economics than I've introduced in the previous chapter (and in the other chapters). I'll briefly discuss how you can learn more in the next chapter. But before I wrap up my discussion of value theory and how you can leverage it to achieve superior empathy and innovation in your entrepreneurial journey, let's follow the logic of the previous chapter a bit further. *How* do some nations develop and unleash an entrepreneurial spirit, while others do not? What changed in ~1775 A.D. that radically altered the economic trajectory of the world (see Fig. 15.1)? You might say it was the Enlightenment, or that it was the Industrial Revolution. Or you might argue it was the founding of the United States of America as a free nation.

All of these answers are, I think, partly correct. But at the fundamental level, the reasons that these changes unleashed entrepreneurship is that they removed inhibitive barriers to the value learning process and to entrepreneurial experimentation. In prior eras, humankind did not fully understand entrepreneurship as wealth creation – i.e., that truly *new* wealth can be created *ex nihilo* through entrepreneurship. Instead, wealth was widely understood as more or less a fixed pie, and that accumulation of wealth was a threat to power. And because entrepreneurship was a means to wealth, it was squelched by the aristocracy and by the guilds. Rules and regulations carefully dictated what could be done and how it must be done. It was not until such rules were thrown off, beginning in the latter end of the 18th century, that entrepreneurship was no longer intentionally suppressed by the political class, and new wealth could begin to be created.

I'm going to make a rather radical and perhaps contentious claim in this chapter – that *all* political regulations hinder entrepreneurship. This goes against the economic mainstream, of course. But I've already rejected the economic mainstream in Chapters 1 and 15. If you don't understand the market as a process, it's perhaps not surprising that you would fail to see how regulations hinder that process. But before I make this case, allow a quick disclaimer. I am *not* saying that such policies are all and altogether a bad idea. All I'm arguing is that such policies innately constrain the value learning process and, as a result, hinder entrepreneurship. Whether such costs are worth the potential benefits of policies is beyond the scope of this book.

The Fettering of the Market Process

As the previous chapter explained, the market process can reproduce the same value state over and over again without entrepreneurs. But *growth* is driven singularly by entrepreneurship. The market process continuously produces new value

https://doi.org/10.1515/9783110750805-016

knowledge and incrementally uncovers new value solution possibilities, and it is entrepreneurs that create and disseminate such possibilities that (hopefully) increase the value state (i.e., well-being) of economic actors.

Economists have shown that market processes work remarkably well in most situations. However, they have also observed various 'market failures' – inefficiencies seemingly incorrigible by the market process alone. These market failures, they argue, may require institutional (e.g., public policy) interventions for their correction. Nicolas Crafts expressed this mainstream view that free markets are largely efficient but can run into roadblocks (e.g., externalities) that require regulatory intervention:

> Regulations . . . can be used to correct market failures through acting to reduce the costs of negative externalities or imperfections on information by providing insurance or public goods . . . . Regulation is central to the efficient workings of a market economy and is a key function of the state. It does, however, typically impose costs on the private sector and so there is a danger of excessive regulation where additional costs exceed extra benefits.[83]

Whereas market standards are institutional market rules that arise spontaneously through the market process, *market regulations* entail the politically institutionalized rules of trade imposed by government mandate. While the intent of such regulations is to prevent socially and economically harmful behaviors, all such regulations are two-edged – they impose costs on the market in exchange for mitigating its failures. These costs include obvious and often explicit compliance costs, such as legal fees, organizational refitting costs, and so forth. At a broader market level, these costs also include regulatory enforcement costs and the taxes that pay for them.

Another important but often overlooked cost is the apparently inevitable corruption of the coalesced political power necessary for such regulatory interventions and enforcement. Political power is a corrupting force that has proved time and again to lead to inevitable misuse. By granting some political power to regulate markets, the inevitable long-term costs include a usurping of more power and, resultantly, additional (over)regulation.

But our value-as-a-process theory implies another significant cost of such interventions, one that is covert and nefarious: the retarding of the value learning process. The protections that regulations are intended to purvey can only be achieved by constraining the options available to consumers and producers. Consumer regulations artificially restrict the range of consumers' value experiences. Because dissatisfactions are a key source of learning, regulations' aim at mitigating such experiences, while perhaps justifiable, would curtail the value learning process. Unregulated markets, of course, allow a greater number of dissatisfactory experiences (including and up to fatal ones), which would diminish well-being. Protections against

---

83 Crafts, N. 2006. Regulation and productivity performance. *Oxford Review of Economic Policy*, 22(2): 186–202, p. 187.

such economic losses should be balanced against the costs of such protections, including the potential benefits of evolutionary value learning and its long-term economic effects.

For example, the U.S. Food and Drug Administration (FDA) enforces rigid clinical testing protocols to ensure new pharmaceutical drugs are safe before they are approved for sale. While this expectedly improves the safety[84] of treatments offered to patients suffering from disease in the future, it also increases the costs of developing drugs and extends their time to market. The average time to market is about 10 years for a new drug. This delays the value learning process. These costs may be bearable for the safety afforded, but Mary Ruwart estimates that 15 million Americans have died waiting for the FDA's approval of drugs that might have saved them. As one example, Paul Rubin documents in a 1995 article that the FDA has placed an ongoing ban on the advertising of clinical research, which shows that aspirin use during a heart attack can prevent death, due to this evidence not being fully vetted through formal FDA processes. He estimated that this has led to tens of thousands of preventable deaths.

Recognition that the terminally ill have much to gain and little to lose from experimental drugs and other medical devices and procedures, many U.S. States have passed 'right to try' laws that partially override the FDA's restrictions. However, the recent pandemic, and the regulatory response therein, show just how tenuous and superficial those laws can be.

Business regulations have similar obstructing effects on the value learning process. Thomas Hazlett's history of wireless telephony in his book *The Political Spectrum*[85] is illustrative. In 1945, the development of 'cellular' technology of "handie-talkies" was already well underway. This technology would communicate wirelessly with their nearest 'cell,' usually mounted on radio towers, which would be connected by wire. In 1947, AT&T's application to begin development and provision of the technology was denied by the FCC on the grounds that it would be a luxury service for the few and wealthy – the FCC wanted to reserve the bandwidth for TV, even though TV already had far more bandwidth than it needed (in 1962 it was using 3.5% of its allocated bandwidth). The FCC delayed granting licenses for cellular service provision until 1982, and then only allocated it very limited bandwidth. As a result, it was indeed, for a long time, a luxury service for the few and wealthy. Landline incumbents, including AT&T and Motorola, lobbied the FCC to prevent bandwidth allocation so that they could continue to enjoy near innovation-less competition for several decades due to prohibitive

---

84 Some research disputes that the FDA has, in fact, reduced harmful drug sales and recalls, e.g.:

   Bakke, O. M., Manocchia, M., de Abajo, F., Kaitin, K. I., & Lasagna, L. 1995. Drug safety discontinuations in the United Kingdom, the United States, and Spain from 1974 through 1993: A regulatory perspective. *Clinical Pharmacology & Therapeutics*, 58(1): 108–117.

85 Hazlett, T. W. 2017. *The Political Spectrum: The Tumultuous Liberation of Wireless Technology, from Herbert Hoover to the Smartphone*. New Haven, CT: Yale University Press.

regulatory barriers that impeded the market learning process. Said more simply, we could have had cell phones decades ago if it weren't for FCC regulations.

The Problem with Socialism

This market process theory, and the learning that takes place therein, underpins the Austrian school's arguments against socialist politico-economic systems. I don't want to dwell on this point, but it is illustrative of why regulations are problematic for entrepreneurship and economic growth.

In socialism, the means of production are owned by the state, and a central planner decides how to allocate those productive resources. Arguments for socialism generally revolve around the inefficiencies of free markets, those 'market failures.' There are problems like free rider problems, or people freely interacting for their own benefit can lead to the richer and more powerful taking advantage of the poorer and powerless. I'll come back to these later. Socialists argued that they could politically engineer a fairer and more productive economy, without any of these market failures, by centralizing economic decision-making and granting the best and brightest experts power to direct their industries.

Austrian economists – Mises and Hayek in particular – leveraged their market process theory to explain why such central economic planning couldn't work.

Hayek focused his argument on the so-called 'knowledge problem.' We are each and all unique in our knowledge of the world – we come from different backgrounds, we have had different experiences, and we interpret our experiences differently. We live in different places, we see different things, we have different interests. In short, we know different things.

A market economy leverages this heterogenous knowledge efficiently. This is called the *efficient market hypothesis*. (Note that 'efficiently' doesn't mean perfectly! Again, the market is a *learning* process, always looking for better solutions to still-remaining problems.) Whatever distinct knowledge we have gets reflected in the prices of things through free market exchanges. For example, let us suppose that there was a global pandemic that severely disrupted the supply chains for lumber (I know, stretch your imagination for this one). This information is exploited by those who know first about the shortage, who buy up the available lumber. This bids up the prices such that, by the time the shortage actually hits the market, the prices are already higher. The knowledge of a select few about particular market conditions is reflected in real-time prices, even if others don't have that knowledge.

Mises and Hayek would explain that market prices contain within them all of this heterogenous knowledge in the aggregate. Thus, prices themselves are vital information for markets to work effectively. If I'm a home builder, I can't know all of the challenges and delays in the lumber supply chain – that's outside my expertise. But I don't need to. I just see that lumber prices have skyrocketed, and so my costs of building homes is too high. I have to either charge much higher prices to my customers, defer homebuilding opportunities until those prices come back down, or else look for an alternative material to use. In short, the lumber shortage is dealt with by high prices, which ensures that only those who desperately need the wood will be willing to pay the higher prices, and most market participants will delay their use of lumber until the shortage is resolved.

But what happens when prices are *controlled* by a socialist central planner? The prices no longer contain the information that the market would imbue them with. So if retail outlets are forced to sell toilet paper at its normal price, despite a spike in demand (say, due to a pandemic), what happens? You end up with an artificial shortage – the first buyers scoop up extra toilet paper to plan for the long haul, and those late to the party are left with nothing. The central planner could ration the toilet paper, but how does the central planner know how much to ration? What if a family is going to need more toilet paper while the grandparents are in town?

In short, the knowledge of the different circumstances of each participant in the economy is beyond the scope and knowledge of the central planner. As a result, the central planner is bound to get it wrong. And getting it wrong means inefficiencies – shortages and gluts.

But Mises goes further than Hayek on this, recalling that the economy is constantly *changing*. It might be possible, per general equilibrium theory, to use synthetic markets to figure out the right 'equilibrium' prices, as Oskar Lange argued,[86] which could solve this knowledge problem. Not so, Mises argues, for the same reasons I have rejected general equilibrium theory in prior chapters. In reality, markets are never in some stable 'general equilibrium.' They are always in motion, and so the prices that are charged are prone to change. In the typical market process, prices of older goods tend downward while new goods are introduced by entrepreneurs into the market.

Because of this, the central planner cannot use any artificial mechanism to ascertain appropriate prices – those prices are impossible to calculate except through the free market process itself. Even then, it's not like a calculation is happening. "The market," again, is just an artificial concept that represents *individual people* interacting, bargaining, and trading with each other for their mutual benefit. Prices are *emergent* from such interactions, and there is never a single, universal price. We all value things differently, so the price I might be willing to pay may be different from yours. Prices will vary from place to place and person to person.

Undermining this price emergence process will necessarily cause inefficiencies and, thus, economic decline. Unmoored from prices and the profit motive, socialist

---

86 Lange, O. 1936. On the economic theory of socialism: Part one. *The Review of Economic Studies*, 4(1): 53–71.

Lange, O. 1937. On the economic theory of socialism: Part two. *The Review of Economic Studies*, 4(2): 123–142.

producers do not know how much to produce, and resources are either wasted in overproduction or else shortages occur.

Why the Great Depression Lasted so Long

Let me return briefly to the economic history of the U.S. and, in particular, to the period of the Great Depression. Different historical accounts tell different stories about how and why the U.S.'s Great Depression happened and why it persisted so long. I favor Murray Rothbard's account in his book *America's Great Depression*.[87] In essence, his argument is that the Great Depression started as a financial market bubble, fueled by rapid monetary inflation. It was then severely exacerbated and prolonged by the New Deal, which tried to fix the problem by central planning and economic manipulation rather than simply letting entrepreneurs adjust to the changing economic conditions and reallocate their resources and efforts elsewhere. Instead, FDR picked and chose industries to subsidize, and taxed the more productive sectors of the economy without abandon. Entrepreneurship ground to a halt as the New Deal tried to allocate productive resources centrally.

As a result, the Great Depression lasted over a decade. In contrast, previous market collapses in the U.S. were addressed centrally with little effort. In 1819, America's first depression, the only thing the government did was to ease the terms of payment to its land debtors. Van Buren did virtually nothing in response to the Panic of 1837. The depression of 1921 was met with only small interventions, including reducing government spending and taxes. Most of these prior recessions concluded quickly, the unproductive resources that caused the crash quickly reallocated by entrepreneurs to productive and growing sectors. Rothbard concludes:

> If government wishes to alleviate, rather than aggravate, a depression, its only valid course is laissez-faire – to leave the economy alone. Only if there is no interference, direct or threatened, with prices, wage rates, and business liquidation will the necessary adjustment proceed with smooth dispatch.[88]

But other explanations of the Great Depression were more popular, especially among the political class. John Maynard Keynes in particular had risen to stardom with his *The General Theory of Employment, Interest, and Money* in 1936.[89] In it he blamed irrational 'animal spirits' for the financial bubble and crash, and advocated that the government borrow and spend to break the vicious cycle of money hording and falling prices to get the economic engine roaring again. Of course, the New

87 Rothbard, M. N. 2008. *America's Great Depression* (5 ed.). Auburn, AL: Ludwig von Mises Institute.
88 *Ibid*, p. 185.
89 Keynes, J. M. 1936. *The General Theory of Employment, Interest, and Money*. London: Macmillan.

Deal's spending failed to bring the economy back to life. The depression only ended with the ending of World War II. Keynesian economists would point to the massive spending as the cause – the New Deal failed because it hadn't spent enough!

The Austrian school's response to Keynes is, of course, that this is nonsense. Economic growth isn't captured by GDP – a measure of economic productivity introduced by Keynes that, of course, includes government spending. It's captured as quality of life and individual well-being. Bringing human welfare back up in a depression is the job of entrepreneurs. And it was entrepreneurs, once the war was over, that finally turned the economy around by moving resources back to more productive uses.

This debate was captured very creatively in a fictional 'rap battle' ("Fight of the Century"[90]) between Austrian school economist Friedrich Hayek and John Maynard Keynes, written by creative artist John Papola and economist Russ Roberts. The song presents the economists arguing over the causes and solutions to the more recent 'Great Recession.' Here are some of the lyrics:

> [Keynes]
> We could've done better had we only spent more
> Too bad that only happens when there's a world war
> You can carp all you want about stats and regression
> Do you deny WWII cut short the Depression?
>
> [Hayek]
> Wow, one data point and you're jumping for joy
> The last time I checked, wars only destroy
> There was no multiplier, consumption just shrank
> As we used scarce resources for every new tank
> Pretty perverse to call that prosperity
> Ration meat, ration butter, a life of austerity
> When that war spending ended, your friends cried disaster
> Yet the economy thrived and grew faster
>
> [Keynes]
> You too only see what you want to see
> The spending of war clearly goosed GDP
> Unemployment was over, almost down to zero
> That's why I'm the master, that's why I'm the hero
>
> [Hayek]
> Creating employment's a straightforward craft
> When the nation's at war and there's a draft
> If every worker were staffed in the army and fleet
> We'd have full employment and nothin' to eat

---

90 https://www.youtube.com/watch?v=GTQnarzmTOc.

That last line really hits it on the head. An economy isn't about employment, it's about well-being. 100% full employment in ditch digging does nothing at all to improve the welfare of humankind – we would all starve, having failed to produce the necessities of life. Instead, the reasons for a recession or a depression are that productive resources have somehow gotten misallocated unproductively. In the recent case of the Great Recession, investors dumped their resources too heavily into housing, and more houses were built than were needed by the market. Those resources could and should have gone toward other consumer needs. But because they went to housing, the housing market overinflated, and when investors finally realized the mistake, the bubble burst and the market collapsed.

The way out of such a collapse is not to prop the collapsed market back up, as the U.S. government did, but to allow entrepreneurs to reallocate those overextended resources to different and more productive industries. By propping up the collapsed industry, the government *delays* this reallocation process and, as a result, prolongs the recession. Government spending is only very rarely truly entrepreneurial and, even when it is, tends to be highly inefficient. Untethered from the profit motive, the government has little incentive to be efficient or effective. In fact, scholars have found that governments are actually incentivized to do poorly. Their reward structure is such that poor performance enables them to request more funding – they get paid more when they fail!

The Great Depression lasted so long because it *inhibited entrepreneurship* through extreme taxation, severe regulation, and government central planning. Entrepreneurs are the ones who can and will move unproductive resources that were poorly invested in the bubble economy into different and productive sectors. By constraining entrepreneurship, this corrective mechanism is impeded and the downturn is prolonged. It was the New Deal that made the 1929 depression 'Great.'

Market Failures as Entrepreneurial Opportunities

Let me now return to the various criticisms of free and unfettered markets. The regular and recurrent complaints of 'market failures' are understandable – there are a lot of social problems that still persist in the world. But what is a market 'failure'? Is the starvation of some in Third World countries a market failure? Is the fact that it still takes me 15 minutes to get to work a market failure? How do we know what is a real market 'failure,' and not just a problem yet to be solved by entrepreneurs? Let me put forward an argument that all market 'failures' are all *entrepreneurial opportunities* for value facilitation, and do not in fact require public policy.

Scholars have levied several particular market failures that they hold cannot be adequately solved by the market (that is, entrepreneurs) alone: behavioral irrationalities, monopolies, public goods, externalities, and information asymmetries. These issues, they suppose, require collective action through public policy. Evidence suggests otherwise. And by using government regulation to solve these 'market failures,' they invoke the inhibitors on value learning that slow economic growth.

Irrationality and Ignorance

First, behavioral economists have argued that individual economic actors often do *not* act in their best interests, that they can act irrationally and, perhaps, even deliberately harm themselves. It's also supposed that actors can act inefficiently and, even, counterproductively due to their own ignorance of (scientific) value knowledge. A science-based policy, they contend, might mitigate such 'mistakes' and, thereby, improve economic efficiency. Behavioral economist Dan Ariely puts the argument this way in his book *Predictably Irrational*:

> We are really far less rational than standard economic theory assumes. Moreover, these irrational behaviors of ours are neither random nor senseless. They are systematic, and since we repeat them again and again, predictable. So, wouldn't it make sense to modify standard economics, to move it away from naive psychology (which often fails the tests of reason, introspection, and – most important – empirical scrutiny)? This is exactly what the emerging field of behavioral economics . . . is trying to accomplish.[91]

Now, there's no denying that we humans are flawed. But judging our decisions from some 'objective' standard, from some god's-eye view, seems hardly fair to humanity. What is this objective standard that we *should* know? Given that we clearly are not omniscient, what is the 'rational' amount of knowledge that we should have? Ludwig von Mises puts it well in *Human Action*:

> When applied to the means chosen for the attainment of ends, the terms rational and irrational imply a judgment about the expediency and adequacy of the procedure employed. The critic approves or disapproves of the method from the point of view of whether or not it is best suited to attain the end in question. It is a fact that human reason is not infallible and that man very often errs in selecting and applying means. An action unsuited to the end sought falls short of expectation. It is contrary to purpose, but it is rational, i.e., the outcome of a reasonable – although faulty – deliberation and an attempt – although an ineffectual attempt – to attain a definite goal. The doctors who a hundred years ago employed certain methods for the treatment of cancer which our contemporary doctors reject were – from the point of view of present-day pathology – badly instructed and therefore inefficient. But they did not act irrationally; they did their best. It is probable that in a hundred years more doctors will have more efficient methods at hand for the treatment of this disease. They will be more efficient but not more rational than our physicians.[92]

---

91 Ariely, D. 2009. *Predictably Irrational: The hidden forces that shape our decisions*. New York: HarperCollins, p. *xx*.
92 Mises, L. v. 1949. *Human Action: A treatise on economics*. New Haven, CT: Yale University Press, p. 20.

Perhaps more fundamentally, what we're talking about are our *preferences*. When consumers make their choices, who is the behavioral economist to say that your preference is right or wrong? Essentially, the behavioral economist is saying "I know better than you what you *should* want." But this is silly – we're all different and we want and need different things. That the behavioral economist *thinks* you want (or should want) A doesn't mean that your preferring B is 'irrational.'

Now, this does not mean that everything we do is effective, optimal, or ideal – we're not always doing what is best for us. In fact, PVT's learning process implies that all action not within the nirvana equilibrium is always and necessarily *inefficient* at any moment given the knowledge that we would have tomorrow or in a decade. Of course we are ignorant and sometimes shortsighted. We often make mistakes and feel regret or remorse. Ignorance or misunderstanding, perhaps even delusion, may lead us to choose actions that are inappropriate *given* our intended aims. So we can even admit that scientific 'experts' may possess better causal knowledge and information that, if we knew it, could lead to better and more productive behavior.

As I've laid out in Section 2, we're each working toward satisfying our *many* needs and switching preferences from one to another as we try to successfully satisfy, at least partially, each of them or as many as possible. Our preferences are hardly stable, and there's no good reason that I can see, other than artificial simplicity for the sake of economic modelling, to suppose them to be.

In short, it is a false presumption that experts can make better decisions for us. Value experiences cannot be objectively observed and so value knowledge is never 'objective.' Any 'expert' can only guess it empathically, just as any entrepreneur must do. Most of behavioral economics is studied in laboratories, where the aims of the experiments are 'given' to participants. But this hardly means that participants' actual goals are those which the researcher presumes.

Imposed regulations intended to restrict our options to the 'objectively better' ones impede value learning and the pursuit and attaining of economic actors' subjective ends. They alter behavior from what people would have preferred had they been free to choose their own actions. There are a couple of problems with this. First, there's a very good chance that the regulator doesn't really know what's 'best' for you since he or she doesn't actually know what you want in life. And second, you learn *nothing*, or very little, about your real value preferences. If a choice is made for you, your real preference is for the thing you would have chosen, so your experience of value is unlikely to affect your real preferences.

While these costs might be worth the benefits gained through regulation to some, such a cost-benefit ratio is individually unique, unmeasurable, and unknowable. Thus, *all regulations come at unknowable and, often, unseen costs* that have to be acknowledged. A more tempered and historically successful approach employs policy as a means of *educating* actors while allowing them to make decisions personally for their own unique situations.

Monopoly

Monopolies are considered inefficiencies in the market due to the seller's 'market power.' Because there is a lack of disciplinary competition, the monopolist can raise prices to excessively high levels. If you remember the VPC framework introduced in Chapter 3, the monopolist is, in theory, able and motivated to set the price at or near WTP, capturing all the economic surplus – the consumer essentially breaks even.

The market process is commonly assumed to tend towards the creation of a monopoly. Success breeds profits that can be reinvested in ways that outpace competitors until only one remains. To counteract this tendency, governments enact and enforce antitrust policies to break up or otherwise regulate companies that have no (remaining) natural competitors.

I can certainly admit that the intuition of this antitrust logic is strong. But accepting PVT's market process theory implies that monopolists are still and always beholden to consumers, and not the other way around, suggesting that antitrust may be unwarranted.

Historical evidence is not kind to monopoly theory. Historians do not treat natural monopolists (e.g., Vanderbilt, Rockefeller, Carnegie, Morgan, etc.) kindly, dubbing them 'robber barons.' But the era of these robber barons was not one of monopolistic price gouging, as economic theory would predict. To the contrary, economic historians have found that prices consistently *fell* throughout their market dominance.[93]

In fact, history suggests that the only monopolies that actually behave as predicted by monopoly theory are those that are politically created and protected by government (such as the USPS and utility companies), being spared threats of competitive entry. This seems ironic to me, as a primary argument for such government monopolies is that consumers have to be protected from greedy monopolists.

Unprotected (natural) monopolies are never truly sustainable. The market process churns on, and eventually the monopolist falls behind in the process. The shackles of bureaucracy that come with growth tend to inhibit the continuous learning processes necessary to stave off industry disruptors, as economic history shows. I always laugh to myself a bit when students remark that Google, or Apple, or Amazon can never be displaced. It certainly seems that way. But people said the same things about Sears a half century ago. They were saying it about Walmart just two decades ago. Now, Walmart will be with us for a while more, but the sentiment that it's invincible is already gone – its future is in question with Amazon's meteoric rise. Microsoft was still in the fray of antitrust litigation over its bundling of Windows

---

93 Folsom, B. W. 2010. *The Myth of the Robber Barons: A New Look at the Rise of Big Business in America*. Herndon, VA: Young Americas Foundation.

and Explorer when competitors like Apple and Google had already eroded Microsoft's dominant competitive position. The corporate powers of yesteryear are tamed or gone, and the new powers – though they now seem imperishable – are only an innovation away from their demise.

As Per Bylund argues in *The Seen, the Unseen, and the Unrealized,*[94] antitrust policies and regulations may come at significant economic cost to the value learning process. Assuming that the market tendency toward monopoly is correct, firms would have to intentionally adopt inefficient business practices to stay clear of the threat of antitrust break-up. And because antitrust policy tends to be highly ambiguous – e.g., what is an unlawful firm size? – conservatism will exacerbate these inefficiencies. There are also potential unseen costs of lost opportunities as more entrepreneurs are pushed into competition with already efficient monopolists rather than pursuing new innovations. It is not at all foregone that those productive activities are better served in competition than in innovation.

Public Goods

Public goods are defined as those that are both *non-excludable* and *non-rivalrous,* which means that the provider cannot discriminate between paying and non-paying users and that one's use of the good does not hinder another's. For example, if I wanted to have a fireworks show for my family, I can't prevent others from watching it also. This can lead to a 'tragedy of the commons,' where resources are overused and not preserved – as exemplified by the overfishing of open oceans – and goods are underproduced due to an absent profit motive. If your productive efforts can be cashed in by others, your incentives to produce are severely dimmed. If producing a good fireworks show costs $10,000, I could charge for admission to cover my costs. But who would pay? Perhaps some would out of a sense of duty or generosity. But others might not. And those that don't pay are just as able to watch as those that do. We have a free rider problem.

The typical solution is the state provision and regulation of any such goods deemed essential or sufficiently valuable to society. Because the state can coercively finance production through taxation, it avoids the free rider problem. A government can tax its constituents to pay for its fireworks show.

There are a few problems with this. First and perhaps most obvious is that it coerces payments from consumers who may not want or need the public good. If my neighbor hates fireworks, I can't coerce him into paying for my show. But he has to pay his part of the government's show, whether he wants to or not. States

---

94 Bylund, P. L. 2016. *The Seen, the Unseen, and the Unrealized: How Regulations Affect Our Everyday Lives*. Lanham, MD: Lexington Books.

spend their taxes on goods and projects that a good many of their constituents find objectionable. Furthermore, the power delegated to governments to make such purchases has historically been easy to abuse, government expenditures going far beyond only public goods.

But perhaps more interestingly, research suggests that the free rider problem may be exaggerated. Historical evidence suggests that most supposed public goods, where government provision is deemed necessary, can be and have been provided by private entrepreneurs. For example, economist Ronald Coase documents that lighthouses – which were one of the most commonly asserted examples of a public good – were historically very often built and maintained by private investors.[95] Economist Elinor Ostrom found in her research that these free rider problems are often, when not politically resolved, solved organically by communities and user societies through voluntary institutions.[96] This type of bottom-up or 'emergent' institutionalism is itself a value learning process.

Again, the value learning process implies that the costs of state-run production are higher than commonly recognized, since the market learning process for such goods is stifled by the non-competitive and non-innovative nature of state monopolies. The recent troubles of northern California's power company, Pacific Gas and Electric (PG&E), is illustrative. Whereas competitive technology markets, such as electronics, continue to push the boundaries of superior technology, PG&E's technology infrastructure went stale and unattended to for decades until it started causing wildfires and blackouts. But the true cost is not the fires or blackouts – it is the unseen 'what could have beens.' While competitive industries are represented by high and increasing rates of innovation, utility markets have little incentive – they are in fact *disincentivized* – to pursue an innovation strategy. How much more efficiently might we now obtain our power if private power companies competed for that market?

Externalities

Externalities are side effects or consequences of economic action that affect a third party, and can be positive (e.g., a beekeeper's business contributing to pollination of farmers' crops) or negative (e.g., pollution from a factory affecting the health and well-being of nearby residents). While positive externalities rarely raise concerns, negative externalities are clearly problematic – the costs of imposed are borne by others, but the profits are not. Traditionally, this problem has been solved by

---

95 Coase, R. H. (1974). The lighthouse in economics. *The Journal of Law and Economics*, 17(2), 357–376.
96 Ostrom, E. 1990. *Governing the Commons: The Evolution of Institutions for Collective Action*. Cambridge: Cambridge University Press.

imposing Pigouvian taxes – government taxation of those creating negative externalities to cover the externality costs.

But following the logic of value as a process, this solution is problematic. First, how can we assess how much should be taxed? Externalities can't be objectively measured as money prices – prices are bargained and relative phenomena, and not approximations of real valuations. Also, it relies on interpersonal *value* comparisons, which are not really possible. Such comparisons would presume that knowledge is sufficient and unchanging over time such that a harmful outcome can be adequately corrected.

Unintended consequences of Pigouvian taxes may end up more costly or harmful than the outcomes they curtail. For example, Schuerhoff, Weikard, and Zetland[97] report on a Pigouvian groundwater tax enacted by the Netherlands in 1995 on the grounds that it would both raise tax revenue and, simultaneously, improve and protect the natural environment by reducing demand for public groundwater. But, due to uncertainties over the tax's impact on groundwater users, especially farmers, various tax exemptions were made to the point that only 10 drinking water companies paid 90 percent of the total tax revenues. Eventually the unfairness and unintended consequences of the tax led to its repeal.

A better understanding of the value learning cycle implies that knowledge is incomplete and that actors learn over time. As a result, both consumers and producers change their behavior, which makes projection of such outcomes very difficult, if at all possible. This isn't to say, of course, that externalities are not a problem. But it is not clear that centrally planned government solutions are or would be more effective than letting solutions institutionally emerge through, e.g., entrepreneurial or common law processes.

The 'Lemons' Problem

A final market problem to consider involves information asymmetries. George Akerlof, in a famous paper entitled "The Market for 'Lemons,'"[98] illustrated this market failure with the example of the used car industry. Where only the dealer knows which cars are good and which are the 'lemons', "the good cars may be driven out of the market by the lemons." The used car dealer might obtain short-term gains through the fraudulent obscuring of known information – and used car buyers, because they know this, would lower their willingness to pay. This would lead to quality used cars being priced out of the market – buyers wouldn't be willing to pay for high-quality used cars, only the poorer quality cars would sell.

97 Schuerhoff, M., Weikard, H.-P., & Zetland, D. 2013. The life and death of Dutch groundwater tax. *Water Policy*, 15(6): 1064–1077.

98 Akerlof, G. A. 1970. The market for "lemons": Quality uncertainty and the market mechanism. *The Quarterly Journal of Economics*, 84(3): 488–500, p. 490.

This argument has led, in the U.S., to state and federal "lemon laws," which require certain warranties from sellers. These laws come with imposed costs of compliance, which include not only the warranties but also legal costs.

But Akerlof's problem isn't as compelling once you incorporate value-as-a-process thinking. The value of goods is uncertain until consumed, which of course is the concern raised by Akerlof. But there is value learning that occurs in the market. If the process proceeded as Akerlof envisioned, what would used car buyers learn? Their willingness to pay would keep falling until the used car market collapses entirely. Is this a good outcome for the used car dealerships? In other words, Akerlof is focusing myopically on the short-term gains while ignoring the long-term implications. But businesses are rarely so short-termist, and when they are they end up in trouble.

In fact, the exemplary problem raised by Akerlof – the information asymmetries in used car markets – has already been almost fully solved by the market process.[99] Their reputations at stake, used car dealers have naturally evolved honesty practices. Allowing customers to have a car inspected by an independent mechanic pre-purchase, the rise of the online review, and car fact trackers such as Carfax, and large-scale used car dealers such as CarMax and Carvana which provide shoppers with car histories, have now virtually abolished the information asymmetry problem altogether in the used car market. We are now still left with the costs of legal compliance to the lemon laws, but with no remaining problem to solve.

Dealing with Regulations

Hopefully, I've convinced you that the market 'failures' that have justified government interventions are actually *entrepreneurial opportunities* that you can solve, if you're clever enough. For example, money is often thought to be a public good – private monies are untrustworthy – so governments typically monopolize the provision of legal tender. But governments have been unreliable in their monetary policies also. But the emergence of cryptocurrencies such as Bitcoin highlight that this stable money problem is an entrepreneurial opportunity. What social or market problem can *you* devise a solution to?

Government activities and regulations tend to crowd out entrepreneurial solutions. Not only are private money solutions difficult, they are *illegal* in most countries. Thus, money entrepreneurship was almost non-existent until Bitcoin emerged. The techno-decentralized crypto solution devised by Satoshi Nakamoto – whoever

---

99 To be fair to Akerlof, he concludes his paper by recognizing several market-based institutions that have already addressed this information asymmetry problem to some extent (e.g., guarantees, brand names, etc.).

that may be – was brilliant and revolutionary. The author's use of a pseudonym, of course, was motivated by the fact that such a replacement money system would be – and was – illegal. But it could not be stopped due to its technological decentralization. Many countries have, since its launch, accepted its inevitability, and recognized Bitcoin and other cryptocurrencies as legal.

My aim here is not to advocate that you skirt regulations. But being aware of how they affect the market and entrepreneurial processes can help you better see how and why current solutions exist and persist in their current form. And it might help you see ways to change these markets for the better, either through political activism or through innovation.

Chapter 17
Continuing Your Learning Journey

I have endeavored to show you a new way of thinking about economic value, what this new value theory means for entrepreneurship, and how better understanding entrepreneurship in this way can help you achieve greater value in your own entrepreneurial journey. Rather than conclude with a summary, let me say a few things about where I think entrepreneurship theory is going in the near future and how you can stay informed and continue your learning journey.

The Future of Entrepreneurship Theory

Let's start with a short discussion of where I think (hope) entrepreneurship theory is going. It's of course hard to predict this. But I can at least tell you where I am going with my own research and where I'm trying to push the field.

I gave you the quick rundown of modern entrepreneurship theory in Chapter 2. Of course, I think that there will be some pivot toward subjectivism and, hopefully, value as a process. But what is the future of this new paradigm?

Entrepreneurship as Process

One of the emerging streams of research in this area is more fully understanding entrepreneurship as a *process* or a *journey*. There is movement in the entrepreneurship discipline toward process philosophy. Philosopher Nicholas Rescher describes process philosophy as holding "that physical existence is at bottom processual; that processes rather than things best represent the phenomena that we encounter in the natural [and social] world about us."[100] In other words, reality is characterized by change and flow rather than substance and stability.

The prevailing realist scientific tradition, including entrepreneurship research, has held to a *substance* philosophy, where 'things' are stable entities and can be studied as such. But process philosophers believe that all *things* are in motion, in process. Many physical things – land, rocks, trees – have the appearance of stability, but in fact are constantly changing, albeit slowly. Most of the things we're interested in – markets, people, social institutions – change much faster.

---

[100] Rescher, N. 1996. *Process Metaphysics: An introduction to process philosophy*. Albany NY: SUNY Press, p. 2.

https://doi.org/10.1515/9783110750805-017

The argument of process theorists in entrepreneurship is that entrepreneurship is a science of *change* – there are no *things* to study, only processes. What we call an 'opportunity' represents the evolving beliefs of the entrepreneur and of consumers. Studying it as a constant *thing* is not only unrealistic but also highly misleading. It suggests to the entrepreneur that their main challenge is execution, diminishing the critical role of learning and adaptation in the process.

Entrepreneurship as Social Reification

Relatedly, a growing and promising literature argues that entrepreneurship entails shifting social beliefs from one dominant value narrative to another. Failure to diffuse, as I outlined in Chapter 14, occurs if the market – consumers – fail to perceive sufficient value, or sufficiently certain value, in the new solution to warrant its purchase at its market price. Consumers' value learning processes, if entrepreneurs are to succeed, must be facilitated by the entrepreneurs' active work to shift others' value knowledge – how people think about and understand their value experiences.

Entrepreneurship is, to a very large extent, a narrative-crafting process, a process of persuasion. In the 1970s, when Steve Jobs and Steve Wozniak were working on developing a personal home computer, the top brass of the computer industry at the time were scoffing at the idea. In 1977, Ken Olsen, the CEO of Digital Equipment Inc., said, "There is no reason anyone would want a computer in their home."[101] It was, at the time, difficult to see how or why people might want a computer – which was at the time excessively big, bulky, loud, and expensive – in their own homes. But Jobs's vision was very different from the way Olsen and many others were thinking about computers.

Jobs's success was not because he was right. He was successful because he persuaded hundreds of thousands of people that he was right, and that the technology establishment was wrong. He succeeded because he was exceedingly charismatic and persuasive, and had a compelling narrative.

In the language of philosophy, Jobs *reified* his opportunity. He had a vision that few others shared. But through active and persuasive argumentation, he convinced others that his vision was right. And only in and by so doing did his vision become reality.

---

[101] http://www.computinghistory.org.uk/pages/3971/There-is-no-reason-anyone-would-want-a-computer-in-their-home.

Innovation and Empathy

Finally, I think that the role of empathy will take center stage in future entrepreneurship work. I've already introduced to you why it's so important. But this way of thinking is still very new to the entrepreneurship discipline. Entrepreneurship scholars still refer to the creative innovation process as the "fuzzy front end" of the entrepreneurial process because we still know so little about how it happens.

I think that's about to change. Seeing and understanding the origins of ideas amid *consumers* rather than entrepreneurs significantly alters the way we think about creativity and innovation. We can finally start to break free from the current paradigm, where creativity is spontaneous and inexplicable, and begin to unravel the *intentionality* that underpins such creativity.

Going Down the Rabbit Hole

I hope you have found the arguments in this book both compelling and helpful. I have focused my writing on those ideas that I thought would be most helpful to you in your own entrepreneurial journey. But there is so much more to know and learn. Most of it entails the 'what it's like' minutiae of everyday tasks you will have to do – finance and accounting, sales and marketing, keeping inventory, hiring and employee management, etc. A lot of this you can learn by doing.

But what you won't easily learn by doing is how to think and understand the economy and the world. Per Bylund has said – and I think he's right – that all successful entrepreneurs are 'Austrian,' referring to the Austrian school of economics that I've introduced to you here. Of course, not all successful businesspeople know and live by the heterodox Austrian school's theoretical principles. But Professor Bylund's point is that success is only achieved by understanding the market in an Austrian way – by treating consumers as individuals and tailoring to their unique, subjective needs. You can get lucky for a time, but unless you adapt to their advancing value knowledge, you will eventually be left in the cold.

If you don't want to learn these principles the hard way, I suggest diving into the philosophy and theory of the Austrian school. Vaults of knowledge are available for free online. The Mises Institute, in Auburn Alabama, offers hundreds of complete books as free downloads, or hardcopies at highly discounted prices at www.mises.org. It has also launched a project, *Economics for Business* (www.econ4business.com), the specific purpose of which is to teach Austrian principles to businesspeople. These principles are packaged in education modules, with application tools to help you put those principles effectively into practice. It also has a community of scholars and professionals that are willing to hold your hand a bit as you learn these things. Hunter Hastings hosts a weekly podcast – the "Economics for Business" podcast – that has expert guests (including yours truly) who share what they've learned.

The Library of Economics and Liberty, at www.econlib.org, has a large archive of free online books also, and the "EconTalk" podcast, hosted by economist Russ Roberts, is excellent.

In short, dive in. Become a perpetual learner. The rabbit hole keeps going and going. I'm nowhere near the end myself. It will change the way you see the economy, and the world, for the better. And that understanding will go a long way in your entrepreneurial journey.

Good luck!

List of Figures

https://doi.org/10.1515/9783110750805-018

Index

https://doi.org/10.1515/9783110750805-019

www.ingramcontent.com/pod-product-compliance
Lightning Source LLC
Chambersburg PA
CBHW081103220326
41598CB00038B/7213